Maker: Here's your step-by-step guide to design, manufacturing, marketing, fundraising, and everything else you'll need to do to turn your dream into a business. *How We Make Stuff Now* is packed with practical advice and inspirational case studies.

—TOM EISENMANN, Howard H. Stevenson Professor of Business Administration at Harvard Business School

There is no one better than Jules Pieri, who has shepherded thousands of consumer products through the keyhole for mass adoption, to write a very practical guide for the dreamers among us, who have an idea for a product and the passion to see it through.

—ROBIN CHASE, founder of Zipcar and author of *Peers Inc*

This is the Maker Bible for starting your business. Read it. Reread it. Dog-ear it, take notes, mark it up.

—CHAD LAURANS, founder and CEO of SimpliSafe

Building hardware products is hard for every company—as evidenced by the countless delayed and failed product launches. With this book and her company, The Grommet, Jules has achieved an ambitious mission to help industry outsiders build both viable products and vibrant businesses.

—HARDI MEYBAUM, founder of GrabCAD, general partner at Matrix Partners, and author of *The Art of Product Design*

This book breaks down what a Maker needs to know into digestible, practical, bite-size gems. *How We Make Stuff Now* is a great how-to guide to support owners on their journey, whether they are just getting started or well on their way!

—TRYNKA SHINEMAN, CEO of Vistaprint

Jules's commitment and experience are an inspiration, and her book is a gift to founders. It's a complete playbook chock-full of tangible, experience-driven insights and advice. Armed with this wisdom and guidance, I predict a whole new class of successful Makers and founders will emerge.

—KIRSTEN GREEN, founder of Forerunner Ventures

Starting a Maker business is hard. The odds are against you. This book literally changes those odds by giving you a road map. I wish I had this when I started my business!

—GAIL GOODMAN, cofounder and former CEO of Constant Contact

As an investor in many of the products The Grommet has helped launched—including Fitbit, Molekule, littleBits, TrackR, and Sphero—I know firsthand the joys of building these exciting and challenging companies. *How We Make Stuff Now* reflects the deep insights Jules Pieri acquired through helping over 3,000 companies.

—BRAD FELD, founder of Foundry Group

As someone who's worked with small businesses for decades, I know how hard it can be not just to come up with a great product but to find, serve, and keep customers. A product isn't a business—no matter how great that product is. Few people know this as well as Jules Pieri. Jules is genuinely passionate about helping independent Makers succeed and is uniquely knowledgeable. In this book, she provides case studies, critical advice, and inspirational stories about Makers who've made it—all based on her years of expertise as cofounder of The Grommet. Jules shows you how to bring your innovative idea to market and create a sustainable business.

—RHONDA ABRAMS, small business columnist at *USA Today* and author of *Successful Business Plan*

This fascinating book by the cofounder and CEO of the pioneering online platform for Makers, The Grommet, is packed with a rich range of invaluable how-to knowledge for the growing community of Maker-entrepreneurs to take their innovative ideas and products to market success. Pieri combines keen observations on Maker culture and its potential business opportunities and challenges. It is essential reading for entrepreneurs, product developers, designers, and business and design students.

—GUNALAN NADARAJAN, dean of Stamps School of Art and Design at the University of Michigan

Stop, drop, and roll: Every kid knows this is what you do when you find yourself on fire. If you want to start a product business (a Maker business), *stop* what you are doing, *drop* into a chair, and *roll* through this book. Read it today, and it will save you months of pain and suffering.

—MARK HATCH, CEO of Maker Partners and
author of *The Maker Movement Manifesto*

A must-read for anyone who loves gadgets and the world of invention.

—STEVE GREENBERG, monthly contributor to the
Today Show and author of *Gadget Nation*

In writing a Grommet case study, I was struck by the many layers of value the company creates. This book is yet another worthy embodiment of its contributions to our economy.

—LYNDA APPLEGATE, Sarofim-Rock Professor of Business
Administration Emerita at Harvard Business School

HOW WE Make STUFF NOW

HOW WE Make STUFF NOW

**Turn Ideas into Products
That Build Successful Businesses**

JULES PIERI

New York Chicago San Francisco Athens London Madrid
Mexico City Milan New Delhi Singapore Sydney Toronto

1 2 3 4 5 6 7 8 9   LCR   24 23 22 21 20 19

ISBN: 978-1-260-13585-5
MHID: 1-260-13585-3

e-ISBN: 978-1-260-13586-2
e-MHID: 1-260-13586-1

This publication is designed to provide accurate and authoritative information in regard to the subject matter covered. It is sold with the understanding that neither the author nor the publisher is engaged in rendering legal, accounting, securities trading, or other professional services. If legal advice or other expert assistance is required, the services of a competent professional person should be sought.
—*From a Declaration of Principles Jointly Adopted by a Committee of the American Bar Association and a Committee of Publishers and Associations*

Library of Congress Cataloging-in-Publication Data

Names: Pieri, Jules, author.
Title: How we make stuff now : turn ideas into products that build successful
    businesses / by Jules Pieri.
Description: New York : McGraw-Hill, [2019]
Identifiers: LCCN 2018051194| ISBN 9781260135855 (alk. paper) | ISBN 1260135853
Subjects: LCSH: New products. | Inventions. | Entrepreneurship.
Classification: LCC HF5415.153 .P54 2019 | DDC 658.5/75--dc23 LC record
    available at https://lccn.loc.gov/2018051194

McGraw- Hill Education books are available at special quantity discounts to use as premiums and sales promotions or for use in corporate training programs. To contact a representative, please visit the Contact Us pages at www.mhprofessional.com.

To my cofounder, Joanne Domeniconi,
who has done more to level the playing field
for innovative products and Makers
than anyone I know

CONTENTS

CONTENTS

ACKNOWLEDGMENTS

I'd always wondered why people fawn over their editors at the end of books. Now I know. Thank you, Casey Ebro, for taking a risk on me.

I disappeared once a week for months while I wrote this book. Thank you, Grommet team, for not missing a beat in my absence. Thank you, Drew, for letting me regularly commandeer your home office, and obsessively stash all your clutter as part of my weekly procrastination ritual.

Bridget Samburg wrangled all the research for these Maker case studies. Imagine chasing down dozens of "one-armed paper-hangers" who are very busy building their businesses. That part was harder than the actual writing.

I'd always wanted to write a book. But I wasn't really doing anything about it until Charlie McEnerney got the ball rolling with a well-crafted proposal backed by his real-world experience in publishing.

My sons are three of the finest people I know and the best cheerleaders a mom could have. That is everything to me, and the thought of their support/judgment/pride fueled this book as much as coffee.

Working closely with over 3,000 Makers gave me a wholly unfair advantage in shaping this book. I hope it saves steps, preserves resources, reduces isolation, and aids success for future Makers who pursue their dreams.

INTRODUCTION

At noon on October 20, 2008, I pressed a button that has since shaped nearly every waking hour of my life. At that moment Daily Grommet's original website went live, and we launched our very first product from a fledgling Maine-based Maker, Bunnytail Blankets.

The night before the launch I looked across our shared IKEA desk at my hardworking cofounder Joanne Domeniconi and said a silent prayer to God, "Please forgive me for what I am about to do." Why? Because from the start, we committed to surfacing an innovative product and company *every single weekday*, supporting each with original research, vibrant video stories, and a nationwide marketing campaign. I knew this responsibility would set a life-altering demand for us both and that the pace in our not-yet-real company would be fast and exciting but also totally relentless.

We were clear about our unwavering mission to fight for the little guy. Over the course of our careers we had seen the odds stacked against innovative products. The United States had lost many of its specialty and local stores. These small retailers historically take bets on new products and develop the market for them, customer by customer. National retail chains were increasingly competing on price instead of sourcing distinctive products. Their buying processes became unwieldy and conservative. The risks of taking on an unknown supplier—no matter how promising the product—were increasingly considered higher than the likely benefits. Still today, that dysfunction in retail threatens to squash product innovation nearly at birth.

Joanne and I decided to build an informative, inspiring, trustworthy place where emerging Makers could "find their people."

We knew that these Makers would have many steep mountains to climb in building their businesses, and that gaining awareness and credibility would be by far the hardest one. New companies do not have built-in audiences or marketing budgets, and if retailers were no longer playing that critical connection role, we predicted there would be a whole lot of worthy products all dressed up with no place to go. We believed that losing those vibrant young companies before they had a fighting chance was an unacceptable cost to our economy and society. It made us spitting mad, and it galvanized us.

So we built a massive community of the very best kind—people from all walks of life who are curious, smart, and looking to support entrepreneurs and innovation. Over time, Daily Grommet became The Grommet, and today we are a powerful and unique market-maker for inspired young products. One of the reasons for our resonance and growth is that our community embraces the age-old human drive to create and invent. Our supporters and customers experience The Grommet as a place to see fascinating passions and talents realized, and to help the intrepid people birthing new companies. And some significant proportion of our many millions of followers cheers for these people because they hope to be one of those Makers someday.

Makers come from all walks of life. Our research across the 3,000 Makers we have partnered with reveals that they are also career changers. Only 10 percent of Grommet Makers have prior experience in the area where they build their business. ER nurses turn into tech device entrepreneurs. Lawyers invent water bottles. So if you secretly believe "I have no qualifications to launch a product," you are in very good company.

It is easier to get into Harvard than to get a product sanctioned as a Grommet. Less than 3 percent of the 300 products that are submitted weekly are accepted. But despite the lack of relevant experience of most Grommet Makers, a guaranteed commonality is that their products are distinctive, innovative, and live up to their promises. Solving a problem in a fresh way or creating an interesting business model does not require domain expertise. It requires tenacity, passion, and energy.

But what became plainly obvious over the years of working with Makers is that creating the product is just the start. The minute your baby gets into the market, your company has to be credible in 16 different other competencies, ranging from logistics to packaging to financial management. And we usually find that any given company is good at about 8 of those 16 competencies. Until we get to know them, we just don't know which 8 areas will be lacking. And we can't fix them all, no matter how much advice and how many lessons learned we share.

Sometimes one particular weakness can be debilitating. In consumer life, people don't really care whether a company is small or large when it comes to, say, delivery time frames and customer support expectations. Running out of inventory, having your shipping packages fail, or not answering the phone can wipe out hard-won sales territory and customer goodwill. The reality is that the under-resourced little guys have to throw their bodies at covering many of the business operations until they can scale enough to bring in a full team or professional expertise. That period between "start" and "sustainable business" can call on a founder's every last wit, resource, and shred of energy, so expert guidance from those who have cracked similar problems is invaluable.

That is the point of this book. If you are an aspiring Maker, this book will help you evaluate a potential product and market opportunity. This endeavor will change your life in the same way pushing the button to take Grommet live changed mine. You will want to be sure that this idea is worth the potential assault to your current sanity and stability. And if you decide to take the plunge and pursue the business, the book will also help you stretch your precious time and resources wisely across all the necessary functions you will build. When you are as "busy as a one-armed paperhanger" building your dream, you want to move efficiently and wisely.

This book is organized in two sections. Part One provides a how-to for getting your business started (Chapters 1–5). Part Two is all about building the 16 necessary competencies (Chapters 6–21). You can read it in any order you like or need. The advice is drawn from our experience with our 3,000 Makers, who work across a couple dozen product categories. We've continuously advised them as they attack new territories, and much of our input is similar from one company to another because people are solving identical problems in isolation. We've also learned and passed along the lessons from Makers who have mastered the 16 necessary competencies. They are the ultimate experts, so I relay their experiences and lessons learned in the form of case studies in each chapter, to bring the lessons to life and to put a friendly name and face to their awesome products.

A whopping 135 million Americans already call themselves Makers. Some are describing the output from hobbies, and others have multimillion-dollar businesses with dozens or hundreds of employees. This will only grow. Thirty-seven percent of U.S. high school students say they want to start their own businesses, as do 25 percent of military veterans. Much of this creative energy is headed toward joining the ranks of existing Makers. Why? Because there is no other thrill or source of deep satisfaction in business quite like seeing a physical product you envisioned come to fruition.

It's an honor to have a young business entrust us with its baby and its story. I hope that this book will help shape the next wave of successful Makers. These are the heroes creating jobs and shaping our economy. Perhaps one of them will be you. Maybe, just maybe, we'll even meet in the happy event of a Grommet partnership and launch.

PART

I

Starting Your Business

1

A BRIEF HISTORY OF CONSUMER PRODUCTS

Before the rise of corporations in the late 1800s, products were invented because people simply needed something for their work or life. They were the results of local ingenuity, put to use on the farm or in the workplace. Some might be shared locally, but there was no easy way for a product to reach people who lived elsewhere—unless the product was distributed by Sears, Roebuck and Company through its mail order catalogs, starting in the 1890s. Retail distribution, as we know it today, didn't exist, so when an innovative product was created, it would take years to catch on, if ever.

After corporations began developing research and development (R&D) departments, they started producing products. The twentieth century brought us an era of company-driven innovation from Ford, General Electric, Harley-Davidson, and RCA, as well as from visionaries like Thomas Edison and his Idea Factory in Menlo Park, New Jersey.

When I started my career as an industrial designer in the 1980s, consumer products were still mostly originated by large companies. For example, I worked at Unisys, Data General, Stride Rite, Keds, and Hasbro—all large corporations. By and large, designers like me had to work for large companies because these organizations had all the resources that enabled us to do our job. Because of that, our expertise tended to exist in a walled garden. Even if I had struck out on my own, an independent entrepreneur would have had a hard time finding someone like me, much less affording my services. Add on top of that the likely need for mechanical, electrical, and/ or manufacturing engineering expertise, and sourcing professional and expensive prototyping. Layer in the massive efforts of commissioning packaging, getting financing, finding manufacturing, and purchasing costly broadcast or print media to build awareness. No matter how committed you were, the vertical mountain in front of an aspiring entrepreneur would have discouraged the vast majority of individuals—until recently.

The only condition better for making a product 20 or more years ago was that retail was much richer, with a far broader variety of local and specialty stores that had not yet been sucker-punched by Amazon and big-box retailers. If an entrepreneur could run the gauntlet of challenges to create a product, there was a healthy network of stores and sales rep organizations that stood ready to welcome innovation from all corners. So other than the very last mile—retail distribution—consumer products were the purview of the powerful and large. The exceptional entrepreneurs who pushed through institutional and financial barriers to get a product to market were truly heroic.

Consumer products are physical items you can see and touch, so it's interesting to note that the main reason for the successful explosion of independent companies and brands over the last 20 years is something entirely invisible: the Internet. Technically, the World Wide Web was created by Tim Berners-Lee (a former neighbor of mine) in 1989. It became conveniently accessible to ordinary people in the mid-1990s with Marc Andreessen's creation of the web browser Mosaic (later Netscape.) That's when I jumped on the bandwagon and joined a startup that scoured early bulletin boards and user groups to glean actionable consumer insights for consumer brands. (There was no Google or other easy way to search for those kinds of conversations and comments online.)

I also became a very early adopter of e-commerce for a great variety of household purposes—driven by both curiosity and the steamrolling time pressures of balancing a career and the needs of three young sons. At the time, my otherwise modern friends were asking me, "Do you really trust getting food and furniture online? Why do you use e-mail? It seems like a pain in the neck." But by 1999 these conversations were largely in the rearview mirror with the dot-com boom roaring and broad participation across personal and professional landscapes spreading.

That's the superficial consumer side of Internet and broadband penetration. Here's why the underground game started changing for product Makers, too: the Internet represents access to the keys to the castle—knowledge previously hidden behind college degrees, large companies, professional subscriptions, societies, and artifacts like industrial component directories. All the know-how and easy access to resources of the Internet became long-overdue fuel to the fire of creative people. A proxy for this expansion in access to creating innovation is patent applications. Since 2002 global applications have grown exponentially, and 2016 set a record with over 3 million applications submitted.[1] China represents the lion's share of applications, with the United States a distant second, but the European Patent Office also reflects a massive 40 percent growth—the biggest increase since 1982.

It is hard to overstate the impact of an aspiring entrepreneur being able to Google "U.S. toothpaste use" or "pet product sales trends," rather than going to the library to scour microfiche of government market data. Compare tapping YouTube to figure out how to use Arduino (easily programmable electronic components)

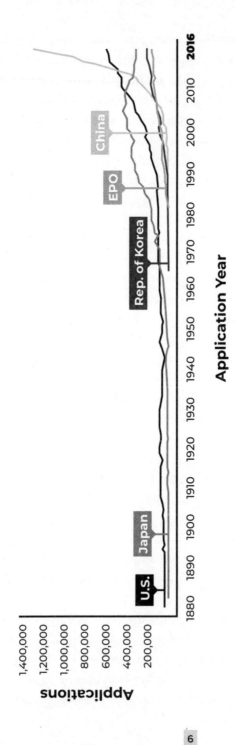

Figure 1.1 Trend in Patent Applications for the Top Five Offices

Note: The IP office of the Soviet Union, not represented in this figure, was the leading office of the world in terms of filings from 1964 to 1969. Like Japan and the U.S., the office of the Soviet Union saw stable application numbers until the early 1960s, after which it recorded rapid growth in applications filed.

Source: World Intellectual Property Indicators 2017 Patents, http://www.wipo.int/edocs/pubdocs/en/wipo_pub_941_2017-chapter2.pdf

instead of going through your Rolodex to find an electrical engineer to help you. Imagine using the Yellow Pages to find a packaging vendor—where you would be restricted to the businesses in your local community—versus using a search engine. For every single business function of a startup there are massive and often superb resources just a few clicks away. The Internet enabled a panoply of new businesses to form around the Maker Movement, too—much like the gold rush birthed the sellers of blue jeans and picks for gold prospectors. And these businesses, along with free information sources, replace what used to be thousands of road miles, work hours, and investment dollars required just to have a first attempt at a new competency or supplier.

The best statistics for illustrating the flood of independent products reaching the market are coming out of the CPG (consumer packaged goods) arena because grocery and drug store brands have always had historically better market share tracking than fashion, tech, or most other product categories. Ryan Caldbeck, the founder of the CPG investment fund CircleUp, succinctly summarized the salient trends in a 2018 tweetstorm:

> In almost every category large brands [are] losing market share to small brands because 1) consumers are demanding products that meet their unique needs, 2) marketing costs [are] switching from fixed to variable, 3) direct distribution [is] becoming more important. Net = higher demand and lower barriers.

Caldbeck continued, "At the same time, large brands are spending almost nothing on R&D. They don't have a pipeline of innovation. They have 50–100 years of R&D-less cultures. Big CPG spends too much on marketing. So you have stale incumbents pumping [millions] into marketing the same products they've sold for 50 years. BTW—kudos to @KITKAT for evolving their tagline from 'Have a break' (1960s) to 'Gimme a Break' (now). Impressive."

Figure 1.2 Seismic Shift in Market Share

Source: CircleUp, Ryan Caldbeck

Caldbeck concludes by illustrating both the market size for consumer products and the rising opportunities for smaller enterprises to be great investments because they have a growing opportunity to be bought by the moribund incumbents seeking a competitive edge and faster speed to market. "Big CPG outsources innovation because they aren't nimble enough to do it themselves. They buy the innovation. Last year the M&A market was >$310 billion. That's with a B. And did I mention this market is absolutely massive? >$15 trillion. That's with a T. Zoom out: So you have one of the largest industries in the world (CPG), with stale incumbents that are losing market share and can't innovate."

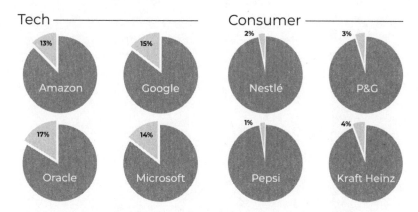

Why does this matter? Big consumer companies are slow to adapt to changing consumer tastes because they spend so little on researching what those tastes are. More investment in R&D could actually save Big CPG a lot of money in the long run because it could keep them from having to pay hundreds of millions to acquire upstart consumer brands.

Figure 1.3 Research and Development Spending as a Percentage of Annual Net Revenue

Source: CircleUp, Data from 2017 10K forms

In today's connected world, entrepreneurs in any field have unprecedented access to market information that can set them up for seizing this kind of opportunity so starkly illustrated in the consumer packaged goods arena. Simply tracking digital news, setting alerts, and participating in streamed events and meetups makes gaining expertise a credible activity.

In parallel to the product development malaise of too many big brands, many powerful technical advances appeared, such as CAD (computer aided design), digital manufacturing tools and online assembly, and additive manufacturing (3D printing.) The first large crowdfunding site, Indiegogo, was founded in 2008, and it and Kickstarter started really gathering steam by 2011. Marketplaces like Etsy (2005) and The Grommet (2008) provided new options for reaching a valuable audience. At every step in the product creation journey, resources have been getting both cheaper and more

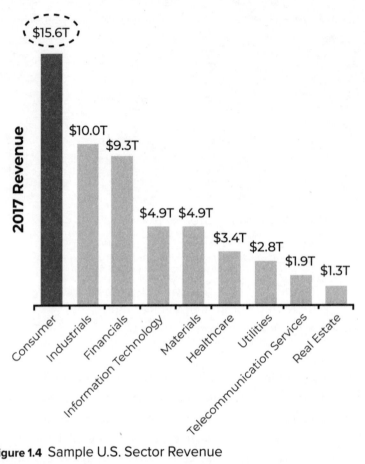

Figure 1.4 Sample U.S. Sector Revenue

Source: CircleUp, Ryan Caldbeck

accessible. These technology trends, along with a massive parallel interest in entrepreneurship, have created the Maker Movement.

Former *Wired* magazine editor Chris Anderson sums it up well:

> I would argue that there have been two major industrial revolutions, with the third one emerging now. The first industrial evolution was about mechanisation; replacing muscle power with machine power and amplifying human productivity by letting machines do the

work. The second industrial revolution was arguably the computer revolution. But it wasn't the invention of computers. It was their democratisation; putting them in the hands of everybody with the PC and the Internet that unleashed a huge amount of talent, energy and creativity which was transformative. The third industrial revolution is just a combination of the first two: it's the Web revolution meets manufacturing.

The reason that this is even more transformative than the Web is simply that the world of physical stuff is bigger than the world of digital stuff. The manufacturing economy is much bigger than the information economy. And if those same social forces that transformed the world through the Web can be applied to physical goods, you would see tremendous social impact.[2]

I am writing this chapter from the porch of the gracious Magnolia Hall at the Savannah College of Art and Design. Beyond being impossibly atmospheric, it's an inspired place to write because John Berendt wrote *In the Midnight Garden of Good and Evil* here. But the location has an even greater significance for me. This is my second visit, my first being in 2009 when SCAD was the place where I first saw 3D printers in a design school setting. It is where I spied the tireless machines—available at $15 per hour to happily chug out student concepts—and knew I was seeing the future. I was only one year into the development of The Grommet. It was an exhilarating but sobering time. The financial crisis was in full bloom, and I had bet my family's security and my career on two predictions: (1) that enough thoughtful and curious people would care about supporting innovative products from independent companies and (2) that there would be an explosion of great products from entrepreneurs. I saw those machines and I knew my instincts were right about this Maker Movement transformation that did not even have a name yet.

In taking my giant leap I was also betting on the simple enduring life force of human creativity. People have an age-old drive to solve problems, to invent, and to create. Because of my professional background I had a sense of the concurring sea change of opportunity for Makers and the expected obstacles. The range of resources for Makers advances every year by leaps and bounds. But this paradox of choice, in business as in life, can be paralyzing. This book will help you navigate those new opportunities and technologies, because even with great resources, you need to have a plan, to know the questions to ask, and to have real-life examples to illustrate the way. Welcome to your future—the one you can now create.

2

WHERE DO GREAT IDEAS COME FROM?

No company or client wants to produce products for yesterday, or even today. They want "Wayne Gretzky" outcomes—to create products that can fulfill where the demand is going. Every product originates from an idea. And great product ideas often exhibit an uncanny prescience for solving a problem, like the "I just want to make a single cup of coffee" solution provided by Nespresso. Sometimes breakthrough products create brand-new behavior the way Fitbit did when it made it a social norm to count steps. Other times new products simply add joy and beauty to a routine activity, just as Method did when it gave pump soap products a contemporary makeover.

So how are these ideas born? How do people who are not professional designers get started?

During my years working at Playskool, advising the company on a product line and packaging overhaul, a trial attorney friend told me he could never do my job, saying, "Sitting down to face a blank screen or piece of paper every day would scare the crap out of me. How do you make something from nothing? Where do you get your ideas?" He envisioned my workday as a mysterious process of actively seeking stop-in-your-tracks lightning bolt inspirations. I told him I could never imagine succeeding in his job, which I simplified down to "getting paid to argue in front of strangers all day." I told my Perry Mason friend that when you are employed to generate good ideas, you develop a definitive and predictable process for being creative. Today people call that process "design thinking."

I will save you the trouble of researching design thinking as an abstract concept and boil it down to its essence:

- **Identifying opportunity.** What is the business or customer area that needs attention? In the case of Fitbit, founders James Park and Eric Friedman saw an opportunity to help people improve their fitness with newfound access to individualized performance data. This breakthrough was made possible because of the advent of new, cost-effective miniaturized sensors.

- **Goals and constraints.** Setting goals for a new product is an iterative process as the entrepreneur learns more via research. But a product like Fitbit could start with a list such as: "This solution must cost less than $100. It has to be convenient to carry at all times. It must be water resistant. It must not interfere with normal daily activities."

- **Research.** Research involves studying the three Cs: customers, competition, and (internal) capabilities, as well as general cultural, social, technological, or natural trends that could influence the business or inform the product. For Fitbit the potential customer need was fairly vast: people who want to set and meet fitness goals. Investigation at the time of Fitbit's founding in 2007 would have yielded very little relevant competition, as existing solutions were cumbersome and required a customer to manually stitch together data from devices such as a pedometer, heart rate monitor, or calorie counter. Products that utilized the Internet to process data were barely emerging, such as SimpliSafe, an apartment security system that eliminated much of the cumbersome nature of existing services. Beyond technology advances, the founders could easily see that people were increasingly drawn to online communities and the gamification of ordinary activities—a big trend to draft off.

- **Ideation.** This involves conceiving and quickly visualizing various concepts (you often see a ream of exciting raw sketches highlighted in the visual history of a product). Some founders draw their own concepts, while others engage a designer at this stage, but fancy renderings are not advised at such an early step. The original Fitbit was a thumb-sized clip, but it is likely that all manner of devices were conceived, such as necklaces, bracelets, credit card–sized devices to fit in a wallet, shoe inserts, and the like. Even if many of these ideas were not technically or economically feasible, the goal during ideation is to cast as wide a net as possible.

- **Rough prototyping and feedback.** Rapidly and roughly prototyping concepts to get customer feedback comes next. Early-stage prototyping for a device like the Fitbit could be as simple as a nonfunctional foam version of a clip presented alongside a static set of graphic screenshots to show the type of data the device could collect. In other words, early prototypes help express the idea to a potential user without needing to be fully functional. Fitbit would have been looking for feedback on core *interest* in these new capabilities, as much as for feedback on form and function.

- **Advanced prototypes.** The entrepreneur repeats the last two steps enough times to commit to testable prototypes that help her lock down on a single idea. Advanced prototypes usually look like the real deal, even if they are not fully functional. But the more functional, the better.

There is nothing in that process that requires long walks on the beach, consuming hallucinogenics, or locking yourself in a dim room with Mozart playing. It's a rigorous and disciplined process you can do right in the middle of a fluorescent-lit office, or in your kitchen, or at a coffee shop. Anytime, anywhere.

There are two deep secrets to this process. Success lies not just in a designer's ability to generate concepts. First, great ideas are entirely hostage to the information and stimulation the designer (or aspiring Maker) gathers to provoke their gestation. In other words, it's all about the goals and research. You can think of this almost like cooking. The better the ingredients, the better the food. Ideas need to be fueled by great inputs.

For example, I was part of a consulting firm team that engineered the famous Reebok Pump shoe, which allowed a user to inflate an internal chamber for cushioning and support purposes. After its wild success we were subsequently engaged to propose ideas for shoes that could help a person jump higher. The research project included a huge range of athlete interviews and observations and then exploration of springy or reactive materials, mechanical systems, and natural systems. It even included the study of what enables the best rebounders on Earth—fleas—to jump 100 times their body height. (That would be like a person jumping over the Eiffel Tower.) Only after that wide-ranging exploration did our engineer, Eric Cohen, sit down and start sketching ideas.

The second critical building block to generating successful ideas actually precedes the research described above. As Eric explains it: "The first step is to define the problem you're trying to solve very clearly. The Harvard Business School professor Clayton Christensen calls this 'the job to be done.' This clarity then narrows down the field of possible solutions and brainstorming activities. If you just start brainstorming, you lack context for deciding which concepts are best. If you can clearly articulate the problem, often the solutions seem to magically appear and become obvious. But getting to that point of clarity is the real challenge."

In the case of step one, "identifying opportunity," Grommet Makers do not approach this step like an established business would. Why? Because they don't have an actual business just yet. They aren't noticing sales slipping, doing heavy R&D that yields opportunity, or responding to competitive threats. They are just going about their lives. As such, they tend to stumble into either (1) a problem that vexes them and needs solving or (2) an emerging technology or behavior that inspires them to improve it or apply it in a new area.

In fact, only 10 percent of Grommet Makers have any professional experience in the area where they end up building a product. In an interesting parallel, in my capacity as an entrepreneur in residence at Harvard Business School, I observe that a great number of the students pursue the well-known degree and credential as a giant, and admittedly expensive, career reset button. Makers often experience their businesses in much the same way. They throw over or work out of established careers to pursue an idea. The business is going to be epic in terms of effort and opportunity cost compared to other easier ways they might have collected a salary. But the idea becomes an itch that must be scratched, whatever the cost. The idea is often the fuel for all of the late nights, financial sacrifice, and occasional skepticism of friends and family.

CASE STUDIES

BluApple

Prior to the 1960s and during cold winter months, produce was often stored in warehouses that were heated with kerosene. The heat kept the fruits and vegetables from freezing before they were shipped to market. As heat sources evolved, these warehouses became equipped with electrical heating systems. With that change came a surprising consequence for growers and commercial produce shippers: the fruit wasn't ripening. It turns out that kerosene gives off ethanol gasses, which help speed the ripening process.

Without the kerosene, fruit could last a bit longer in transit and in warehouses. And with the discovery of the unique relationship between kerosene and produce ripening came an understanding of how to slow the ripening process as well. If the ethanol gasses released from produce could be captured or absorbed, fruit sitting in a bin or box would ripen less slowly. So the cucumbers, lettuce, and peaches sitting in your fridge could last a bit longer if only the ethanol gas could be absorbed by something other than that same fruit or vegetable.

You may have seen those "eggs" that go inside produce bins, the ones that keep fruit and veggies fresher longer. Eric Johnson was part of the company that developed the egg-shaped gadgets that worked the magic. Inside the egg was a combination of naturally occurring elements that slowed the absorption of the ethanol gases and therefore slowed the ripening process.

The only downside was that the egg wasn't very popular; the shape was throwing off consumers. People were returning the eggs to the store, thinking they had mistakenly bought an Easter decoration. But Johnson knew there had to be interest in the actual function of the egg. He had hoped that the company would reconsider its design, but when that didn't happen, Johnson and his now cofounder and partner, Timmy Chou, started BluApple.

Johnson says he knew the components of the product—potassium permanganate, a bit of water, and volcanic ash—were essential: "It's a product everyone needs and no one knows about." Johnson and Chou designed their gadget as a small blue apple "because it's odd enough that it stands out. Your mind doesn't come across that very often," says Johnson. It's something people easily remember, and it certainly can't be confused with an actual fruit. Plus, Johnson says, "the apple is an iconic symbol, one that represents life, freshness, and growing."

Launched in 2009, BluApple is now in major retail stores such as the Container Store, Albertsons, and Bed Bath & Beyond, and in more than a thousand smaller shops that sell housewares. They sell nationwide in the United States, as well as in Canada and Australia. Johnson says the company is expanding internationally. "We do best where people are actually shopping," says Johnson, explaining that when people are rushing through a grocery store with a quick list they are less likely to stop and browse and consider a new product. Online sales are also growing. Johnson says the company started with just the simple BluApple and has grown to include other produce storage solutions. "We're looking for things in the same space; that is fruit and veggie storage," adds Johnson. The company is working on four other products to launch in the next few years.

Peeps

A self-described serial entrepreneur, Daniel Patton was working in the optic industry and knew about a carbon-based technology developed by NASA that was responsible for cleaning the camera lenses at the International Space Station. In space, it's impossible to use sprays because of zero gravity, low temperatures, and the fact that cloths often damage lenses. The technology became essential as standard cleaning options were a liability at best. If you destroy a lens in space, you're in pretty big trouble.

Working on product development within the optical industry, Patton knew there had to be a way to take the same technology developed by NASA and bring it to the everyday eyeglass wearer.

There hadn't been a lot of changes in the optical cleaning world in about 30 years. After much research into how the carbon technology worked and how it could be translated into the consumer market, Peeps was born: it cleans glasses and lenses perfectly without any scratches, smudges, or the need for wiping away a wet solution.

The product was launched at the end of 2016 and is sold in nearly 30 countries and is considered the number one eyeglass cleaner sold in optical practices in the world, according to Patton. "The industry really supports us," he adds. Peeps is in more than 12,000 stores and thousands of Walmart Vision Centers.

The company is working with luxury brand eyewear companies for co-branding opportunities. And they can customize the Peeps product to match fashion glasses in texture and design. "Our revenue is in the 10s of millions annually," says Patton. The company later added mobile cleaning products: a small device to clean the screens of iPhones, laptops, iPads, and more. While Peeps has been exploding, Patton says the team is working more on marketing the newer device cleaner.

Nuheara

David Cannington had been an executive at Sensear, a hearing technology company that specialized in industrial headsets, the sort that looks like earmuffs with large coverings over each ear and a bulky headband. Only this one was unique because the headset blocked out loud industrial noise and amplified the relevant sound. The technology enabled people in industrial zones to remain situationally aware because dangerous and distractingly loud noises were filtered out.

The main customers of this product were mining, oil, and gas companies. The users were people in rugged, high-noise environments. "When we put this on people's heads, they could not believe it," says Cannington. "They said, 'I want to wear this in my personal life.'"

That's where the idea for Nuheara originated. Cannington quickly left his first company and created a new one, based in Australia and San Francisco. "We really did start the company to make an impact on people's lives." To him, it was just about selling to different consumers for a different reason. Nuheara consumers are primarily people with mild hearing loss, and the product enables them to separate speech from background noise. The other audience is people who simply love new technological innovations and want great earbuds.

"It makes an immediate improvement in your life," says Cannington. "There's a pretty compelling wow aspect." This was something Cannington saw firsthand while working on industrial headsets, so he knew the interest and the appeal of the product was there. He simply wanted to convert that big, bulky headset into earbuds, a complicated process. The first prototype for Nuheara was made in January 2016, and the product went to market in 2017.

Nuheara launched with one earbud and by April 2018 had brought to market a second version. The latest product allows users to do their own hearing assessment, and the buds adjust accordingly. There is an internal calibration system. "It's a huge evolution in the sophistication of wireless earbuds," says Cannington.

The company has taken off, and Nuheara is sold around the world, including in well-known shops such as Brookstone and Best Buy and through Amazon. The earbuds are also available through audiology clinics, and Cannington says they are constantly in talks to help expand into new markets. As for growth, the founder thinks constantly about ways to improve technology and user experience. "We have to continue to bring new hearing experiences to our audience."

EDUCATING THE NEW ENTREPRENEUR

When I read Walter Isaacson's book on Steve Jobs, I delighted in learning one simple insight about Jobs: his methodology for starting difficult projects. I had imagined Jobs as an obsessively focused and solitary genius who pursued new ideas in isolation. Instead he began every project by finding experts to teach him about the new area he was entering. He was an energetic and enthusiastic student, and he consistently asked for help from other people, especially at the outset of a project. He said, "Most people never pick up the phone and call and that's what separates, sometimes, the people who do things and the people who just dream about them."[1] This revelation changed my understanding of Steve Jobs because he displayed an efficient and highly social playbook that anyone can borrow when entering new territory.

The fundamentals of his "just ask" playbook will make you successful too. In fact, you can likely lap Jobs because it is a far easier time to educate yourself today than it was in his time. The young Steve Jobs could only dream of the educational tools that are available to anyone with an Internet connection. Like Makers of earlier eras, he was limited to the scope of (1) traditionally published resources, (2) his personal and professional network, and (3) his ability to laboriously research and uncover expert sources outside his network. But Jobs was exemplary in his boldness—famously calling Bill Hewlett, cofounder of Hewlett-Packard, when he was only 12 years old, asking for spare parts and landing a summer job.[2]

One of the reasons that so many new and unexpected Makers are emerging is that combining old-fashioned chutzpah with tech-enabled resources speeds up the entrepreneur's education and ability to execute. Here's a simple example of how the game has changed. When Ben Cohen and Jerry Greenfield started building their eponymous ice cream company, they wrote to the Small Business Administration and bought a variety of how-to pamphlets (which cost about 25 cents apiece) and dutifully followed the prescriptions for activities such as creating a financial plan or looking for good real estate sites.[3] Obviously, it worked, but the pace of their progress had to be glacial. Today the SBA's vast resources are available at the end of a few keystrokes.

Before you start asking *anyone* for *anything*, you need to do some basic research from the comfort of your own couch or chair. Below are the first-step resources to give you a working knowledge of just about any topic, technology, company, or person.

- **Google** (google.com): The omniscient Google has become everyone's go-to place to start for basic information, resources, and articles on just about everything.

- **Quora** (quora.com): An online question and answer site that allows users to post and answer in real time. With 100 million monthly visitors, the site is a great place to get crowdsourced answers and discover the pros and cons of anything you can imagine.

- **Wikipedia** (Wikipedia.com): This free online encyclopedia is a great place to get background details, dates, or a general understanding of a company or person. Not all information on Wikipedia is verified, so it's best to use it as a jumping-off point or to discover original articles, which are listed in the Reference section.

Once you have your first blush questions answered, you will find yourself in need of the type of *people* Steve Jobs tapped. You will have learned which organizations or people have the keys to the castle in terms of resources or knowledge. Now your job is to get to them. One way to find those people is to attend a trade show in the area of interest for your business. Susan Tynan, founder of the online framing service Framebridge, was making the leap to a man-ufacturing business—an industry about which she knew nothing. One of her first steps was to attend a framing industry trade show. To this day, a few years into her business, some of the people she met at that first show represent her best suppliers.[4] Eileen Fisher tells a similar story about how she moved from "I want to design a line of clothing" to "I want to make it a business." She made her first great strides by going to a trade show for small fashion design houses sell-ing to boutiques.

Imagine trade shows as a friendly, live version of an encyclope-dia. These events have long aisles of booths staffed by people ready and eager to explain their products and share their expertise. Ide-ally, you want to approach and ask questions when a booth is not too busy. Be honest about your research. If the people in the booth have paying customers competing for their attention, politely ask for a card and follow up later with a second visit or e-mail.

When I was forming the idea for The Grommet, one of my biggest concerns was figuring out the production capacities of embryonic companies that we sought to feature. I had built a basic (really, really basic!) financial model that proved we could have a scalable business if the average company we featured could supply 1,500 units in the first 30 days. But I had to test the reasonability of that number. So I went to the MIT campus for a local holiday fair where a mix of manufactured and crafted products from small local companies was being sold. I found the most manual and laboriously produced product on display and asked the Maker, "If I gave you a couple of months' notice, what is the maximum number of units you could produce?" She pondered and then answered, "600." I knew that if she could make that many of her handcrafted products, a manufacturer would not blink at 1,500. We had a business!

Let's say you've done some desk research, and you may have attended a trade show or two. But you still have huge gaps in knowledge or need specific resources, professional services, or mentors. Run, do not walk, to LinkedIn. This business-oriented social networking service represents the fastest way to build and grow a network of contacts and community. Its power cannot be overstated. I should know. I was president of a social network that competed with it, and lost.

Buy a LinkedIn Premium Account. It's worth it.

Having access to a robust professional network is half the battle. The other half is how you use it. When I worked in large corporations, I usually had the resources and expertise I needed at hand, and if not, I could usually buy the information and services required. It's a topsy-turvy, humbling new world when you become an entrepreneur and you have none of that. Virtually everything you need is outside of your immediate control, and you have little to no ability to pay. So your top skill becomes asking for help, often through expert networking. Don't think of networking as that sales guy in a cheap suit collecting business cards. Sincere, real-world networking is simply finding people whose expertise you respect and asking them to share a bit of it. Expert networking is also fundamentally a two-way street—you have to have something to offer to the person you are tapping. And you do. People get energy from hearing about new ideas or helping up-and-comers. Done right, you will rarely be turned down.

The best networker I know is Mike Troiano of G20 Ventures. He is generous with his time, his contacts, and his insights. I will never forget him making a very valuable introduction for me after our very first meeting. He says he thinks of business relationships (he hates the word *networking*) as working much like the beginning of *The Godfather*. In that first scene, Vito Corleone has to school a supplicant in the art of asking and giving favors. Vito makes sure that the asker knows that if and when he complies with the request, then his guest will owe him. My friend Mike's stock in trade is not in any way related to organized crime, but he explains that the core principle is the same: "Someone who builds a great network is someone who has done a great deal of kindness for other people. They don't do it to build up debts, but people owe them and will happily repay a kindness."

Obviously, when you are reaching out to a stranger you are a bit on the back foot, but you can still succeed if your outreach is done right. When I network for help via LinkedIn or other online resources, I deploy my tried-and-true playbook. Highest and best, I try to get an introduction via a friend or acquaintance who is linked to the person I need to know. (Remember, giving you an introduction means your friend is tapping his or her own social capital—do not use it lightly and be ready to repay.) I am extremely disciplined in building my LinkedIn network—adding people I meet in my travels so I can get back in touch with them later. And the Kevin Bacon six degrees of separation factor means about half the time when I need to reach out to a stranger I can get an introduction from someone I know.

A key tactical point is I only ask my contacts to make introductions to people *they* really know well. The quality of the actual relationship has a lot to do with both their comfort about reaching out and the likely success. Well-matched intros usually work, but I have to admit I was pretty shocked with a recent failure. I wanted to have a prominent CEO review this book because it is extremely relevant to his business and his customers. I studied all our mutual contacts and asked an even *more* accomplished business executive for the intro. She gladly complied. The first CEO passed on the connection, saying he was too busy and had to focus. She persisted, and he still put up the proverbial hand. This rarely happens to me. Not because I am such a hot ticket, but because I have a great network I use thoughtfully. What the rejection-happy CEO does not understand is that he was disappointing our mutual acquaintance more than me, only a stranger. He really dissed *her*. This is a big faux pas. She will be very hesitant to help him when he needs her. And he will. (Geez, I sound like a business mobster with this ominous prediction. But I believe it.)

These behaviors matter in your personal life, too, and can have unexpected influence on your professional reputation. One of my favorite yoga teachers was excited to be making her first trip to Dublin. She was a little intimidated about touring the new city by herself, and she enthusiastically accepted my offer to introduce her to a local Irish friend. I made all the connections. My Dublin friend cleared some time. But the yogi never followed up, despite my pinging her. A few months later when my company was looking to hire a yoga teacher to provide a weekly evening class, I had to reluctantly pass on offering the job to the no-show. She lost my trust.

But let's say you haven't yet rocked LinkedIn, and your business network is just getting started. I get requests all the time from people I don't know, and about one in 10 crafts a message that elicits my response. I want you to be the one in 10.

The keys are:

- Using real, textured language that makes you sound human and also shows that your message is tailored to an individual and not a form letter

- Being brief—long messages signal a time-wasting person

- Showing you did your homework and are not asking for information you could find on your own

- Having a clear ask

Here's an example. I once wanted to meet a Boston-based CEO with whom I had zero connections. I wanted to get an informational interview. I was living in Dublin and read about him when the *New York Times* Sunday magazine did a cover story on his business. He revealed that he was considering opening an office in London, and I knew that would mean I could easily meet him during one of his visits to the U.K. (Airline tickets often went for as low as $15!) But I also thought writing from Ireland to someone in the United States would seem kind of random. The CEO came across as a quirky, funny guy, so the first line of my e-mail was, "I am not a nutcase." I quickly went on to explain who I was and what I wanted (a meeting). I don't recommend doing risky and attention-getting openers, but I had done my research on this man and was pretty sure it would land the right way. It did. I met him in London a couple of weeks later.

Here's a template of a compelling message that nearly always gets a positive response from strangers:

Dear Ms. Company CEO,

I am so inspired by all of your accomplishments at XXX, especially how you have done [name something specific that is fairly current.]

I am in the early stages of building a company to do XYZ. I am making a leap from my current career as a dog catcher to a whole new field, and I am reaching out to you to advance my business knowledge. My profile is here. [Insert your LinkedIn URL—you need to give the person comfort in your sincerity and truthfulness.] I have scoured all I can about your work from a distance, and I still have questions about A and B. I suspect you can answer my questions very easily and would greatly appreciate the chance to have a 15-minute phone call.

I can propose a few times over the next month for a brief call. I promise not to waste your time.

Warmly,

Your name here

P.S. [Put those suggested times in a P.S. just to keep things moving.]

Through every "cold" message or phone call to a stranger you should be working very hard to establish your credibility and make it seem really easy for the person to help you. A 2015 Harvard Business School study illustrated that people who ask for help are perceived as more competent,[5] so don't let your own insecurities stop you. Simply asking makes you smarter.

Just as you would not go into a school exam without reading the course material, you are in a massive student phase at the very beginning of your business. Although it never really ends, the early weeks and months are a fun phase of dedicated exploring that can really open up your understanding of the business world and expand your network at the same time.

CASE STUDIES

BRUW

A high school kid who loved coffee, Max Feber one day was reading a novel that featured cold brew coffee. His interest was piqued, and Feber decided to give it a try at home. After researching how to cold brew online and watching a few YouTube videos, Feber experimented in his kitchen. Although it seemed simple enough—grind the coffee, steep it in cold water, filter out the grinds—it turned out to be a total mess. "I thought there had to be a better way," says Feber, who was just 15 years old at the time. So he started trying various methods that people claimed were the best, but he wasn't wowed. That was when he decided to try making his own mechanism for cold brewing.

Out in his garage Feber got a hot glue gun and some Mason jar lids and rigged together a filter-type gadget. While Feber was tinkering with the idea of making his own cold brew filter, he was simultaneously given an assignment in one of his high school classes to create a prototype and pitch it to the class. Feber said it was completely coincidental with his foray into entrepreneurism, and the class helped him think through some of the steps more quickly than he might have.

When he considered manufacturing his filter, he turned to his father, who had worked in the plastics industry and was able to connect him with some engineers. One was particularly helpful and worked with him to translate his ideas into a 3D design so it could be made into a prototype.

Feber taught himself all he could about plastics so he would be able to communicate with the manufacturer. And since he couldn't drive yet, he had his mom drop him off at the factories near Detroit, where he's from, to meet with manufacturers. When he needed to come up with a logo, he taught himself all he could about graphic design, too.

For Feber, research was key when it came to figuring out how to turn his idea into a product. He launched his idea on Kickstarter in November 2015, raised just over $10,000—more than his goal—and started manufacturing in January 2016. Since then Feber says he's sold tens of thousands of units, and he's pushing for more. He's working to get BRUW into more stores and has begun talks with a few big-box ones. BRUW sells through

Amazon, The Grommet Wholesale, and on Feber's own site. Most sales come from online, although BRUW is in many small boutiques. "We're finding people through social media," adds the founder. Feber is looking to add products "that will help the customer" and is considering some new, unusual uses for discarded coffee grinds. "There's a certain person who will always be thinking of new ideas," says Feber, about himself.

The Butterie

When Joelle Mertzel was at her friend's house, she noticed there was butter sitting out on the counter. "Why isn't your butter in the fridge?" she asked. Mertzel always hated hard-as-rock butter that was impossible to spread. You know, the kind that rips the bread as you try to spread it from edge to edge.

"So you keep your butter out?" Mertzel asked. "For how long?" She learned that her friend always kept her butter out. Mertzel was intrigued. She started leaving her butter out, too. It was sort of revolutionary to have soft, ready-to-spread butter any time of day.

Except the traditional butter container, the one with the lid shaped like a stick of butter that always ends up covered in butter, was annoying. It was greasy and far from attractive.

Mertzel thought she could come up with something much better; she was thinking of a ceramic dish that could be on the counter, wouldn't need to be put away, and would look nice enough to be brought straight to the table. That was assuming it was hygienically acceptable to leave butter out and that people—all across America—would adopt the practice.

First, Mertzel knew she had to find out if there was any scientific reason not to keep butter out. Did it actually have to be refrigerated? She went to the Food Safety Lab in Los

Angeles—there are many all over the country, but this one was close to her home—and enlisted its services. Mertzel went to the supermarket and bought lots of butter, drove it to the lab, and had scientists test the butter for shelf life. She brought a variety of brands, organic butter, and even margarine.

The lab tested the butter when it was initially brought in and then every 24 hours after that for bacteria, mold, yeast, and rancidity. Mertzel kept waiting to hear that the butter had gone sour, but nothing seemed wrong about keeping the butter unrefrigerated. At Day 23 the tests showed "some tiny little somethings popping up" on the butter. "Great," thought Mertzel. "We'll call it 21 days, or three weeks."

With her research complete, Mertzel just had to convince potential customers that you don't have to refrigerate butter. By her estimate, half of America needed convincing. Mertzel launched the Butterie in January 2016 and since then says, "I've been moving the needle in the kitchen. People can enjoy soft butter anytime."

The Butterie is selling in more than 1,000 Bed Bath & Beyond stores, was featured in the *New York Times*, and has launched in more than 500 Ace Hardware stores. "Enjoy Soft Butter Anytime" is promoted on the front of every Butterie box, and on the back there is a message that goes into further detail about the scientifically proven shelf life. Mertzel is working to grow the Butterie's distribution and has some plans to launch additional products. But for now, her dream is that instead of saying, "Please pass the butter," people will one day say, "Please pass the Butterie."

Force of Nature

While working at Boston-based razor company Gillette, Sandy Posa had come across technology that created electrolyzed water. It was a cleaning and disinfecting solution that had a commercial use. Only the equipment used to make the water came with a nearly $20,000 price tag. Posa was intrigued and even tried to buy the company that was making it. When that didn't work out, he decided to design a consumer product that would feature electrolyzed water as a cleaning product.

Posa says the science—which is a combination of vinegar, salt, and water that is processed at a low level of electricity—was well documented about the benefits and uses of electrolyzed water. The solution is a powerful disinfectant, without any dyes or unnatural, harmful ingredients. It had been invented in the 1950s but was a new and revolutionary idea as a consumer product. Posa says he wanted to be able to present this product as something that was just as effective as bleach but without any of the chemicals or harmful side effects. He knew it was a bit of an uphill battle since no one had heard of it.

First, he'd need proof of all of his claims. Posa took the electrolyzed water to a lab for testing. He needed to know if it killed bacteria, mold, and viruses. It did. Then he had a third-party lab test for whether it cleaned as well as anything else on the market, including Windex, 409, and Lysol. It cleaned as well as if not better than those products. "We checked that box," says Posa. And then he had it tested for killing odors, and it did that, too. At that point, Posa had to figure out the rest, including manufacturing, pricing, and how to educate the consumer.

Force of Nature hit the market in the spring of 2016. "We have a big, audacious goal: it's to eliminate unhealthy cleaning products from homes and businesses," says Posa. "We are in the very early stages of doing that." At the point that the cleaning system had been on the market for just two years, Posa said there were 50,000 users. "We want it to be millions in the next few years."

All Force of Nature sales originate online—through the company's website, The Grommet, and Amazon. Posa says the company's next strategy is to work into new markets around the country, including senior centers and restaurants as well as internationally. The company has raised capital for a next-level marketing push and for continuing to develop new products.

Orange Mud

"I like to run, but I hated carrying a hydration pack," says Josh Sprague, founder of Orange Mud. The water packs were always sloshing too much, bouncing uncomfortably, causing blisters and chaffing. You name it, they never really worked. As a runner and participant in many multisport events, Sprague would often find himself staring at people's backs for miles on end while running behind them. He noticed that there is a lot of movement in the body while running, except for high up on a person's back between the shoulders. "You don't move much there," says Sprague. That's why he decided to try to create a hydration pack that would rest on the high back between the shoulders.

Sprague went home and started putting together his first prototype from a fanny pack, bottle rack, and gun holster. He sewed together his vision of the first Hydro Quiver, an actual product that launched in 2012. "We've grown a ton," says Sprague. "Every year has been enormous." Orange Mud launched with that one hydration pack and now has 80 SKUs. Some include T-shirts, but others are hydration systems, quick dry towels, and other sporting equipment. Sprague says that about 70 percent of sales come from online, and about 15 percent from international markets. They're in 15 countries as well as 400 small retail shops around the United States.

Orange Mud sells on Amazon as well. "They take 18 percent, but they cover the hassles," he says, referring to shipping, returns, and payments. Sprague designs everything himself and is constantly working on new ideas and products for the company.

4

TAPPING ESTABLISHED EXPERTISE

Let's say you've done enough research and networking to validate your business idea, and you've gotten started. Now you are looking to move to the next gestation phase of the business, during which you will pursue a variety of product development and business activities simultaneously. It's a phase in which it is hard to see around corners and anticipate what must be done or where the hidden pitfalls of your chosen path will be. It's a phase in which it is easy to stall out or overfocus on one area.

Phone calls, meetings, and Google alone are not enough for this stage. Instead, this is the time to try to build reliable, accessible sources of expertise. Of course some of that can be assembled through a constant trawling of publications and gatherings that represent people pursuing relevant ventures. For instance:

- **Maker Media** (makermedia.com): The team behind Maker Faire publishes information to help Makers share ideas, build community, and introduce new technologies.

- **Maker Faire** (makerfaire.com): Created by *Make:* magazine, these events are part science fair, part crafts fair, with DIYers who are branching into arts, engineering, and crafts.

- **Meetup** (meetup.com): A social networking site that enables members to join in-person or online groups around the world. Members can find others with common interests and tap into knowledge and expertise either locally or virtually.

If you still crave more assistance and expertise (and you will), here are some relatively new and vibrant sources to fill this need:

- Maker and hacker spaces

- University startup labs and incubators

- Libraries

- Business accelerators and incubators (general)

- Hardware accelerators (dedicated to physical products)

- Custom advisory boards or peer groups

MAKER AND HACKER SPACES

Think about the typical private health club. You go there to get fit or stay fit. It's membership based. For your fees, you gain access to expensive and up-to-date equipment, staff to supervise and facilitate your visit, private training instructors, group classes, and a like-minded community of people who are there for a similar purpose.

This is exactly what Maker and hacker spaces are, except the goal is to create a project or viable commercial product, using the professional level of resources housed under one roof. They can help you prototype a product, learn new skills, meet like-minded people, and take some of the steps to start your business.

For example, Peachtree City, Georgia, has Creative Fuel Studio, to which one can purchase an unlimited six-month membership for $300. This gives a member access to classes and equipment to learn woodworking, CNC routing, and 3D printing. Master Maker Gregg Lehman runs the studio and says, "We are one of 14 small Maker spaces in Georgia, and part of the Southeast Makers Alliance."

These spaces have become so mainstream and accessible that the furniture retailer West Elm covered the phenomenon on its company blog: "In upstate New York, Etsy cofounder and former CEO Rob Kalin recently started The Catskill Mill, a community of ceramicists, woodworkers, leatherworkers and textile artisans all under one roof in a former furniture factory. In San Francisco, a group of feminist activists founded Double Union to support women within the Maker movement. In Nashville, Fort Houston is an incubator for 70 local artists and designers—it even includes a motorcycle shop! And in Portland, design destination Beam & Anchor reserves its second floor studios for local designers and craftspeople. The common thread between all these organizations is an interest in sharing space and knowledge to help grow local economies."[1]

Some of the spaces are commercial, for-profit enterprises. Others are subsidized by corporations, foundations, or municipalities to foster local entrepreneurship. Their models are so wide and diverse that they can be hard to decode. For instance, the nonprofit Ponyride in Detroit has a 30,000-square-foot urban space dedicated to "facilitating the growth of social missions within artists, entrepreneurs, makers, and nonprofits."[2] One of its more prominent "residents" is The Empowerment Plan, a nonprofit focused on creating jobs that lift people out of poverty. Its product is a "sleeping bag coat" designed for homeless people, made by 45 formerly homeless women. Since 2012, more than 30,000 of the coats have been distributed in 49 states and 10 Canadian provinces.

Also in Detroit, Jeffry Aronsson, a former luxury goods and fashion executive, is forming Treadwing, a fashion hub where

founders can find comprehensive resources for design manufacturing and marketing their lines. He was inspired by what Henry Ford
did in creating the legendary River Rouge complex, which handled
every aspect of car manufacturing from producing steel and glass
to assembly of final vehicles. At its peak, it employed 100,000 people
and is still in operation today.[3]

There are accelerators that also cater to certain populations,
such as women, students, or people of color. Bunker Labs is a
national nonprofit helping veterans, active-duty service members,
and their spouses start and grow businesses from the idea stage
when active-duty service members are thinking about what to do
post-service, to the growth stage when successful companies are
looking to hire, raise capital, and expand into new markets. One
of its portfolio companies is Rumi Spice, a Grommet we launched
with a team of veterans who had served in Afghanistan with the
U.S. Army. During their service in that country the four founder vets
saw an opportunity to grow and cultivate the world's best saffron
while providing farmers alternatives to growing Taliban-controlled
opium poppies. Rumi has since become the largest private sector
employer of women in Afghanistan.

These spaces and organizations are increasing, so the best way
to find a local one is to search online or refer to the ever-expanding
Hackerspaces wiki (https://wiki.hackerspaces.org/List_of_Hacker
_Spaces) that catalogs these endeavors across the world.

UNIVERSITY STARTUP LABS
AND ACCELERATORS

These facilities are just as diverse as Maker spaces. Their focus is
also to foster entrepreneurship but in a wider variety of forms, from
software to life sciences to social enterprises. Their typical constit-
uent focus is on staff, students, and alums, but they are increasingly
permeable and open to entrepreneurs with no affiliation. The first

port of entry for the general public is typically the frequent startup competitions that these labs and accelerators host. If you live near an institution of higher education, especially one that is publicly funded, don't assume that it is a walled garden. Successful ventures that spin out of these institutions are valued, and many of these schools have a commitment to giving back to their local communities through these activities.

Janet Napolitano, president of the University of California, says that at her institution "research has led to roughly 1,300 startups since 1968, three-quarters of which were launched since 2000, according to a new Bay Area Council Economic Institute report. In 2015, our research spawned 85 new startups and 1,756 new inventions. That's nearly five inventions a day."[4]

I grew up in a working-class neighborhood of Detroit and would never have imagined my alma mater, the University of Michigan, having a facility in my neighborhood. Yet, it is partnering with Detroit public schools to create the Brightmoor Maker Space as a give-back activity to help one of the most impoverished areas of the Motor City.

Universities and colleges have traditionally seen one of their central societal roles as being a provider of access to opportunity. Educational institutions are now extending that mission to Maker spaces.

LIBRARIES

Public libraries have been among the most ambitious entities to embrace the Maker movement. Because of their deep commitment to fostering learning in local communities, many library leaders naturally saw how this mission could extend to building and running Maker spaces. "MakerSpaces and the Participatory Library," a public Facebook group with over 4,000 members, is a good place to start to search for a library-based Maker space near you.[5]

BUSINESS AND
HARDWARE ACCELERATORS

Technology startups have long had the benefit of a vast array of established resources for tapping expertise. Startup incubators and competitive accelerator programs like Techstars and Y Combinator have been cloned and reproduced across the country and world. Until recently these programs tended to exclusively focus on software and core technology companies. When we started The Grommet in 2008, none of the conventional accelerators would consider companies that dared to make things. With the success of breakout companies such as Casper (mattresses), Warby Parker (eyeglasses), and SimpliSafe (security systems—and the first Internet of Things product launched by The Grommet), some startup accelerators have broadened their areas of interest to embrace companies creating a physical product.

These programs can help to accelerate your venture thanks to their established network of mentors and intense programming of educational events. They also provide the helpful catalyst of structured deliverables. Because they often provide shared office space and a local residency requirement, the program lets you focus exclusively on your venture. And many of these accelerators provide a legitimacy and demo day showcase that can provide a faster path to funding. If you consider applying to one of these programs, it's essential to study their list of mentors and past portfolio companies to ensure that they really do have a significant cohort of physical product expertise to help you. Just having local businesspeople signed up is not enough—look at their track records and specific expertise to make sure it is relevant to your business.

An offshoot of these accelerators is a smaller subset of them focusing exclusively on physical products. They call themselves "hardware" accelerators, carrying over the old computer industry term that distinguished the "boxes" from the software. Side note: this term makes me crazy. Would the average person who conceives of the next breakthrough consumer product featuring sleek industrial design or home-friendly materials really aspire to create a piece of "hardware"? Anyway, HAX, the world's first hardware accelerator, incubated its first teams in 2012. HAX can go further than some accelerators in sourcing offshore production because it is based in both San Francisco and Shenzhen, one of the consumer products manufacturing hubs of China, It has been fast followed by a number of other physical product accelerators.

Sculpteo, the Paris- and San Francisco–based 3D printing company, has started to publish an annual list of the "18 Best Hardware Accelerators" that is worth checking out.[6]

For a broader view on the performance of startup accelerators, there is a trio of university researchers out of Rice University and the University of Richmond who have been rigorously evaluating the various accelerators since 2014 and publishing their "Seed Accelerator Rankings" (www.seedrankings.com). This work focuses on the most prominent accelerators, of which 150 are invited to submit their data. This data is supplemented by additional research on their startups' survival rates, financial outcomes, and founder satisfaction with the accelerator programs. This information is like gold because that kind of insight is very hard to glean from the outside as a potential applicant.[7]

NETWORKS AND ADVISORY BOARDS

Among Grommet Makers, many have tapped into the resources described here. Others have carved an independent path and assembled a thoughtful network or advisory board to provide expertise and help create accountability. In addition, accelerator spots are very limited, so a founder cannot necessarily count on admission. A network is very different and more flexible than an advisory board. It simply means finding and engaging people who have expertise you need to advance the business. The art of this is in the finding, which leads back to the all-important art of asking. If you are efficient with their time, people in your network will readily share their expertise.

Advisory boards come in two flavors. The first and more common is to make your relevant advisory board publicly attached to the business. You see this especially in highly technical, educationally oriented, or regulated businesses (food, supplements, juvenile products, IoT) where a founder needs to borrow the credibility of scientists, engineers, doctors, and other industry experts. Sometimes these people do virtually nothing but offer to be on call and publicly attached to the business. But their association has value in itself, and the wise founder will of course ask them to help when and where they are needed.

An active advisory board is a bit more formal. You may ask the board to regularly assemble as needed or at a regular cadence such as quarterly. The advisors tend to have a mix of technical and general business expertise. Their association with the business is far more oriented to the inside operations of the business than to its public face. They advise on specific functions as well as help with recruiting of talent, fundraising, and business development. They tend to also get some form of compensation such as equity in the venture. Membership tends to be somewhat fluid with people cycling in and out as the business scales and the leadership team expands to cover the functions an advisor might have provided.

There are two words to the wise regarding relying exclusively on advisors. First, the main downside I have seen is that the commitment can be rather casual on both sides and can correlate to an overly slow pace for businesses that don't have the benefit of external deadlines and rigor. An ambitious and aggressive founder will still move quickly despite a relatively distant set of advisors and will work to create frequency of contact as well as accountability. A fast-moving founder will then find the second downside of an advisory board: a startup's advisory needs will change from year to year, so founders need to continually refresh their advisory circles and not give too much equity or other long-term commitments to advisors.

The core reason for any of the above opportunities is that building a business is a race against the clock. It's hard to get it to scale fast enough to survive the startup costs. Getting help from a "pit crew" in the form of accelerators, advisors, and other external experts makes you both more efficient and faster.

CASE STUDIES

Flic Button

Amir Sharifat, founder of Flic Button, had a mentor in Sweden who recommended that he check out a San Francisco–based incubator. In 2013, that was the place to be. Although Sharifat says the tech scene in Sweden is now booming, back then it wasn't. There were some startups and exciting things happening, but he didn't get a strong sense of community there. "We saw it was going to be valuable for us to get the connections and see how things are done," Sharifat says of being in San Francisco. He then applied, with his two other cofounders, to Highway1, a startup hardware incubator. They were further along than many of the startups chosen as Flic Button already had working prototypes.

Flic is a small Bluetooth-connected button that can be used as a shortcut for apps, devices, and to control your phone. With the click of the button you can turn on music, track a workout, make a call, set a time for tracking billable hours, and more. With the help of the incubator, Sharifat did a whole redesign of the product.

The Highway1 program was a four-month stint, which included two to three pitch sessions every week, a trip to China to visit suppliers, and constant hands-on assistance from mechanical engineers and electrical engineers. "It felt like being back in school," says Sharifat.

Highway1 brought in potential investors, partners, suppliers, crowdfunding campaigns, and industry leaders. Sharifat says about midway through the program, production engineers were brought in to talk about how to manufacture products as well. And all the while, Sharifat says he and his team were surrounded by other startups and entrepreneurs who became sounding boards.

While at Highway1, Sharifat also formed a relationship with some of the people at Indiegogo. He and his team were looking for a crowdfunding platform and liked that with Indiegogo you can go live instantly and you don't have to meet a certain fundraising goal.

Prior to launching on Indiegogo, Sharifat says his company had received a grant from the Swedish government, plenty of media attention, and social media traffic, and had gathered a long list of e-mails. Sharifat saw a big opportunity in reaching out to people through direct e-mail. He had a goal of collecting 100,000 e-mails before going live with the campaign. "The campaign is 80 percent what you do before the campaign and 20 percent what you do during the campaign," says Sharifat. By the time the founders launched they had nearly 40,000 e-mails and raised $150,000 on the very first day. Their goal had been $80,000. By the end of two months Flic Button was at $650,000. "It was of course, unbelievable."

As Sharifat says, "Any campaign that raises this much on Day 1 and 2 will get attention." And get attention it did. The company was on the front page of Indiegogo, was mentioned in e-mail blasts, and "millions of people are now seeing this."

Flic Button has been very successful ever since. "We went global from Day 1," says Sharifat. The product is most popular in the United States and Europe, and Sharifat says the company sells equally online and in retail stores. It launched with one product and now has three. Flic Button did a trial period in 500 Best Buy stores and did well with that, but Sharifat says it's expensive to stay in some of those larger stores, so it pulled out. Now it mainly sells through Amazon, b8ta—a new technology products site/popup store—and other tech sites. Flic Button generates substantial traffic to its own site and sells a lot business to business.

Sharifat says he and his team are always innovating and thinking about new things. The company recently invited customers into their office and asked what they would like as a next step or a next feature with Flic. Through this they came up with 30 new product ideas. Many of them had already been floated as possibilities internally, but Sharifat says it's a great way to hear new ideas and validate already established ones. The company will use much of this information to work on future products, he adds.

Cleverhood

After meeting the criteria for number of employees, years in business, and annual sales, Cleverhood, the maker of waterproof bike-friendly ponchos and rain gear, was selected to participate in the Goldman Sachs 10,000 Small Businesses program, an ongoing accelerator-style opportunity. Susan Mocarski, founder of Providence-based Cleverhood, says the high-quality professors who were brought in and the number of people "who are really dialed into the industry" were extremely helpful. It was time-consuming for sure, and Mocarski says there were rigorous accounting classes, something she wouldn't have had exposure to otherwise. "You just have to know so much," she says of starting a business, adding that she doesn't have a large math and accounting background. "That turned out to be the best part," adds Susan. "It made it more accessible."

Goldman offers the six-month program at various locations around the country. The one Mocarski was selected for was in Providence, not far from her home. With three full days a week, plus homework, the experience was intense, says Mocarski, who was one of 35 owners and CEOs selected to participate.

Mocarski launched her business in 2012 and participated in the Goldman program starting in the fall of 2016. She says participants stay connected with Goldman, which is committed to helping the fledgling entrepreneurs grow their businesses and to working with incubator participants long after the actual program is over.

Cleverhood has worked hard to keep its manufacturing in the United States and appeals to a specific demographic, mostly an urban biking crowd, says Mocarski. Cleverhood launched with one poncho and now has 26 SKUs. "We came to understand our buying audience is very specific." The rain gear does well in the United States, Canada, New Zealand, Germany, and the United Kingdom. Initially the company worked with retailers, but Mocarski said the products do better when they can be explained to the consumer, and that happens more effectively through online sales.

The company has mostly expanded in styles and colors and has added items of dog apparel as well. "As a smaller company you have to zig and zag," explains Mocarski of constantly being aware of your audience and determining their needs and wants and willingness to buy. The company has additional lines, including a trench jacket (which I cannot live without—it is my go-to travel outerwear) as well as styles for children and even dogs. "We keep touching on a deep lane but a narrow lane," says Mocarski about the target consumer audience. Cleverhood grew steadily 80 to 100 percent for the first few years and around 20 percent annually more recently, a pace with which Mocarski is quite happy.

Guardian Bells

Adam Hizme bet a stranger a coffee in a Starbucks that the New York Giants were going to lose a big game to the Arizona Cardinals. Instead, his team ended up losing. It was easy enough to find the winner of the coffee since the Giants fan was at Starbucks every morning along with a group of men. Hizme was invited to sit down with the group of eight—all ages, all backgrounds, but each with some significant experience in business. "There are some who have bought and sold huge companies. Some are young." Just around the corner from his Phoenix home, this is where Hizme goes most mornings.

It's been immensely helpful as Hizme has built his business, Guardian Bells. Anytime he's had issues or questions that come up, he can bounce ideas around with the group. As an entrepreneur who often works on his own and learns things as he goes, this has been invaluable. The group has been meeting for about 10 years, and Hizme says he can show up and just listen, offer advice, or ask for guidance.

Guardian Bells was launched in 2002 as Hizme saw a market for the pewter, bell-shaped charms with a variety of designs and symbols that were popular among motorcyclists and later the general public.

Fifteen years after launching his business, Hizme says his company now sells close to 650,000 bells each year in roughly 18 countries. "We battle with staying relevant and launching new products and designs," he adds. Because it's expensive to cast new bells—although with 400 different styles they are constantly doing so—Hizme says if the company ends up sitting with a design too long that hasn't sold, they will melt it down and start over.

Hizme says Guardian Bells routinely asks customers for input and takes their feedback on new designs. He keeps track of requests the old-fashioned way: by jotting down ideas and suggestions in a notebook. "That's my high-tech research and development," he says. About 60 percent of the company's sales are online, and he's always looking for new ideas; the latest is that Hizme is considering a machine that can engrave the bells for custom orders.

The Negg

Bonnie Tyler had been invited to a cocktail party and was planning to bring deviled eggs. Fed up with trying to peel all of the eggs, she figured there must be an easier way. But when she looked online and couldn't find a simple egg peeler for the home cook, she decided to make one. "I didn't start out to make hundreds of thousands of these," she says. "I just wanted one."

Tyler and her friend Sheila Torgan had been in business together before, teaming up in marketing and web development. The two set out to produce a consumer egg peeler. There are some industrial egg peelers out there, but they peel 40,000 eggs at once. Not exactly something you need in your home kitchen.

Tyler took a two-hour course at her local library in Connecticut to learn how to use a 3D printer. The instructor was 11 years old. Seriously. He was working on how to create a prosthetic hand and teaching others how to use the equipment as well. Torgan worked on the CAD drawings. Once the women were happy with what they had, they took the design to a local plastics manufacturer, near where they live in Connecticut.

When they first started out Torgan says she had 5,000 units of the Negg sitting in her garage. Since then they've sold nearly 300,000 units. "It's been a bit of a rocket ship ride," she says. They're selling on Amazon, through The Grommet wholesale division to get into retail shops, Ace Hardware, and more than 400 retailers across the country, including Sur La Table.

MARKET RESEARCH

We look at 300 new product ideas a week at The Grommet and have worked with more than 3,000 companies to help them get discovered. You could rightly say we have "seen it all." The one thing that makes me cringe is when a new entrepreneur pursues a product or business that has no market. We once saw a perfume promising to make women smell younger. I could be wrong—I did not do the market research—but that idea struck me as an uphill battle.

A common "too small market" entrepreneur is a new parent. Kids put us through a continuously changing cycle of fresh problems and challenges. These issues are often emotional and upsetting, so parents naturally seek product solutions for the sleeping/dressing/eating/bathing/traveling problem du jour. When no solution exists, they sometimes want to invent one. And therein lies the problem. Many "hair on fire" childhood problems last no more than a month or two. So even though there are *plenty* of parents in a target market, by the time they start seeking a solution, the problem is almost gone. That slice of life is just too narrow to support the potential solution.

Nothing I said indicates a problem with the product itself. The perfume probably does what it promises or at least smells wonderful. But is there a market for it? It would suffer from a lack of *accessible demand* if women do not know or believe that a perfume could make them smell younger. (And more than that, would enough women even care?) In other words, this perfume could be a solution looking for a problem. I expect it would cost more to find women who are willing to believe a perfume could make them smell younger than the typical startup company's budget could afford.

On the other hand, the kid problem-solver product could be remarkably effective. It could be the best solution in the world to a real problem. But the problem is too fleeting. The company or product would simply suffer from a very different lack of accessible demand.

Smart market research tends to divide into two categories. First, there is up-front research to assess the size of a target market. Second, there is research to determine customer responses to your concepts, prototypes, brand position, or packaging. To be fair, I rarely see would-be entrepreneurs do a thorough job on market sizing. And as I already said, this makes me cringe. Why? Because unless you are just looking for a side hustle, and not a full-time endeavor, building a small business will take you just as much effort as a big one. So go for a big market.

People skip this step for a variety of reasons. First, they think just talking to friends and family is good enough. It is *not*. Unless you are directly related to millions of people, friends and family will not be your full customer base. You need to talk to strangers who do not love you and will tell you the truth about their needs and desires and willingness to pay for your idea. The second and more valid reason people skip the market sizing research is that this task ranges from mildly difficult to almost impossible.

For instance, when I started The Grommet, I needed to understand the potential number of new products coming from small companies, as they would be one side of my marketplace. Try Googling for that number. You won't see anything credible or useful. The good news is I had enough specific market knowledge to be confident in the supply side of my business. The harder part was assessing the demand side. Would there be enough consumers who care about innovative products from small businesses to support The Grommet? This research was darned near impossible. I did learn that since 1980 the share of sales controlled by the 20 biggest manufacturers was on the decline.[1]

I knew that any survey would be flawed: people would express positive intent for independent products, but I really wanted proof via market data. But because our customer could be anyone, and because our product could be just about anything, market data was elusive. So I did my best. I used the staggering growth of farmers markets as evidence of an interest and willingness to pay for higher quality, locally relevant products. But I knew that buying locally grown lettuce was not a proxy for buying a better-designed dog toy, fitness product, or wine storage carafe. I was keying into the inconvenience, effort, and expense people were expending to buy at farmers markets as a leading indicator of interest in better products from small producers.

My lame efforts aside, if you are lucky enough to be considering a market with a good data trail, follow it. Start with Google Trends (www.google.com/trends). It provides the latest data and trends for search terms, allowing users to examine the popularity of subjects and interests. A friend of mine is considering creating a product to respond to the exploding new uses for home laser cutting machines. She did a targeted search for the brand names of the machines to help her understand how many people online are looking for the solution she is considering offering.

One of the most thorough (though impractical for most) approaches to market research I've ever seen was demonstrated by Lara Merriken, the founder of LÄRABAR, a popular raw fruit-and-nut energy bar product. She developed a personal interest in the category and discovered a wide-open gap in the market for simple whole-ingredient bars. But she had two problems: she was a social worker looking to change careers, and she knew nothing about the food business. She solved both problems elegantly by getting a job in the nutrition department of her local Whole Foods. She spent three years on the floor of the store learning about the business and her future customers, but also eating humble pie when her high school friends would come to the shop and wonder what happened to her lofty career aspirations. I suppose she had the last laugh because she created a wildly successful company that was bought by General Mills five years after launch.[2]

Looking at offerings on Amazon can give you a sense of the relative demand for products that might be similar to yours. The reviews are a gold mine for both gauging the existing volume of purchases and figuring out what people think of available products. (Just take them with a grain of salt as Amazon reviews are reported to be at least 50 percent fraudulent paid fake ones.)

One of the favored tricks of the Harvard Business School students I advise is to allocate a very small budget (under $1,000) to running Facebook or Instagram ads for a potential product. Even before the product exists, you can send people, via a single click, to a basic website where you describe the product and offer to follow up with more information. You can measure the traffic to your website and send visitors to a variety of different simple pages dedicated to different product options shown in ads. Just be sure to collect e-mail addresses. This gives you a self-identified group of people to use for your own market research.

Let's say you've sized the available market for your product. One of the trickiest things is to figure out what share of the market you can capture. To do that really does require a full business plan because you need to estimate your customer acquisition costs and think out a plan for finding customers. As a very rough cut, if you are excited about the financial potential for your business with capturing just 1 percent of the market, you are in a safe zone to proceed. If you need to capture double-digit percentages, proceed with caution. You will need a very powerful marketing and sales engine to achieve that kind of penetration—something the average Maker does not possess.

When estimating the size of your potential market, consider using the Small Business Administration (sba.gov), the federal government (https://nces.ed.gov/partners/fedstat.asp), and industry associations as resources. There are many estimates of market sizes and other helpful statistics already available. This may also lead you to associations or organizations that can provide even more granular information. By researching the companies that already sell to your target audience, you may also be able to find additional statistics on the market size and other helpful data.

The second form of market research is aimed at getting feedback on your product's features, design, prototypes, packaging, or messaging. I will cover this more extensively in Chapter 8.

If you are not ready to test prototypes, yet you already have high-level customer behavior or product concept questions, consider running a survey through Survey Monkey (www.surveymonkey.com). It's an online survey generator for anything under the sun.

When you get to the stage of user testing, visit www.usertesting .com to get on-demand user feedback from your target audience. This is mainly relevant for digital products (your website, an app) and will be discussed more thoroughly in Chapter 8.

At this stage of your business (getting serious, but you are not yet fully committed), consider this research primarily as an effort to minimize risk. You are trying to figure out if the market is big enough to merit your efforts, and to get early indicators of customer responses to your product or solution. Taking this effort seriously will provide a good foundation for the more expensive and scarier commitments that lie ahead.

CASE STUDIES

Click n Curl

With a master's in counseling and 20 years spent in management, Kim Nimsgern didn't exactly have experience with product development. Although her parents were small business owners and her husband runs his own commercial painting company, she hadn't launched a product from conception to market. But she was determined to see to fruition an idea she had for a detachable roller brush hair dryer, a product she thought every woman should own.

Nimsgern is now the CEO and founder of Menomonie, Wisconsin–based Click n Curl, a clever barrel brush with a detachable curling mechanism. Nimsgern credits the Small Business Administration with helping her get started. She spent plenty of time online using its resources, becoming knowledgeable and learning as much as she could. She sought workshops and met with a small business counselor. Through the SBA, Nimsgern says she figured out how to do a feasibility study and where to go to develop a prototype for her product.

Going to trade shows has been extremely beneficial as well. For a while, she set up demos and would show anyone willing to listen how to use the Click n Curl. Laughing, Nimsgern says, "People are very willing to give feedback." She says she's relied on feedback about everything from the company name to the color of the product itself. Originally Nimsgern had planned for the dryer and curler to be white, but that choice was a total bust with potential clients. Now you can find Click n Curl in four sizes and colors, including green, red, purple, and blue.

When she launched the prototype, she would routinely go to the "cash and carry" fairs and trade shows to solicit the advice and input of prospective buyers as well as fellow presenters. Nimsgern also hired a firm to conduct market research, through the Small Business Administration in Wisconsin. Nimsgern quickly learned that she couldn't just rely on her own instincts or preference. "I can't do just what I like," she says, adding she now knows she must rely on feedback. She tested the name of the company as well and ended up with a name that was popular with focus groups but wasn't even her favorite. And, Click n Curl was originally in one size, but thanks to feedback, it's now in four different sizes.

Launched in 2013, Click n Curl is now on shelves at Bed Bath & Beyond and online at Target, Walmart, Kohls, The Grommet, and Amazon. Over the past five years, Nimsgern says she has seen a huge shift toward online sales. As Click n Curl grows, Nimsgern says she's turned her entrepreneurial eye toward other ventures and was launching an upscale campfire tool and a beer caramelizer. "It's the alcohol version of roasting marshmallows," she says. Nimsgern is excited about launching other products as a means of branching out and building off what she learned while creating Click n Curl.

Daytrader

One day, as Samir Lyons was looking over his Fidelity account, he felt vaguely like he was playing some sort of board game. That's when he thought it might be fun to actually create one based on day trading. At first Lyons considered an app, but friends convinced him that he should explore the traditional board game option. His first iteration was on a pizza box. It was ugly, he says, but people liked playing it. So, he thought, if an ugly game was fun to play, then a well-designed, beautiful game would be even more enjoyable.

Lyons tested what would become Daytrader on his friends and family. He would invite groups of friends over for pizza and ask them to play the game, get feedback, listen to suggestions, and make changes to the board, the rules, and the design. He joined board game clubs on Meetup and began testing a more refined product on total strangers, but ones who were interested in games. He even gave out gift cards to thank participants, although Lyons says he didn't tell them in advance they'd be receiving one.

Ironically, he can think of only one board game he ever played before creating Daytrader, and that was Monopoly. He may have had little knowledge of board games, but he was confident in his knowledge of finance. "I wanted to make a game that quenched my thirst for finance," he says. And that he did. After testing the game with 20 to 25 groups of strangers and approximately double that with his friends and family, he launched a Kickstarter campaign in 2013 to fund the business. Lyons quickly sold out of the 5,000 games he initially manufactured.

He then went on to redesign the game and make it smaller without losing the creative and appealing graphics. The biggest reason for the redesign was to reduce packaging and shipping costs. "I'm working with designers to fit under certain restrictions," says Lyons.

Today, Lyons is beginning to design additional games and would like to build new products as a way of offering more than one item to buyers.

Livliga

Sheila Kemper Dietrich holds three patents associated with dishes and dinnerware that integrate portion control into the unique patterns and beautifully designed plates and bowls. While working at the American Heart Association, Dietrich became acutely focused on data and research on obesity and how it can trigger other diseases, including cancer. She was determined to know more about how people could be living more healthily. She spoke with cardiologists and researchers, and read extensively on behavioral economics, all of which helped her to accumulate the knowledge she needed to tackle portion control in a unique way. "What do we need to do? What do we need to change?" Dietrich asked herself.

She also did extensive research on the effects of colors on people's perceptions of hunger. "Our eyes make all of the decisions," says Dietrich, explaining that the more excitable colors you're presented with at mealtime—say the glowing yellows and reds of McDonald's—the more likely you are to eat quickly and therefore overeat. Livliga's line of dishes features subtle, calming earth tones.

Dietrich even wrote her own white paper to delve into the concepts behind Livliga dishware. The size, shape, and color of each product have been thoroughly researched and include a subtle design element that indicates portion size for various categories of food. Livliga launched in 2013 and began selling dinnerware in 2014.

It launched with two sets of dishes and now has many. It also sells serveware, flatware, and more. Each year the company has added multiple items to its offerings. Dietrich says it's also added a bariatric line, which has become increasingly popular. "Online platforms were the way to go for us," she adds. A good proportion of the company's sales come through social media channels and other online avenues that deal with eating, wellness, bariatric surgery, and health. Dietrich says she and her team are constantly planning for additional products that can enhance sensible and healthy eating and serve their customers.

Ooni

When it came to determining whether there were any competitors on the market, Kristian Tapaninaho realized quite quickly that there weren't. A thorough online search revealed that a personal-sized, wood-burning pizza oven just wasn't out there. "There were plenty of people spending thousands of dollars on wood-fired ovens, but no one was spending hundreds." That's because there wasn't one on the market selling for just hundreds.

"In the beginning, I was a focus group of one," says Tapaninaho. He didn't really think he needed to test his idea much at all. He knew he wanted to make better pizza, and he knew that most everyone loves pizza and you can't get that smoky, wood-fired flavor in a conventional oven. So Tapaninaho was confident about taking the next step into prototyping.

"Outdoor cooking was becoming big," he says.

Kristian's wife, Darina Garland, says her husband's background revolves around a very practical and outdoor lifestyle, so something like this seemed like a natural fit. Once they had a prototype of the Ooni (formerly the Uuni), they went to Kickstarter. It was the early days of Kickstarter in the United Kingdom, and within two weeks they raised $10,000. To Tapaninaho, it was a strong indicator that people would buy a portable household pizza oven. Although a modest amount now, in 2013 this was a wildly successful run on Kickstarter. Blogs and mainstream press started featuring the Ooni.

"Who doesn't love pizza?" quips Tapaninaho. He attributes the near-universal love of dough, sauce, and cheese to the reason the company took off so quickly. "It captures people's imagination."

Since the beginning, sales surged quickly. Sold through Williams Sonoma, Ace Hardware, The Grommet, and Amazon, Ooni has added a larger "pro" model, many accessories including pizza peels and oven mitts, and bundles to include multiple products. And the company's site (Ooni.com) has evolved to include recipes for a variety of diets and palettes—the perfect place to go as a cooking resource if you're an Ooni owner.

PART

II

Building the 16 Competencies for Success

6

DESIGN AND DOCUMENTATION

Being an industrial designer, I've encountered the lack of familiarity people often have with the profession. My own father, a toolmaker at a Ford plant, asked why I would use my expensive new degree to "just design factories? With all that education, why don't you become a lawyer or a doctor?" To help him understand, I replayed one of my college project presentations to him and my mom in our tiny living room. Back in 1981, I had designed a portable computer that looked a lot like a contemporary MacBook. Seeing that futuristic model, and all the research and thinking that went into it, he finally understood the intersection of business and creativity that had me so excited about the profession.

But confusion about industrial design persists to this day, and I encountered it throughout my career. A case in point: after several months of working with a talented new product manager at Keds, I was both surprised and even a little amused to hear this very smart MBA ask me, "What exactly is industrial design?" We were on a plane—she must have had a glass of wine or two to release her inhibitions. I showed her the fork in my hand, the mechanical features

63

and surfaces of the tray in front of her, the contour of our seats, and the controls on our armrests and said, "This is what an industrial designer does. Every product has to be designed. It is just a question of whether it is done well and deliberately—or by default."

I want to be sure your product falls in the former category, the thoughtful and successful camp.

Say you've done the "napkin sketch" phase of ideation to capture the essence of your product. Let's assume you are not a trained designer or engineer fluid with product ideation or documentation. The home-grown sketch (or rough model, as the case may be) is more than adequate to communicate your concept. But even if you manage to get something fancier like a formal rendering, CAD (computer-aided design) drawing, or realistic-looking model, your product is likely still far from truly designed or optimized.

To be fair, a very tiny segment of products are so simple that no industrial designer is needed. I am thinking of Whooz, a clever system of stickers created to help customize the ubiquitous white Apple power cords and chargers. Its creator, Sativa Turner, was tired of having hers mistakenly swiped or left behind, so she solved the problem. No industrial designer needed. (But a good graphic designer was essential!)

Most products are more complex, and that's where a designer can be invaluable. Industrial designers tend to focus on physical products and complex services design. User interaction/experience designers are their necessary counterparts when it comes to orchestrating the specific flow and nature of a person's interactions with a product, system, or application.

At a minimum, an experienced industrial designer and user experience team (occasionally, they are a single person) will address the following areas:

- **Human factors and ergonomics.** You know the difference between a well-balanced pair of scissors and ones that pinch your fingers or do not give you great leverage for the task? The knowledge of human ergonomics is part of what a designer brings to the table.

- **User experience (UX).** Think about driving your car or using an app on your phone. Every time you push a button, use a keyless entry pad, or swipe on your phone, you are interacting with a product. In a successful execution, every element of your interaction has been designed. If you have not been behind the scenes to see a product designed, you would be floored by the amount of deliberation put into the shape or color of a button, or the location of information on a control panel. Strong UX design is rarely noticed. If users are not actively thinking about whether or not it's difficult to do something, it's because the UX is so smooth they don't have to think about it. Most users only stop to think about their experience when it's bad. For instance, consider your visit to a restaurant. If everything goes well—you are seated promptly, served seamlessly, the food is good, and you are able to pay your check and leave when you wish—then you've just had the equivalent of a good user experience. Conversely, when you get on a site and can't figure out how to search, or delete an item from the cart, or update your account, you notice bad user experience design. When it goes right, it is invisible.

- **Materials and finishes.** As an inexperienced product creator, you will likely not know what materials are feasible for your product. When it comes to plastics alone, there is a panoply of choices. For instance, when Joelle Mertzel of Butterie received the first prototypes of her butter dish, they were executed in a material that she noted "just felt cheap." She showed her manufacturer a completely unrelated product she admired and was told "Oh, that is made from ABS. We can do that." Instant quality upgrade. The same goes for finishes—simply put, those are textures that can go a long way to enhance the usability and appearance of a product. Think of the difference between matte and shiny, ribbed and smooth, coated or uncoated. The fastest way to get what you want is to give a designer or your manufacturer examples of products that represent the materials and finishes you want to use and then use their expertise to narrow down your choices according to cost, manufacturability, and ultimate expected function.

- **Manufacturability, durability, and cost effectiveness.** An experienced industrial designer who has worked in your product category can get you pretty far in terms of developing realistic and affordable concepts. But you will ultimately need to tap mechanical, electrical, and manufacturing engineers to finish most jobs. Sometimes a manufacturer has those professionals in house. In other cases your designer should be able to refer you to trusted contracting colleagues or firms.

- **Form and function.** There is a myriad of choices in the shape and function of everything: from a teacup to a shipping-worthy product package. Just think about a chair. Every chair has the same function, but the actual execution could not be more radically different, from a fold-up tubular aluminum and plastic webbing lawn chair, to a Chippendale dining piece, to a corduroy beanbag.

Good user experience design is about removing everything that comes between the user's objective and the actual fulfillment of that objective. Computers, buttons, control panels, menus, and the like are all tools designers use to help them achieve these objectives. The simplest tool that does the job well is always preferred.

Even though I run a very, very lean, high-growth company, I have never compromised on hiring design talent. At first, our public face was only a website, so we worked with just two firms: one to design our visual identity (logo, color palettes, type, imagery) and an interaction design firm for the website. Our customer-facing activities grew to include social media, e-mails, packing slips, and advertising. As our business became more complex, we brought our web and graphic design largely in house. The small team of five is now designing everything from our website and mobile experiences to physical catalogs, retail signage, Facebook ads, and shipping boxes.

But we still outsource our office design, trade show booths, retail stores, and display fixtures to an expert, Vince Pan and his team at Analogue Studios. Nothing gives me greater joy than to hear our hard-charging vice president of wholesale, Jason McCarthy, who does everything in the fastest and most resourceful (i.e., homegrown or cheapest) way possible, say, "We need to call Vince." Jason has learned that an up-front investment in Vince's concepts and designs will save both time and money over the course of a project.

Designers can also be useful nodes to finding other professional resources, such as packaging or manufacturing firms, prototyping facilities, research and testing tools, and mechanical and electrical engineers.

Design and "documentation" are often confused. It should be noted that starting out on paper, on the back of a napkin, or in some other nontechnical format is not just a cute scrappy way for first-timers to make a product. It's an essential first step for any designer to quickly get ideas out of his or her head and onto the page. Dan Schults, the head of user experience design at The Grommet says, "This is in fact how the pros work, too. In this fast, low-fidelity format, you can rapidly refine and iterate at almost no expense of time or money. There's no need to break out the CAD software or the rapid prototyper until you have a good sense of the direction you're heading in."

So how do you find a designer? LinkedIn is your friend, but you can also benefit from trawling a host of online resources.

DESIGN TALENT RESOURCES

- **Behance** (www.behance.net): owned by Adobe, Behance is an online portal for showcasing and discovering creative work.

- **99designs** (99designs.com): online graphic design marketplace for marketing, logos, packaging, and more. After submitting your needs and some guidelines, you can tap into ideas from more than 1 million designers from around the world.

- **Office Depot** (www.officedepot.com): the ubiquitous office supply retailer has introduced a variety of services to aid small businesses, including access to design resources, especially for online and print projects.

- **Guru** (www.guru.com): a freelance marketplace where companies can find freelancers from just about any industry.

- **Zurb** (www.zurb.com): a product design company that often works with fledgling companies to help create digital products, websites, and integrated service. They focus on capturing the personality and uniqueness of companies.

- **Upwork** (www.upwork.com): online, global platform company that connects professional freelancers with companies looking for talent.

One of the keys to working with a designer successfully is to clearly articulate a project brief. At a basic level, a brief should be written and not just a hand-waving oral exercise. Don't cut corners here. In my five years working at the innovation and product design consultancy Continuum, I learned the value of a great brief. And here's a secret: very few big company teams even know how to deliver a good one, so *any* brief is fantastic in comparison to, well, nothing. Time and time again, I found myself in meetings with the heads of engineering and marketing that were disorganized and unclear. My potential clients may have had plenty of passion, but they delivered it in a pile of problems, competing goals, aspirations, and data. I found that translating that corporate mess into an intelligent proposal meant I had a huge success rate in landing projects.

Do yourself a favor and write a brief. Designers are understandably wary of startups. Startups don't pay well, and default accounts are always a risk with this class of company. I was happy to sort out the project brief complexities for an established company, but I would not have had that luxury or trust with an emerging one. As a startup you can distinguish yourself from the pack with a coherent brief that describes an interesting project. It may make the difference between being dismissed and being taken seriously.

A brief should include:

- **An overview of the market opportunity.** What product gaps and market opportunities do you see? Talk about existing solutions and potential competition.

- **Distribution.** How do you foresee distributing your product? There is a world of difference between retail-ready packaging and an e-commerce only product.

- **Basic product features, including ideal retail pricing.** This specification is more complex if the product is largely digital or app-enabled. You will likely need some early brainstorming with a UX designer to help you adequately specify a project such as an application.

- **A discussion of your expected customer.** This is where you describe your user research and any target demographics for your customer (age, geography, gender, profession, education, user scenarios).

- **Time frames and deliverables.** Are you searching for rough concepts to attract investors or fully developed designs that are appropriate for mechanical, electrical, or manufacturing engineering? Are you looking for rough prototypes or user testing? How much research and customer/field exploration are you willing to fund, or do you expect the designer to use your own research as a base?

This brief can be anything from a couple of pages to a full dossier with inspiration images and market research findings.

DOCUMENTATION

The core role of documentation is twofold. The first wave of documentation is simply to communicate a concept. But the bulk of what constitutes documentation is elaborate and detailed articulation of a product or package so that it can be manufactured. Like industrial design, this is generally a task best left to the pros, in the form of engineers.

When it comes to documenting their designs, some Grommet Makers do indeed decide to go it alone and master the tools of the design and engineering trades. If your product is either so simple it does not require design expertise, or you decide to sidestep my advice to hire a designer, you will find yourself learning about how to document your own ideas and designs. Here are some of the tools you will need.

I am not addressing software coding tools as they fall outside the scope of what could be reasonably expected of a founder. In other words, if you have an app or other digital interface and you don't want to hire a software engineer to design your product, you will have an individual journey. You will determine which coding languages and tools you wish to learn, and that may require a more extensive investment in your own training than most founders would take on.

IDEATION AND DOCUMENTATION RESOURCES

- **Autodesk** (www.autodesk.com): creates software for Makers in the engineering, 3D design, and entertainment industries.

- **National Instruments** (www.ni.com/en-us.html): producer of automated test equipment and virtual instrumentation software.

- **SketchUp** (www.sketchup.com): producer of 3D modeling software, creator of tools that help engineers, designers, and makers bring visions and ideas to a more concrete space.

- **Rhinoceros** (www.rhino3d.com): this commercial 3D CAD modeling software program allows users to model designs and prepare them for manufacturing.

- **Tinkercad** (www.tinkercad.com): online 3D design and printing app, which is free, easy to use, and allows quick modifications to existing designs.

- **Balsamiq** (https://balsamiq.com): is an inexpensive option for 2D wireframing.

- **Omnigraffle** (www.omnigroup.com/omnigraffle): is a Mac-only tool for wireframing, flow diagrams, and vector graphics.

- **Invision** (www.invisionapp.com/): is a freemium web-based tool for making basic clickable prototypes.

- **Axure** (www.axure.com/): is a tool for making flow diagrams, wireframes, and robust prototypes with more advanced logic.

Documentation tools change regularly, so as for previous chapters, please consult my regularly updated resource list at www.howwemakestuffnow.com.

Beyond the technical documentation of the product per se, be sure to document the building blocks of your end result. There is a lot of documentation that can occur before you even whiteboard your first mockup. Gathering and processing unbiased data from your users/customers is an art and science in its own right, but interpreting that data in a useful way is an essential early step. User flows, decisions trees, and journey maps will help identify the needs and existing processes of users regarding the problem you are trying to solve. They are also useful for identifying the strengths and weaknesses of your idea before going too deeply down a given path.

Save all your sketches, photograph your mockups, and preserve your early prototypes. Believe it or not, we have saved a sample of every Grommet ever launched because they are useful for telling our history as well as serving as relevant props in our current photos and videos. These development steps in your business are part of your story, and with success you will be very proud to share them, whether with future employees, investors, business partners, advisors, journalists, or your family.

Working on the design of your product will be one of the most rewarding parts of your journey. A professional designer will take your concept to new levels of form and function and make it both more effective and more commercially viable. This is not a place to cut corners.

CASE STUDIES

eyn

Frustrated that she couldn't put her phone and a few credit cards or a bit of cash into one neat, convenient place without having to carry around a bulky wallet or bag, Linda Connolly set out to design just that. She wanted to be able to close a case so that no one could see whether she was carrying a credit card, an ID, or a few dollars. "I was confident it wasn't out there," says Connolly after doing much online research.

She sketched some ideas on paper. She had a friend who was proficient in Photoshop. This was back in 2010 when Photoshop was the fanciest software available. Her friend helped her after work. They would sit together and tinker around with the design. "I didn't have someone doing CAD drawings," she says.

Connolly ultimately got a utility patent for the hinged door on the back of the phone case. She worked to make it sleek and easy to use, and added improvements along the way. Her friend would adjust the drawings accordingly. "Erase this, color this in," Connolly would say.

"I'm very creative, but I'm not a salesperson." She did some minimal focus groups. By March 2012 eyn (Everything You Need) was selling like crazy. Connolly had an initial run of 5,000 cases that sold almost immediately.

Thanks to a mention on the *Today* show, sales were given a big boost. The case has been sold through Amazon, eyn's site, and The Grommet. Connolly says business is strong since the company's potential audience is simply massive—anyone with a smartphone. Connolly says the case can accommodate credit cards, medication, hair ties, shopping lists, lip balm, mints, and assorted other things people want to carry around when not wanting to lug a large bag.

Get It Right Ultimate Spatula

Samantha Rose's love of design, experimenting, and cooking came together one day when her go-to spatula broke while she was cooking. It had one of those well-loved, slightly burned, and cracked wood handles. "Why not make this all one piece of silicone?" she wondered. After all, the silicone portion of the spatula was in perfect condition. It was the annoying wood handle that just wasn't cutting it. "It was a lightning moment," says Rose.

That's how Get It Right started. First Rose looked to see if there was anything even similar to what she was imagining already on the market. When she found nothing, Rose used Sculpey to mold her own version of what she wanted. From there, she ordered a silicone modeling kit to create her own prototype. She cast her own spatulas to prove the one-piece design was plausible. Rose worked through various iterations of the design. From there she needed to make sure the silicone was really long lasting, high heat–resistant, and without any harmful by-products.

Rose gave herself a massive education in silicone and other heat-resistant materials. As she searched for a core that wasn't metal (which would conduct heat too quickly), she found a heat-resistant fiberglass that would last just as long as silicone. "I wanted to make 10 for Christmas," she said, laughing now that she knows few manufacturers are interested in an order for less than 10,000.

Rose introduced that spatula in 2012. Get It Right now has more than 50 silicone utensils and products. Get It Right doubled sales in 2017, and Rose smiles gratefully, "It feels like we've made it." Get It Right has seen enormous wholesale growth and landed in Target. "That was a huge validation for us," says Rose, adding that she plans to carefully balance their Target account with the smaller shops. "Independent, gourmet retailers are our bread and butter."

Yoga by Numbers

When Elizabeth Morrow was in the midst of a scary medical experience, with a collapsed lung and on blood thinners, she was told she could do only gentle exercise, nothing that could cause her to bruise easily. That's when she turned to yoga.

"Yoga was really helpful," says Morrow. But it was also expensive to go to studios, and the set times didn't always work with her schedule. And as a beginner, she was struggling to find the right pace. At the same time that Morrow was recuperating, her father was healing from having broken his femur. He, too, could do yoga.

But between the physical therapy appointments, trying to get her life back in order, the time, and the expense, it just wasn't going to happen. If only she could practice at home. Morrow tried yoga videos, but found those a bit hard to follow. She thought yoga at home should be easier. Surely people living in rural areas and parents juggling children and various schedules faced similar challenges. Morrow assumed that there were plenty of people who would benefit from doing yoga at home.

As she practiced, Morrow imagined her mat as a piece of graph paper, with a grid that could help with cuing. Every time she followed along with an on-screen instructor, she was craning her neck to look up rather than assuming a pose.

On a notepad, she started sketching the idea for a mat that would allow yoga positions to be called out by numbers and quadrants. She also decided to make the mat a bit larger than the standard-sized ones.

Morrow printed out circles, painted them various colors, and glued them to her mat to test the outcome. She researched colors and sizes, considered which colors were pleasing, and found out that manufacturers' fees depended on colors. She settled on color combinations that were gender neutral and soothing. Morrow used PowerPoint to create her final design. Her first prototype was done on a piece of canvas.

Five years in, Morrow says, "The business is chugging along." As a solo, first-time founder, she says it's taken a lot of sacrifice, but she's stuck to her values and hasn't compromised, even when the money was attractive. She says one investor offered her a significant amount of money and resources if only she would "sex up the videos" that accompany her mats. "We're not selling sex," Morrow says, especially annoyed given that her company was founded as a way to help those who are managing health problems.

Morrow says she knows there are ways she could have the business take off, but she's more comfortable with the current state and pleased that she has not compromised the mission. She says many sales come throughs social media and word of mouth, and there is a consistent flow of orders. Yoga by Numbers sells on The Grommet, Amazon, and Uncommon Goods.

Lovepop

Friends Wombi Rose and John Wise were in Vietnam on a business school trip when they discovered a beautiful paper-cutting art. It was a pop-up style with intricately cut lines. As engineers who had studied boat building together, Rose and Wise could envision how the three-dimensional creations had been made and sliced into planes. "It's exactly how you make a ship," says Rose.

With backgrounds that melded arts and engineering, the two knew it was something they could recreate. The company has an in-house design team of 20. "We combine some modern engineering tools with old-school classic design." In the initial design process, Rose says it was very tricky because they needed to have something that was beautiful, but also something that would pop up consistently. Paper can be finicky. The designers at Lovepop had to create art as well as a functional product.

Lovepop solicits requests and suggestions for new designs, and in 2017 it received 100,000 responses. Many were duplicates. The company currently has 120 designs. The design process starts as concepts that are sketched by hand, then transferred into the 3D CAD system.

Each design is crafted by hand. No computer could do that, says Rose. "But without the computer, it would take months to design." All pieces are then cut on a laser cutter, but every card is assembled by hand.

When Lovepop made it on *Shark Tank*, cofounder Wombi Rose says it catapulted the company in many ways. "It's amazing to share your story with the country," he says. "Nothing shows who you are as much as when smart people ask you all these questions in front of everyone."

Entrepreneur and investor Kevin O'Leary, who has starred on *Shark Tank*, invested in the company, and Rose says he's been instrumental in working with Lovepop on strategy and planning. And after their *Shark Tank* appearance, Rose says the company was flooded with people reaching out. "There are so many ways people want to talk to you," he adds. "It's important to treat everyone as an individual. Our mission is to be sure they feel appreciated."

"Any way you can get in front of customers, do it," says Rose. In order to know more about your product or ideas, it's important to decide whether you're looking to have a sales strategy, a word-of-mouth strategy, or a marketing strategy. This will lead you toward how you can scale. Ultimately, he says you want to know that people want your products and that you can scale it and execute on meeting deadlines while balancing the right levels of growth.

In January 2018, Lovepop announced a $12.5 million Series A financing. The company has 15 of its own brick-and-mortar shops and sells at hundreds of specialty retailers and online.

INTELLECTUAL PROPERTY

When entrepreneurs are in the early stages of forming their businesses, I often find they are overly wary of sharing their ideas with people who can help them. The bottom line is that very few people you might ask for help are going to throw over their current livelihoods to take on the grueling work of copying your undeveloped napkin-sketch idea. People rarely fall that deeply in love with someone else's baby. So by all means, take the teeny tiny risk of sharing your idea with individual advisors, experts, and potential investors. Your early job, as outlined in prior chapters, is to figure out if you have a viable business idea in the first place. Lawyering up or fiercely defending a bad idea is just a waste of time, so realize that the benefit of outside assistance far outweighs the threat of experts and advisors stealing your stuff.

On the flip side, in contrast to seeing expert advisors as potential competitors, inexperienced entrepreneurs can be too trusting of potential business partners. Founders will engage a distant factory in China who might easily knock off their idea, or list their product on Amazon and expose it to a world of counterfeiters without even taking the steps to protect their product. So the art of managing intellectual property is more about risk assessment than anything else.

Intellectual property protections roughly fall in five camps. I list them in order of both necessity and degree of difficulty to attain:

1. **Nondisclosure agreements (NDAs).** From the very start of your business you will want to deploy this protection. At Grommet we use it for all employees, consultants, board members, and service providers. I never asked a potential investor to sign an NDA, because that would have put us out of the running for investment consideration. (Venture capitalists and other professional investors tend to take great offense to the notion that they might steal entrepreneurs' ideas.) The core idea behind an NDA is to enable the company to share internal data and intellectual property freely with someone who is working within or for the enterprise. Its second and equally important role is to assure that work done on behalf of the company will be assigned to and owned by the company. An NDA will also cover what marketing promotion or disclosures a consultant can make about its work for the company. Another name for these agreements is a confidentiality and inventions assignment agreement. Whatever you call it, this protection is fundamental to working with any internal or external party. Never neglect getting one executed, and keep excellent digital files of final signed copies.

2. **Copyrights.** While typically used to protect creative assets like photos, videos, artwork, and written pieces, the one copyright use you are certain to need is for your company's website. I remember being quite annoyed and surprised when a loosely competitive business actually lifted whole lines of copy off of our site. It was reassuring to have that website copyright protection. I merely indicated my

displeasure in an e-mail and the other business resolved the issue, but the legal protection was extra insurance. Our website copyright also nicely covers all of our original photos and videos. Copyright.gov has a helpful compilation of frequently asked questions to learn how to copyright your work (https://www.copyright.gov/help/faq/).

3. **Trademarks.** This is the mechanism you use to protect, at a minimum, your logo and company name. But a trademark can have surprisingly broad applications for business assets, like the shape of a Coke bottle, or even a color such as "Tiffany blue." The computer processor company Intel trademarked its distinctive "Intel Inside" sound as intellectual property. At The Grommet we purchased the website URLs in countries where we would wish to do business in the future. That step was relatively easy. We also secured U.S. trademarks for our company name, logo mark, "Discover What's Next" tagline, and the phrase "Citizen Commerce." This work has had to be repeated every time we change our company name (once) and logo. Far more laborious has been the effort to secure protection of those assets in international markets. This is work we could not have pursued on our own, and we have relied entirely on the advice and work of our patent attorneys at Lando & Anastasi. One "gotcha" I did not anticipate was the effort to defend our international intellectual property. We must demonstrate concrete trademark usage in each of the countries where we own such property. In some countries, where we cannot prove a commercial presence, we have let those trademarks lapse.

4. **Trade secrets.** The most famous example of this is the formula for Coca-Cola, but trade secrets can extend to business processes, customer lists, and a myriad of other business assets as well. For most practical purposes, your NDA agreements should cover you for this area.

5. **Patents.** One of the first questions our Discovery team asks when they talk to a new Maker is "Do you have patent protection?" We think about this exactly like any investor would: If I dedicate my company's assets and expertise to building this business, what is the risk of that investment being destroyed by a copycat or counterfeiter? What are patents? According to the United States Patent Office, "A patent for an invention is the grant of a property right to the inventor." Patents can apply to a myriad of product features and functions, from the shape of a water bottle lid to a core website functionality (like Amazon's One Click feature.) The key issues in determining whether you can get a patent are: (1) just the concrete embodiment of an idea, formula, or product is patentable; (2) the invention must be new or novel; (3) the invention must not have been patented or described in a printed publication previously; and (4) the invention must have some useful purpose.

The U.S. Patent and Trademark Office site has resources for filing for a patent (https://www.uspto.gov/patents-application-process/file-online). I've seen some Makers go it alone in filing for a patent, but the vast majority work with a skilled attorney for these filings. Just getting advice on what is worth filing for is valuable in and of itself.

On a purely practical basis, the two places where we most frequently see Makers encounter intellectual property infringements are: (1) on Amazon and (2) from nimble copycat companies releasing similar, counterfeit, or knockoff products. The minute you put a product on the market (and not just on a napkin sketch), the competition does come sniffing. In particular, we have seen devastating infringements from the "As Seen on TV" companies, and from Makers being knocked off by their own offshore factories. (I will address this issue in Chapter 11: Manufacturing.) More rare is for a larger established brand to knock off a product, but that does happen as well. The protections listed above are your best defense in these product knockoff or counterfeit situations.

Legal expert Andrea Evans formerly worked as a U.S. patent examiner and trademark examining attorney before forming her own Baltimore-based firm serving small businesses. Regarding defense against international counterfeiters and copycats, Evans explains, "The beauty of federally protecting your inventions, brands, and written works with patents, trademarks, and copyrights, respectively, is that trademarks and copyrights can be recorded with U.S. Customs and Border Protection (CBP). If a U.S. patented product is illegally imported into the U.S., the U.S. International Trade Commission (USITC) investigates these claims to determine if there is a violation of Section 337, which makes it illegal to import items that infringe on patents, trademarks, and copyrights."

Click n Curl founder Kim Nimsgern says her sales are suffering because of copycats. "I'm not selling at the pace I want because of knockoffs." Although still growing, Nimsgern says she's been online when an ad for what looks like Click n Curl pops up; even the name is the same, but it's not her product. She's received complaints from people about faulty Click n Curls. Again, not hers. And she has a patent. Nimsgern tries to find out where people have bought the knockoffs, but it's an exhaustive process. Shopify makes it easy to file complaints against copycats, says Nimsgern, but it's not always worth the time or the money to chase down all of the companies purporting to be hers. She even found a knockoff of Click n Curl being sold through Sephora. Once she alerted Sephora it no longer sold the hairstyling product.

In researching this book I found both a disturbing level of emotional trauma and a very high level of conflicting advice when discussing protecting intellectual property. I observe this issue to have vastly accelerated over the last five years as well. Few Makers escape challenges in this area, and even fewer agree on the best approaches to defending a business. Most do agree that a patent is only as valuable as your resources to defend it. Makers also agree that while proper, professional legal work and patents are the essential foundation to protect your business, your attorneys are not going to be the main combatants in those agonizing midnight and weekend hours. You and your team are.

Josh Malone is an example. Malone discovered his company Bunch O Balloons, which offers a quick and easy way to fill dozens of water balloons at once, had been completely copied. Although he had a patent on his invention, which required a certain device for inflating and filling the balloons, he wasn't able to stop the other company from copying his ideas, manufacturing, and selling.

Malone was one of several inventors featured in *Invalidated: The Shredding of the U.S. Patent System*, a documentary about companies whose patents have proved useless. Many people, Malone included, have ceremonially burned their patents, since they've become in essence worthless. He's also been involved in public lawsuits and court cases against the infringer. Although Malone has been involved for years fighting the imposter company, Bunch O Balloons still generates about $125 million in sales. Malone admits that about $20 million in legal costs have protected that business, but he also says the business would be much bigger if the copycat did not continue to operate with impunity.

I discuss the risks of selling on Amazon in detail in Chapter 14: Retail Distribution. The best protection from Amazon's many dark sides regarding IP protection is to make your business big enough to matter to the digital oligopoly. This, alas, is the only way you can get them to take steps to enforce your IP. But now you have a chicken and an egg problem. By definition, when you are just starting out, you are not big enough to get Amazon's support. And I really mean support from a human being who works at Amazon. These are the people with the power to remove hijacked listings, counterfeit products, and rogue sellers. As a general rule, Amazon staffers are just too overwhelmed with fraudsters to help any but the largest sellers. In 2018 Amazon even revealed that some of its own employees are contributing to the proliferation of fraud on the marketplace by selling access to data and taking down select reviews.[1] But the catch-22 with Amazon is that you can lose all control of your IP in the process of growing to becoming a large-enough seller.

A common new Maker solution to deal with the very prominent Amazon threat is to hire a rep/service business that specializes in managing Amazon listings. You sell your products at wholesale to this rep. It manages the Amazon listings for dozens or hundreds of brands and can get nearly immediate intervention from Amazon when a counterfeit listing or rogue seller is damaging your brand, overriding your pricing, or stealing your IP. It will take a margin cut, of course. This detailed and highly laborious forensic work alone makes the revenue you give to your agent well worth the price. The rep's additional business-building services can go well beyond "compliance and enforcement," and I will discuss this a bit more in Chapter 14.

In summary, taking steps to mitigate known risks to your hard-earned intellectual property is fundamental to protecting your broader investments in the business.

CASE STUDIES

Negg

After visiting a few manufacturers, Negg cofounder Bonnie Tyler ran into someone who directed her to a manufacturing plant in Marlborough, Connecticut, not far from where she lived. She and partner Sheila Torgan were able to drive an hour away to have a mold manufactured for their egg peeler. Although they had hoped to keep manufacturing in the United States, they didn't know what would happen in the end. Sure enough it worked out, and Tyler says the manufacturer was extremely helpful in coming up with a clever way of holding the Negg contraption together.

Despite manufacturing in the United States where she could protect her product a bit better, Tyler was appalled when she started seeing knockoffs and counterfeits of her hardboiled egg peeler populating Amazon and eBay. She laments, "They were all junk. They had no seals and were made of cheap materials. They didn't work. But they used our trademarked name, our ASN [ID number], the Grommet video, and even my own photo. We have patents and they just ignore them." These hijacked listings prompted Tyler to seek legal help. The first attorney she reached told her she would have to pay him $20,000 for a court order that would get Amazon's attention. And it would require a separate court order for each of the up to 150 businesses listing fake products. Bonnie said, "What small business can pay that? I was starting to see all of our hard work go up in smoke and it made flames come out of my own ears."

Tyler kept trying to find someone at Amazon and eBay to help her take down the counterfeit listings, but to no avail. Meanwhile, she maintained an active search to find a responsive legal firm. Tyler finally found one that heard her story and jumped in with both feet, never asking for a $20,000 court order, and working fast and furiously to join her battle. Tyler says this attorney has been effective in getting the listings taken down. But she shares, "They just keep coming back. It's like playing Whack-a-Mole. Whether from China or the United States, they just keep reappearing. It's like standing outside your own home looking in the window watching someone blatantly steal everything you have ever earned. We have an intern in the business who says she can always tell when I am trying to deal with counterfeits because my mood goes way down."

Tyler says she has learned a backdoor route to getting Amazon to answer her concerns. She calls the normal customer service phone number and then tells her business story. She is usually connected to the fraud department. But Tyler says, "Amazon doesn't care. We have to band together and stop what they are doing. This is a great country. We need for other people to be able to do what Sheila and I have done to start a business. I have been told to just keep my head down, but I will be darned if I am going to let Amazon take away my hard work. I am shouting this from the rooftops until people start to understand what is happening on the big online platforms like Amazon and eBay."

Gleener

It all started when Kim Cole tried to get the fuzz off her beautiful merino wool turtleneck. She used a battery-powered shaver, and within minutes, there was a hole in her sweater. Seven months pregnant and feeling overwhelmed, Cole started crying. She figured there had to be something better.

Cole happened to be watching Oprah one day, which she says she never watched, and the show was about everyday millionaires. "People like myself, who had ideas and saw them through." At the end of the show, Oprah leaned toward the camera and said, "For anybody out there with a great idea, go for it." Cole said, "It was an aha moment for me."

Cole started planning out the sweater de-fuzzer at her dining room table. Her background was in commercial design, and she made various sketches before hiring an industrial designer to do the CAD drawings. And from there she learned more than she ever thought she could about aluminum molds, inventory, and how to get a product to market.

It took many iterations before Cole was able to figure out how to create a product that could work on many fibers, not just on wool. As hard as it was to get her product perfected and into market, Cole reflects that the single hardest thing about building the business has been defending her intellectual property. She asserts, "It's almost like a bunch of us need to file a class action suit against Amazon and Ebay because they provide the perfect runway to copycats and criminal counterfeiters. It's become a discouraging game of Whack-a-Mole."

North Country Wind Bells

Jim Davidson was a lobsterman in Round Pond, Maine, where he spent hours on the water listening to the familiar and haunting tolling of the buoy bells. He loved the sound and wanted to recreate it for people to hear back on land. Davidson spent time recording various bells and then worked to shape steel bells just so, in order to mimic the sounds he was hearing while on his boat. He started the company in 1975, and his daughter Connie now runs it.

Connie Davidson says she and her family have been fending off copycats since the 1990s. The company has an attorney who works with them to protect the original artwork and designs. The attorney advises them routinely on how to handle copycats. Davidson says this typically involves a cease and desist letter, which is often all that is needed to get someone to stop selling the knockoff.

North Country Wind Bells has patents and trademarks on the bells. Davidson explains that there is specific engineering and design that goes into each one. "You have to protect your work," she says. While at a trade show in Rochester, Minnesota, years ago, Davidson saw an exact replica of their bells. She was shocked. "It was a blatant copy," she adds. Another copycat she came across had even created an end display similar to North Country Wind Bells'. Davidson says future copycats are something you have to watch for at trade shows—people taking photos that are then used to recreate what they see on display. She's mentioned it to security before and had people removed from the trade show floors.

North Country Wind Bells has grown exponentially since Connie's family founded the company. There was one design when the bells went to market. There are now more than 50 bells and more than 100 wind catchers. The company sells nationally through gift shops, museums, nurseries, art galleries, and trade shows.

Ruppert Garden Tools

Jon Ruppert had been in the electronics industry for 40 years, largely designing circuit boards, and has patents in voice activation systems. He'd also been gardening since he was 10 years old and realized not much had changed with gardening tool technology in a long time. "Shovels are shovels," he says. "People haven't come up with a lot of innovative things in gardening."

Ruppert was inspired to work on what is now known as the Dirt Snatcher, a bulb planting mechanism that makes digging holes quick and simple. He received a utility patent for the tool and was selling on QVC and in Brookstone. That was in 2001. The next one he worked on, the Weed Snatcher, helps to rip weeds from driveways, patios, and sidewalks with its hook-like attachment that is good for getting into narrow spaces. That has sold on The Grommet and QVC.

"If you're going to invent something, you need to do a lot of research," says Ruppert. For him that research included Internet searches for gardening tools similar to what he envisioned and asking around for what he wanted. When he realized it wasn't out there, Ruppert knew he was on to something. The more unique the product is, the faster the patents come through, he says. "If you don't have something that is really novel, it will be a struggle." If an inventor is continually fielding questions from the patent office about how his or her product is different from the many other similar ones out there, it's bound to take time and maybe never happen at all. For Ruppert, the products he was inventing were so far from what else was on the market that his patents were issued fairly quickly.

Ruppert advises people to get a provisional patent as well. Once you have a solid idea, this allows you to work on prototyping and iterating without worrying about someone coming along and taking the idea before it has fully come to fruition. A provisional patent can cost between $900 and $1,200 and an official patent upward of $6,000. Ruppert says it's also important to find a patent attorney who understands the field in which you're working. When he was seeking electronic patents, he had an attorney who understood that industry. He's not using the same attorney for his gardening tools.

Ruppert says his patents have protected him against copycats. He says he's seen many knockoffs of the Weed Snatcher. "If you have a patent, you can do something about it," he says— meaning you can sue the company or shut it down.

Ruppert says he's very cautious about sharing his ideas. He never tells anyone except for his family about his next idea. He has more garden tools lined up, both ones he's only started to think about making and another he's received a patent for already. For now, he'll only say he's looking to reinvent the shovel.

8

PROTOTYPING

irst, a word of caution. If you are intending to make your business your full-time gig and you haven't started prototyping, don't quit your day job yet. Even if the size of your available market and business plan are giving you dreams of someday owning a small private island. Even if your test Facebook ads or focus groups yield a fantastic and encouraging market response. Even if you hate your boss and can't spend one more minute filing TPS reports. One of the critical parts of assessing the viability of your venture will happen in the prototyping phase.

Consider the riddle about the chicken and the pig.

> **Question:** In a bacon-and-egg breakfast, what's the difference between the chicken and the pig?

> **Answer:** The chicken is involved, but the pig is committed!

You will morph from being the chicken to the pig soon during the process of prototyping. Having said that, try to stay in the fowl category as long as possible before you sign up to give it your all. Prototyping, which is simply creating a physical or visual sample of your product, is the central part of the active design phase, so try to think of it in that context. Most (not you, of course) will approach prototyping as the next step *after* designing a product. Nothing could be further from the truth. Prototyping is one of the most essential steps in the design process. One of the biggest differences between professional designers and "civilians" is the pro's commitment to many cycles of concept iterations and prototyping.

Designers do not fall in love with their ideas until *other* people do. Lots of them. Dan Shults, our Grommet UX lead, admits, "My brain knows this is true, but it hurts my heart to hear it." He explains, "This is a great ideal, but it's worth noting that it can be hard, even for pros. The best designs are reached using real data derived from testing your concepts at each stage of the design funnel. Exposing weaknesses in your work is much more useful than patting yourself on the back prematurely. Egos, consequently, must be checked at the door. Bottom line: compliments breed complacency, but criticism yields improvement."

Prototypes range from cardboard mockups and wireframes (simple blocking out of the content of an app or website) to 3D-printed solid forms that show the shape and parts of a product and to preproduction units that come very close to the real thing. In other words, they are physical manifestations that help you move from just thinking about an idea into shaping it just enough to share it with others. This helps you learn enough about your concept alternatives to move into the next step of creating more refined designs to express your idea.

Nothing yields clearer customer responses than giving people something to play with, whether it is a clickable prototype of a mobile app or a foam model of a golf club grip. It's important to stay open-minded about your product for as long as possible before making any major commitments to your business, including making the career leap. This is the critical point in the process when you can make absolutely certain you are *not* building a solution looking for a problem, or a great solution that is not viable from an execution standpoint.

The good news is that prototyping is fun. It is the first time you see your concept taking life. Your initial rounds will be mainly for your own edification. You are just trying to figure out if your idea is roughly in the right zip code. You may be really surprised by how a 3D expression of your product is radically different from what you had imagined or conceived on paper. You will immediately find new opportunities to make the product better. Take it from one of the most famous design firms, IDEO, whose team frequently says, "If a picture is worth a thousand words, a prototype is worth a thousand meetings."[1]

Your first prototype can be made of virtually anything. Lisa Fetterman made the first prototype of her Nomiku sous vide cooking device in a single mad-genius, all-nighter binge. The prototype was put together from chopsticks and a PID temperature controller. But I've seen prototypes made out of everything from oven mitts to hangers to duct tape.

Whether your prototypes are extremely basic or fully realized preproduction (i.e., close to the final look and functionality of the product), you want to think of this phase as iterative. In other words, each prototype is an opportunity to learn, revise, and refine your way closer to a viable product. Prototyping can also prevent a premature commitment—honest assessments of prototype testing may lead you to abandon your concept if it does not hold up to user scrutiny.

Prototypes can help you in three ways:

1. **Exploring.** You can explore various aspects of a problem and a variety of solutions so much faster than if you stick to words or even drawings. A physical object will move you farther and faster.

2. **Learning from potential customers or users.** If you put your prototype in the hands of a relevant potential user and genuinely seek feedback, you will quickly escape the founder's ivory tower. The key is to really listen. Or have an impartial third party (a researcher you press into service) walk a person through the use of your product without you (the eager creator) being present. If you do conduct your own

research, bite your tongue *hard* to avoid selling your idea or overexplaining the product functions. You will bias your test results and obviate the benefits of prototyping.

3. **Inspiring others.** The reason the Pump shoe got resources and attention from Reebok's founder, Paul Fireman, was because an employee had hacked a fake "pump" button onto an existing shoe. You will be surprised by how important a prototype is for recruiting new team members and getting funding or other forms of support. It separates you from the legions of people who have vague ideas on which they will never execute. Prototypes represent action. Prototypes are made by people who are committed.

Joelle Mertzel of Butterie took a highly creative approach to testing her prototypes and doing some basic market research. On the day of a planned family trip to Kentucky, she arrived at the airport four hours early. She spent that time going from one gate to another showing people her prototype and asking them to fill out a survey. It had a few simple questions:

1. How do you store your butter?

2. Would you use this covered butter dish?

3. What color would you like it in (multiple choice)?

4. What price would you pay?

5. Where would you expect to see it for sale?

Of super importance was that she did not reveal that she was the inventor until the surveys were completed. She said, "I will answer any questions you have after that." There were many benefits to this guerrilla style of prototype testing: Mertzel lives in Los Angeles, but she got a national cross-sampling. It was highly productive. By the time she had walked down a corridor in the airport and finished getting her surveys, all the gates changed over and she had fresh subjects. It is a methodology she returns to when needed. She learned that she didn't even need to take a flight: she just buys the cheapest plane ticket she can get and spends the day in the airport. Mertzel laughs, "You'd be surprised how eager this captive audience is to be included. When they see me talking to other people, passengers are almost primed to talk to me. But I do look entertaining, juggling my prototype, a raft of clipboards, and clean and filled surveys all the while." It sounds a bit zany, but these surveys told Mertzel what she needed to know about the demand for various colors and prices, and they gave her effective and clear language to help her describe Butterie.

One of the biggest mistakes I made in the early days of The Grommet was not creating a clickable prototype of our website. My reasoning was as follows: I internally committed to not spending any of our investor money—not one dime—until I had reached my initial seed funding target. I collected all the checks and kept them in a home file folder. I did not want to start using funds if I could not support our first investments with the security of a full funding round. But here was the flaw in my thinking: it would have been so much easier to raise the full round if I had spent $10,000 on an initial prototype of our website. With greater visual understanding of my vision, subsequent investors would have come in faster.

I didn't do it because of my commitment to protect my investors. It was stupid. The other thing that held me back was that I knew our business would depend on excellent brand building, and the website would be the first and most central example of my vision—and I did not want to show a half-formed prototype. But I now know that the point of my prototype was not to show a beautifully realized brand—but to exhibit commitment to the people I was asking to commit to me and The Grommet.

Now that I hopefully have sold you on the merits of prototyping—and lots of it—another word of caution. When you set out to test an idea or expose a prototype, remember the basic scientific method you learned in eighth grade. It can be unwise to alter and test too many facets of your design at once. If I am designing a checkout experience that is supposed to reduce shopping cart abandonment, and I change the address entry, credit card entry, and cart review screens, how do I know which of those created the positive impact? How do I know that one of my changes isn't having a negative impact, which is being overpowered by another positive change, and is therefore still suboptimal? Approach things scientifically. Controlling the number of variables in your tests will allow you to draw firmer conclusions. Sir James Dyson is famously rigorous about applying an empirical approach to prototyping: he produced 5,127 prototypes of his first vacuum. Each iteration reflected the change of a single variable, which allowed him to prove the function and form of his firm's bagless vacuum. It's hard to justify rushing the prototype stage when you know the outcome: Dyson was pursuing this work while in debt and on the verge of bankruptcy. Today Dyson produces some of the bestselling vacuums in the world, and Sir James's net worth has been estimated at over $7 billion.[2]

When you are ready to begin prototyping, here are resources:

- **Protolabs** (www.protolabs.com): rapid prototyping (3D printing in a wide variety of materials, CNC machining) and low-volume production including injection-molded products. This resource could also be viable for your first actual production units, beyond your prototypes.

- **Ponoko** (www.ponoko.com): turns 2D designs into actual products, often within just a week. Uses distributed and on-demand manufacturing.

- **Dragon Innovation** (www.dragoninnovation.com): simplifies manufacturing and provides the framework and tools to move out of prototyping.

- **Shapeways** (www.shapeways.com): offers 3D industrial printing from user designs, and there isn't a minimum number of items required for any order.

CASE STUDIES

Up Dog Toys

Michelle Moy was working as a practitioner in healthcare, but she didn't love her job and wished she could find a more creative outlet. That's when she decided to start her own business, selling the Odin Dog Puzzle Toy, a geometric puzzle made of soft rubber in earth tones. Moy was tired of ugly dog toys for her young corgi named Odin. She wanted her pup to have toys she didn't mind looking at. Most existing dog toys were primary colors and rather unseemly looking. Moy imagined a toy with cleaner lines, materials that didn't scratch the walls and floor, and something her dog would truly love.

Moy started off by cutting holes in tennis balls, working her way through ideas on how to create the perfect puzzle toy. She'd let her dog bat it around the apartment and refined the design many times. She tried a Wiffle ball and tape. Moy was very focused on incorporating clean lines and geometry, two things she says were trending at the time and still remain popular. She tinkered with other household items as well to help her narrow down the design. Ultimately, Moy used a 3D printing shop to create a toy of thermoplastic rubber (TPR). While it wasn't the material of the final product, the 3D-printed prototype allowed Moy to save time and money getting closer to what she wanted. She says there were several back-and-forths with the designer and various iterations of the CAD drawings before she was satisfied.

The Odin was on the market by June 2015, and the company has been selling on Amazon, The Grommet, and in many small shops in the United States and Canada, especially pet boutiques. It's developed additional colors, and Moy says, "sales are great." Moy is working with a distributor in Japan and Taiwan, and Anthropologie will be carrying the dog toy during the 2018 holiday season.

Moy says she's working on a new product. "We need to keep working on it. It's not ready for release," she says, adding that she's confident she will soon have another puzzle toy on the market.

Food Huggers

Adrienne McNicholas and Michelle Ivankovic came from the old-school style of business. Ivankovic was the creative lead, and McNicholas was the marketing manager. Together they were a freelance team. Companies hired them to come up with products and pitch their next big ideas.

In 2013, as Kickstarter grew in popularity, the two friends decided to start making their own products. They took Food Huggers to Kickstarter, and it was the first time they were responsible for all of the steps themselves.

Knowing that there's an excessive amount of food waste—to the tune of nearly $1,600 per family per year in the United States alone, as 48 percent of all produce gets thrown away—they were looking for ways to keep food fresh longer. Their idea was to protect one side of the food—the end of a cut banana or the cross section of an orange—given that the rest is naturally protected with a rind or peel. Food Huggers emerged as "the cover for the missing piece," says McNicholas.

When thinking about the old vs. the new way of doing things, McNicholas says the biggest difference she experiences is the speed to market. When she and Ivankovic would present ideas to clients—between showing the idea, discussions within the companies, budgeting, planning, and manufacturing—it would often take six to nine years before that product launched. Compare that to Food Huggers. The duo had the prototype for Food Huggers in March 2013. By June of that same year, the company started selling its product.

As the industrial designer, Ivankovic developed the 3D files for Food Huggers and sent those to a prototyping house to have a set of molds made. They tested and tweaked them several times—in size and shape. The first set of rubber prototypes was a few centimeters too tall, and McNicholas says they tinkered with colors as well. These adjustments were made on CAD files.

McNicholas says 10 or 15 years ago, it was so much more difficult for a small business to get started and to get in front of the market audience. Now with more marketplaces and options for selling—micromarkets, Amazon, big-box stores, small shops, and sites like The Grommet—it's far easier. Online retail has changed everything, says McNicholas. "Where people drive to and park is not as much where they buy things" anymore.

When Food Huggers launched on Kickstarter in 2013 with a few products, the team raised $184,000. Food Huggers is now in a variety of online and more than 100 brick-and-mortar independent retailers. McNicholas says they open accounts with a few new retailers every week. The avocado Hugger is sold at Williams Sonoma, and their products are featured on Home Shopping Network as well. The Huggers sell on Amazon as well as on the company's website.

"Selling online is an important piece because it puts us in touch with customers," explains McNicholas. Through customer contact, she says, the company better understands consumer needs and challenges. "That's how we get to take the temperature of how the product is doing."

The company has continually added products to its line with recent additions including bowl huggers, wine huggers, and cheese huggers. McNicholas says growth is planned around products and tools, and they are always working on new options for sealing and wrapping products for storage—"anything to reduce food waste."

Masontops

When Mike Bacher and his friend Phil Baron started Masontops, it was because they noticed a resurgence of interest in and use of mason jars. It was 2014. At the time, Bacher says 99 percent of jars were promoted as canning materials. "But we knew that people were using mason jars for things other than canning." It turns out that fermenting was one of those things. That was the niche Masontops focused on.

Traditionally, fermenting occurs in huge barrels, but Bacher and his partner knew that the home cook did this in smaller batches. They developed three main products: a glass weight that fits inside mason jars (to help press down food that is being fermented), a simple wooden muddler, and a pickle pipe. The first two products were quite simple to design. Bacher says he could describe them to any manufacturer with the materials, and they could make the muddler or the glass weight without a prototype.

But the pickle pipe, which allows carbon dioxide to escape from the mason jar so fermentation can occur without too much of a buildup of gases, was a more complicated design. It required many iterations to get the size, shape, material, and valve construction just right. At the time, Masontops didn't have a 3D printer, and Bacher says he and his partner went back and forth for about six months with the manufacturer. Some of the pipes were venting too much, others not enough. Once they finally had a product that worked, they turned to Kickstarter, raised almost $200,000 in 30 days, and were off and running.

But Bacher and his partner knew that they had to get from ideation to production much more quickly, especially if they were going to continue developing products. So, they agreed to hire a product designer and buy a 3D printer. It changed everything for Masontops. "We could have a sample from prints in one day," says

Bacher. The in-house designer and printer enable them to tinker with ideas without feeling they need to commit to them.

Those three initial products of Masontops have grown into nearly 40 SKUs. And the company is launching three new brands: one is playful construction-themed utensils for children; another is innovative and simple hand tools for making bread (without a bread machine); and the third is a line of modern tools for rustic applications such as log splitting. "At every stage we look and decide, what are the next things we need to do to grow," says Bacher.

When the company launched in 2014, they were almost exclusively selling on Amazon. But over the past several years Bacher says it's been important to diversify and to be sure that they reduced their dependency on the retail giant. Masontops has seen a lot of growth in brick-and-mortar stores, including Bed Bath & Beyond and Ace Hardware. While they don't see a significant amount of sales through their site, it is a place where customers and interested buyers go for more information on canning. Bacher says the company is working on turning the site into more of a resource center with content.

TripleLite

One night, as Ron Pritchett was walking down some steps in the backyard of his home in California, he tripped. He had been holding a flashlight, but he turned it away from the steps and toward the side. That's when he lost his balance. Fortunately, Pritchett wasn't hurt, and he didn't think much of it until the following week when he was out jogging in the evening. He came across a couple, out for a walk. They were swinging a flashlight back and forth in front of them as they walked so as to light up more of the road.

"There must be a better way to engineer a flashlight," thought Pritchett, realizing that flashlights only project light in one direction rather than casting it in a more helpful arc. Pritchett started sketching out his idea for a 180-degree flashlight, one that would cast light to the front and sides at the same time. He talked to a patent attorney and started researching Chinese manufacturers. Once he settled on a factory, he and the team there faxed drawings back and forth until he was finally sent an actual prototype. It took two to three months to get the prototype drawn and manufactured. It took a mere 18 months from the concept to finished product on the market.

Pritchett said he remembers when the box arrived. He opened it, took one look at the flashlight that he had conceived of months earlier, and had one concern. "I didn't even know if it was going to work when I put the batteries in it," he recalls. Well, it did. He and his wife stood in their bedroom in the dark, and when they turned on the TripleLite, "It lit up the whole bedroom," says Pritchett, recalling that moment.

TripleLite was launched with that one flashlight. They started on Home Shopping Network, and "we did really good," says Pritchett. He now wants a mini version of the flashlight and is working on prototypes for one that would fit on a key chain, and instead of the small, singular light beam that some small flashlights have, this one will offer a wider scope and better light for people needing light while using their keys.

Pritchett is putting together an official sales team, something that is new for the company, and he is in talks with several large companies, and the flashlights are sold online at Target and Home Depot as well. TripleLite upgraded the lights in the original product to make them more powerful. The flashlight is now offered in four colors, and Pritchett expects the key-chain version to be available in seven or eight colors.

9

INDUSTRY ACCESS AND EXPOSURE

efore becoming a parent, many people would exit stage left at the prospect of changing a dirty diaper or cleaning up someone else's throw-up. And then the real live baby is born, and those unpleasant tasks become honorable sacrifices made for the well-being of that fragile little creature. So it goes with your business. I mean pitch competitions, speaking engagements, and other low odds–high rewards activities. Few get into the product game so they can prostrate themselves in front of a panel of judges at a trade show. They do it because they love their product and see it as an investment in the future.

Cracking open doors by putting yourself out there is not an academic exercise. These activities can yield key customer awareness, retail distribution, employees, suppliers, investors, and invaluable media coverage. It's a crowded world and everyone is busy. External validation is a universal shortcut for people to determine who is worth their time, partnership, or money. Everyone loves when others do the hard work of vetting for them. This is why you see awards badges prominently displayed on packages and on the home page of websites.

In the first four years of The Grommet I begged anyone who was organizing an event to put me on a speaking panel. Sometimes I showed up for an audience that was smaller than my immediate family. I did Friday night talks when I was almost comatose after putting in a 60- to 70-hour week. For the first New York Maker Faire I spent many tense hours in Saturday traffic driving from Boston to Queens. My gig happened on a small outdoor stage. I spent 30 valiant minutes trying to keep a small audience's attention while situated between a loud three-story-high fire-breathing mechanical dragon and a small business giving out free chocolate samples.

I scrutinized every startup competition and showcase that came my way. Because we were building a tech and media company, our choices were broad. We competed to be considered for a panoply of spotlight activities. Two of the early ones are indelibly burned into my brain because they caused a lot of nerves and physical drama.

Being new to the founder game, I was initially unaware of these activities, but a fellow entrepreneur and CEO recommended we apply for an upcoming Springboard Enterprises event in New York. The focus was on grooming and presenting 15 digital media companies at a pitch day to an investor-heavy audience. While this event led to meeting two of my most impactful backers, the real benefit was the training and polishing Springboard provided in preparation for the showcase day. I was assigned a handful of committed mentors, and we had two prep events, during which we refined our pitches and received coaching on a variety of topics from experts. (One of the mentors ultimately became one of our two lead angel investors.) The night before the big event, I did not sleep a wink. Not a wink. I spent the night "floating" above the bed, in our tiny cheap New York hotel room, listening to my cofounder Joanne's steady breathing as a backdrop to my own palpable anxiety. Joanne is blessed with the ability to sleep through anything. I am nearly the opposite. After all that angst, I did fine on stage—my adrenaline did not peak too early and I was forceful and determined. I got the job done. I even attracted a prominent investor and future supporter: Gerry Laybourne, the creator of Oxygen Network and Nickelodeon. And thanks to my black jacket and jeans, no one could see how drenched in sweat I was—be careful what you wear under those hot lights.

By the time our second competition rolled around at South by Southwest (SXSW), we sprang for two hotel rooms in the distant exurbs of Austin. We were selected for a Microsoft BizSpark Accelerator competition. Giddy with excitement, we went out for big, cheap burritos the night before. I don't know what was in that food, but it came up all night long in the bathroom. Two hours before my assigned pitch time, I was still upchucking and unsure of whether I'd be able to make the event. My stomach finally settled, and I entered the convention space a wan and spacey figure, looking at the ground and hoping no one would talk to me. I curled up in a corner of the auditorium awaiting my turn. And then, like a parent who finds the strength to lift a car off his trapped child, I sprang from my chair and pitched my heart out. We lost.

I share these stories because when you watch videos of this sort of event, you see only the end product, and you can't know the pain and suffering that might have paved the way to that sparkling and smart presence on stage. Anyone who is new to this is going to have a learning curve on both the business and emotional sides of conquering a pitch. Just start putting one foot in front of the other, ask for help, and don't judge yourself too harshly. There are many ways that your business will force you outside of your comfort zone, and public competition means putting on the big boy or girl pants, accepting the internal challenge, and the external stumbles. Apropos of this (and entrepreneurship in general), we have a big quote on our company kitchen wall from Burt's Bees founder Roxanne Quimby: "I really believe success is just getting up one more time than you fall."[1] After years of "just getting up" and just showing up,

I cannot count the number of times someone applied for a job at The Grommet, or recommended us to a friend, or contacted us for a partnership, or submitted a promising product for consideration because they saw me speak. Just this month a man I did not recognize came up to me to tell me he had seen me pitch at SXSW. I have always thought of that event as a valiant fail, but he remembered The Grommet quite positively.

After these somewhat traumatic early events, I entered the company in the esteemed Ernst & Young Entrepreneur of the Year competition—we were a regional finalist—and for numerous MITX awards. We never won a MITX award we applied for, but we won two big ones they bestowed on us without applying! The latest was "Disruptive Genius Company" in 2016.

When it comes to gaining industry attention for physical products, there are a variety of outlets and opportunities:

- **Trade shows.** New products are the lifeblood of every industry, and show organizers love the fresh energy these up-and-comers bring to their events. Often you will find a showcase or competition event at a trade show. We are frequently asked to judge them and find ourselves next to journalists and buyers from credible companies. The way The Grommet uses trade shows is instructive for new Makers. At some shows, our wholesale team has a booth, the primary purpose of which is to give our Makers a showcase to retailers, but it also is a great new product sourcing tool. Outside of that, our Discovery team attends every major trade show relevant to our product categories. They skip right past the big booths and find the lonely entrepreneurs manning tiny booths next to the bathrooms and hot dog stands. While most attendees are ignoring these unproven ventures, our Discovery team finds many diamonds in the rough. For instance, at the annual International Home and Housewares show in Chicago we discovered Negg, Butterie, and Frywall, among hundreds of our Makers. For many of these Makers, the best outcome of the show was a Grommet launch.

- **Alumni competitions.** Entrepreneurship is trendy, and chances are, your educational institution is eager to affiliate itself with alumni enterprises. This often takes the form of competitions and mentorship networks.

- **Traditional media:**

    Shark Tank is the most prominent expression of this opportunity. Many of our Grommet Makers go on from their Grommet launch to gain a slot on the show, having been validated by our curation. The financial deals on the show can be crazy greedy, but the media exposure is undeniable.

    Make48 is an up-and-comer geared toward providing an intense 48-hour boot camp experience that gives a TV audience (and potential supporters) exposure to the process of bringing a product from a gleam in the eye to a viable prototype. The Grommet team acts as mentors to the teams during each season.

    The Mark Burnett series *America's Greatest Makers* was a 2016 reality show with the goal of sourcing a new wearable device. The winner received cash as well as support from Intel. They are casting for subsequent seasons.

    The Science Channel series *All American Makers* with Marc Portney is a vehicle for Marc to source investable ideas. There are three Makers in each episode: two get consultants on product design, and one gets Portney's investment and industry introductions (QVC, The Grommet ,etc.). See https://www.sciencechannel.com/tv-shows/all-american-makers/.

- **Retailer programs.** Some retailers recognize their size has started to work against them because their buying processes and requirements are largely geared for the capabilities of big suppliers. They are counteracting that with streamlined submission processes to get exposure to new entrepreneurs. QVC has its Sprouts program, and both Staples and Hasbro have Maker outreach programs. The Hasbro one is notable because when I worked there, there was a policy of not opening unsolicited packages. The risks of unintentionally seeing an inventor idea and provoking a legal claim were too high. In a more digital world, Hasbro has better options for seeing new ideas without taking on unneeded risk. Women's apparel retailer Title IX has started a Movers and Makers Pitchfest to source gear and performance apparel for its rabidly loyal community.

- **Mashups of retailers and digital platforms.** The community-led invention platform Quirky, in partnership with entertainment and lifestyle retailer HSN, has launched The World's Greatest Party Host Invention Challenge on Quirky.com. Quirky and HSN ask Quirky community members to submit their ideas for game-changing party products, and select a winner who will have the opportunity to present live on HSN's show *American Dreams*. Ace Hardware invested in The Grommet partially, so this giant co-op of locally owned stores could have access to validated, de-risked, distinctive, and locally relevant products. This opportunity originated from my speaking at a Women in Retail conference, after which an Ace employee in attendance, Karin Schlueter, came running over to discuss a juicy business need. And truth be told, I did not want to go to that event—it was inconvenient and I had to dress up in girly clothes (not my comfort zone.) Because of that conference experience alone I have learned to trust that *something* good comes out of almost every effort I make to expose The Grommet.

- **The Grommet.** We've held local and national competitions to uncover new Makers. Our largest one was a product pitch held at Fenway Park, of all places.

- **Regional events.** I've emceed a pitch competition at Detroit Homecoming, a gathering of 250 Detroit expats who are invited back to reconnect with our hometown. This pitch event is terrific exposure for the local startups that participate, many of which have a physical product.

Every time you see a chance for exposure, grab it with both hands. Over time you will start to separate the wheat from the chaff, but in the beginning it is great practice to start small and humble while you get your sea legs for speaking and pitching.

CASE STUDIES

Articulate Gallery

Colin Gilchrist and his wife were tired of sticking their kids' artwork to the fridge or watching it curl in the humidity of a doorway. They designed simple, practical, and classy picture frames to house rotating (or permanent) works of art.

Gilchrist thought *Dragons' Den*, the Scottish version of *Shark Tank*, might be a good way to get in front of a larger audience. He pitched his idea at a local business event and won a slot on the show about a year after the business had launched. Articulate Gallery had only sold 300 frames at that point.

Gilchrist says the frames weren't quite the success he had hoped they'd be on the show, but since two of the show's investors each bought one (totaling 30 pounds altogether), the local paper ran a tongue-in-cheek headline about the Articulate

Gallery's appearance on the show. "Glasgow Couple Secures Record Investment from *Dragons' Den*," read the headline. Gilchrist laughs about it still. It was a record, all right. A record low investment. But, it gave the couple bragging rights. "As seen on *Dragons' Den*" and "Purchased by *Dragons' Den* experts" is something Gilchrist could now say about his product.

There was an uptick in sales after the TV appearance, and Articulate Gallery was off and running. Helpful, too, were appearances on Britain's *Next Big Thing*, the morning news show that featured the frames as a best buy for the holidays, and *I Want That*, a show on the DIY Network. "It's free advertising," Gilchrist says. "Industry access and marketing go hand in hand."

But Gilchrist says trade shows have been especially helpful for business in the long term. After three visits to U.S. trade shows, Gilchrist says two-thirds of the company's business now comes from the United States. Amazon is the largest of all retailers, but others include Bed Bath & Beyond online and Target online, and they do well at trade shows. Amazon in Australia and France have helped the company reach into Europe and other markets. They also participate in flash sales through sites such as Zulily.

Gilchrist says the company launched with three products, and the idea was to expand into so many more. They now have four frames and offer them in "any color you want as long as it's white," laughs Gilchrist. He said they tested other colors and people weren't much interested in anything other than white. He's happy with what they have to offer and with the scope of the business. "If it ain't broke, don't fix it," he says.

ChargeHub

Cable Hub, which kept wires and cables neatly aligned on a tabletop or desk, came first. Then came ChargeHub, a multiport charger that was launched at the Consumer Electronics Show in January 2014. The company had won an innovation award and was getting great feedback from that show. It was there that Rock Smeja, one of the principals of parent company Limitless Innovations, met a team from QVC. Smeja says his company was immediately interested in learning more about being on QVC, but there were a lot of logistics to understand and work out. They ended up hiring a consultant to coordinate the details of the QVC relationship.

QVC stands for Quality, Value, Convenience. "It sounds so simple," says Smeja. "But it's so important." QVC opened a whole new world for ChargeHub, which meant Smeja and his team have been more focused on those three attributes. They've bundled ChargeHub with cords, car adapters, and other items to create more value for the consumer. They've come to better understand their demographic (90 percent are women making the buying decisions for their homes) and making sure that convenience was still a need the product satisfied.

ChargeHub was first launched on QVC in early February 2015 and sold 1,200 units in under 10 minutes, says Smeja. He has a photo of the "SOLD OUT" sign that flashes on the screen when inventory is gone. He was really floored by the success. QVC quadrupled its next order. Since then, it's continued to order more and more. Approximately 60 percent of the company's sales are now through the channel. Smeja says one of the advantages to being on television is the opportunity that it affords to visually explain a product. "That's very special to have that," he says, adding that videos and online tutorials can be invaluable when selling a product.

The company added another four chargers to its line in 2018 and now has 50 products. "Every two years we make a big jump," says Smeja, explaining that they are constantly working on designing and creating new products and customer opportunities. The latest big named product is JumpSmart, a self-contained vehicle jump starter, and sales of the tool now account for 50 percent of the company's business. Smeja says it's been an exciting and sometimes overwhelming ride, not to mention a successful one, as the company has grown 34 percent each year since its founding.

PocketMonkey

For Nate Barr, founder of PocketMonkey, which produces credit-card thin pocket-sized multitools, going on *Shark Tank* isn't the be-all and end-all. He says he's constantly asked if and when he'll be on the show, and many people he encounters think it's legitimizing for a business. He's been approached, but he isn't that interested. At least not yet. Barr sees it as a double-edged sword. You may be chosen to film a segment, but that segment won't automatically air. So if you prepare to be on *Shark Tank* by building up inventory, you may never even be on TV and could end up with surplus inventory you've paid for and can't sell. On the flip side, if you don't have enough inventory you could ruin your reputation and future by not being able to meet the demand these shows often produce.

And Barr says that while finding a mentor through *Shark Tank* has long been appealing, the reality is that "the sharks are stretched so thin" that he doesn't expect he'd actually be receiving that much one-on-one time anyway.

For him greater success, "is having progress from one product to a portfolio of products." PocketMonkey now has more than 800 SKUs. The company also makes state-specific shaped multitools, beer can openers, necklaces, and more. The company's leaders used to rely on outsourcing the manufacturing of most of their products. Today they have nine laser systems that allow them to cut their own thin pocket tools and gadgets. Most all of what they sell is made in-house, and the company built new warehouse space to accommodate its growth and business model.

Most orders flow through the warehouse in a few days, and the company keeps very little inventory since production time is quick and the bulk of orders are are custom-made, taking into consideration the pairing of state shapes and tools. "We're using the Agile methodology to develop new products," says Barr, explaining that they work in an efficient, cost-effective way. By manufacturing in-house they can also test new products and designs without becoming overcommitted.

REI is one of the biggest retailers that carries PocketMonkey, says Barr. Others include The Grommet as well as many museum stores.

10

FUNDING

The topic of funding is near and dear to my heart. I postulate that each young company is going to be severely tested in one area more than any other. While I hope your challenges are vastly different than that of The Grommet, funding (or lack thereof) was the continual wolf at the door for our first four years. Did I mention that we launched days after Lehman Brothers collapsed in 2008 and the financial crisis was reaching full devastation?

Beyond financing, in the case of consumer product companies, the biggest existential threats often come from illegal counterfeiters selling on Amazon or eBay, or good old-fashioned competitors who improve product features or lower pricing.

Alternately, the numero uno challenge could be people-related: conflict between founders or dealing with the destruction that just one bad-apple employee can bring to a new company. It might be legal threats or manufacturing glitches.

In the case of The Grommet, there were plenty of battles in many areas. They all presented adversity and pushed me to new limits and learnings. But the bigger battle in our early years was far and away the challenge of funding the business.

I devoted at least 75 percent of my time to finding the resources to keep the company alive. It was soul-sucking, hard work that took a toll on me in every way. And it was only possible for me to manage this high-demand focus because I had a strong cofounder in Joanne Domeniconi, who was building our core product discovery and content operations successfully and largely independently.

SOURCES OF FUNDING

While it would be cathartic to write a whole chapter, if not a book, on my four years of pounding the pavement, suffice it to say that if you find cash to be your major problem, I feel you. The good news is that there are some interesting and dedicated options for addressing the specific needs of a product company, and many Grommet Makers are navigating these waters better than they ever could have when we first started our company.

There are many kinds of funding:

- **Funding from internal operations.** This is the happiest scenario, in which you self-fund the business only long enough for it to generate enough cash to cover all of your business needs. The odds of this are low, unless you have (1) a decent personal bankroll to last a couple of years without a salary; (2) long margins on your product; and (3) miraculous speed in gaining customers.

- **Partner financing.** Sometimes you can work a version of the above, while some of your partners advance you what you need. This would largely be retailers prepaying for inventory or a contract manufacturer offering you generous payment terms that allow you to sell inventory before you have to pay for it. It's a bit of a chicken and egg, but the larger you become in terms of importance to a partner or supplier, the more leverage you have to get financial support. When we were in the middle of a funding project at The Grommet, I went to one of our largest vendors to renegotiate our pricing. Our business success mattered to the vendor, and they understood why I needed to show better bottom-line results. They agreed. I was grateful, and my loyalty was both rewarded and enhanced.

- **Loans.** There is a huge range of sources here. The most common are friends and family, banks, and economic development programs through nonprofits and government agencies such as the SBA. There are more tech-enabled solutions such as Kabbage, the assessments of which are based more on algorithms and big data rather than a meeting with a loan officer or long credit applications.

- **Invoice financing.** NOWaccount is one option that was built to address the common problem of financing inventory to meet big orders. Oddly enough, success itself can kill you in the form of new retail accounts. Home Depot makes 75 percent of its profit from the "float" period between the time it sells goods to consumers and the time it pays its suppliers. Big manufacturers can finance big-box stores, but this scenario is a terrible mismatch for a young company's cash resources.

- **Lines of credit.** This is similar to a loan, but the difference is you use it only for short-term needs and repay the loans regularly and rapidly. These instruments can be a lifesaver.

- **Crowdfunding.** Kickstarter and Indiegogo are most often used to build a first production run while assembling a small cohort of curious early adopters and supporters. Some Makers treat these platforms as a form of intermittent financing and go back for a second or third round.

- **Equity.** This is giving part ownership of the company in exchange for capital. *Shark Tank* dramatizes this and brings it to life. Sources of this capital can be friends and family, professional angel investors and angel funds, and venture capital and private equity funds. These funds can also come from strategic partners, such as a retailer, media company, or manufacturer with a strategic partnership interest in a business.

- **Incubators and accelerators.** Examples would include:

  Y Combinator (www.ycombinator.com): a seed accelerator that twice a year invests in a large number of early-stage startups.

  Bolt (www.bolt.io): a venture capital firm that invests in pre-seed, early-stage companies and focuses on hardware.

  HAX (www.hax.co): an investment company and hardware accelerator.

  Highway1 (highway1.io/): a hardware startup accelerator.

  Hardware Club (hardwareclub.co/): a community-based venture firm for hardware startups.

  MassChallenge (boston.masschallenge.org/): the largest startup accelerator in the world, with operations in the United States (Massachusetts and Texas), Mexico, Israel, Switzerland, and the United Kingdom.

- **Competitive pitch events.** These tend to be put together by an industry organization, accelerator, university, or group of sponsoring entities looking to create media awareness for themselves or "deal flow" for investors. Prizes range from in-kind services to meaningful no-strings checks. Chances are there is one (or several) in your region.

FUNDING NEEDS

Before you jump on any given source, let's review the basics of what kind of funding needs you can anticipate. Your capital requirements are likely to fall into three buckets:

- Business operations

- Inventory

- Capital equipment

Business Operations

The first bucket, business operations, is the only one in which you might consider taking on equity investors, or people who expect part ownership of the company in exchange for their capital. Selling equity (as opposed to, say, taking loans, running a crowdfunding campaign, or securing short-term financing from a customer or a line of credit) is the most expensive form of funding. Why? Every percentage of investor ownership is a percentage you give away. If and when you sell the company, or if and when you use stock options as a way to attract top-notch employees, you will be very protective of the equity pool. Equity ownership percentages will move from simply being a pie chart diagram to real economic incentives for employees and real money in a transaction.

First, despite this caution, let me acknowledge that many founders are too protective of company equity in the early stages. They often believe they have a billion-dollar idea and overvalue the idea itself. Ideas, especially those without patent protection, are a dime a dozen. They have little to no value. You create real and increasing value with each step you take to turn that idea into a thriving business. Going from no prototype to a working prototype creates value. Hiring your first employee creates value. Getting your first production run from a factory creates value. Securing packaging and nailing fulfillment and delivery operations creates value. Most of all, securing repeat customers and growing revenue creates value. When you only have an idea or business plan, you are not offering much to potential investors, and they will rightly expect a huge share of the company in exchange for capital—if they invest at all. They are taking on three kinds of risk: funding risk because you may not be able to attract enough capital to make the company viable; market risk if the product is not fully developed and proven; and executional risk because you are promising to run a well-oiled machine but you haven't shown you can do it yet.

Just watch two episodes of *Shark Tank* to see that reality writ large. The founders who just have a prototype and a dream are proposed usurious offers by the Sharks, who expect huge ownership stakes in an embryonic business. The founders serving real customers and who have impressive sales trends are the ones who can go toe-to-toe with the investors and negotiate a healthy deal.

When you can show investors that their capital will help you grow the real business operations you already created, then equity makes sense. This means that you can demonstrate how you will use the investment: perhaps you will make sales soar by hiring sales reps, or pursue marketing activities you have already tested and proven successful, or fund future product R & D to keep the product line extensions rolling. Sometimes it can feel like the only time you can get an equity investment is when you don't really need it. But dems da apples.

At The Grommet we see many Makers who never take on equity investors or who have a very limited close set of friends and family as investors. It is exceedingly difficult to convince traditional venture capital firms to invest in physical product companies. They tend to have little to no experience in those areas (having come from a banking, tech, or software background) and perceive the risks to be larger than the rewards. Beyond that, they like to believe that lending their expertise to a company can double the value of their investment. They are rightly cautious about approaching the magical, mystical world of consumer products. When I was raising money for The Grommet, which had more to do with building a tech company than a product, I was hampered by this investor insecurity. They saw the focus on consumer products and took that as a compounding of risk. I distinctly recall one investor telling me, "Jules, what I myself know about your business would fill your little finger. I have given you the sum total of what I have to offer you in this single conversation. There is no more there." Another said, "I can't invest. I like you. I believe in you. But I know so little about e-commerce and consumer products that I just can't get comfortable in the space. It's no knock against your business. It's probably brilliant and I will regret passing. But I am just not able to evaluate it."

Having said that, there are positive trends creating increased venture and private equity funds for consumer products. This is due to the fact that consumer products far outweigh the tech industry in our economy. They represent a whopping 70 percent of our GDP!

One of the tech-enabled venture capital platforms that has been unique in addressing early-stage funding of the consumer products sector is CircleUp. Founded in 2011 by Ryan Caldbeck, its interesting machine learning–powered marketplace has sourced $390 million in funding for over 250 companies. CircleUp portfolio companies typically raise $1 million to $5 million from a combination of institutional investors, family office funds, and companies such as Kellogg's, General Mills, and Unilever. In 2017 CircleUp also raised its own $125 million fund to complement the marketplace investments already in operation.[1] Its portfolio includes a few early Grommets such as Back to the Roots, Soma Water, Hickies, Nomad, Rumpl, Sunski, and Urbio. Sarah Endline, founder of all-natural chocolate and snacks company sweetriot, successfully raised funds on CircleUp and says, "CircleUp creates a seamless platform for consumer entrepreneurs to quickly and efficiently find capital and support for their companies. I found their team quite committed to building a community and ecosystem to lift emerging consumer product companies."

Here is a sampling of the more established and traditional venture capital firms, plus some up-and-comers that have made a strong and concerted effort in consumer products:

- Forerunner Ventures
- Trinity Ventures
- Lerer Ventures
- Silas Capital
- General Catalyst
- NEA
- BBG (Built by Girls)
- Maveron Venture Capital
- Beechwood Capital
- XFactor Ventures
- Female Founders Fund
- The Helm
- SheEO
- Backstage Capital
- Upfront Ventures

These conventional VC firms fund a tiny fraction of the deals they see. Entrepreneurs run the gauntlet of a rigorous partnership review and diligence process to gain the small number of (large) checks a year that the partnerships write. Leverage all your networking skills to get an introduction to the right partner at any of these firms and read up on the extensive online advice about how to approach a venture capital firm. Venture capital fundraising is a full-fledged founder activity, and it comes with a set of processes and language all to itself.

In the right place at the right time, equity financing represents a boost to both the credibility and bank account of a company. Knowledgeable investors such as savvy angels and venture capitalists can be amazing allies for your startup.

One final thought on equity: If you take a check from a friend, a family member, or anyone who is not an experienced investor, *your* decision to take the money has to run through two gates. First, be sure this capital is not important to the person's balance sheet. You do not want the burden of carrying anyone else's financial pressures and security beyond your own. These should be funds the investor can totally lose without undue suffering.

Second, you need to have this conversation every time you take a nonprofessional's check: "I value this relationship. I intend to work as hard as humanly possible and do my best to give you a terrific return on your investment. Your trust in me is meaningful. But if typical startup odds come true, there is at least a 50 percent chance this business will fail and I will lose all your money. I need to be 100 percent sure that if that happens our relationship will survive as it is more important to me than the funds. Can you give me that assurance?"

Getting a yes to this question is the difference between sleeping at night (at least when it comes to investor responsibility) and not. You are going to need your sleep. Ask the question. Listen to the answer, and watch the body language. No investment is worth putting your relationships at risk.

Inventory Financing

While many Makers finance the business operations by hook or by crook, and never pursue the high effort/high reward activities of an accelerator or competition, virtually all successful Makers find funding inventory to be a pressing need.

Many use Kickstarter and Indiegogo for the first run up that hill. A successful campaign is a business in itself and not for the faint of heart, and there is a whole cottage industry of advisors and resources for crowdfunders to tap. Don't go it alone without studying the best practices and devoting substantial time and energy to the campaign. The rewards can be high in that a successful campaign is like a friendly low-cost loan against your first production run (much of which you typically use up to repay the funders). Compared to meeting the needs of retailers or online customers, this community is patient and supportive of the ups and downs of delivering their inventory, as long as you are highly communicative during the whole process.

Let's say the business is operational and you funded your first production run yourself or via an Indiegogo campaign. Let's say you are starting to see some retailer traction and the orders are growing. That's when things get interesting and growth presents an unexpected and sometimes impossible challenge. For an example, when Kate Spade got some great editorial coverage for a new line of handbags, its existing retailers such as Neiman Marcus decided to expand the bags from just a handful to their full line of stores. Happy day, right? Not exactly. That's when founder Kate Brosnahan had to beg, borrow, and steal the capital to front the inventory costs because department stores pay 30 or 60 days after you ship them the goods.[2] Add on all the time to get the goods manufactured with a producer who will probably require a hefty down payment on the work, and you've got a several-month financing pinch. It can feel ironic to have growth and success present one of your biggest problems.

Lara Hodgson experienced this very problem with her water bottle company, Nourish. When Nourish received its first big order from Whole Foods, Hodgson's team celebrated. But "it was that very success that almost put us out of business," she recalled. Selling to small boutiques had been simple. Those stores paid immediately with a check or credit card. Large companies, on the other hand, paid anywhere from 30 to 90 days after receiving a bill. Hodgson had to scramble to keep up with the growing demand, not wanting to strap the young company with debt that might hinder future access to capital that would be needed for tooling and not wanting to raise equity that required her to give away half the business.

"This just doesn't make sense to me," she moaned. "The reality was we were growing to death."[3]

This experience inspired Hodgson to found NOWaccount Network. Its core benefit is that a small company can sell its retailer invoices to NOWaccount for a 3 percent fee, to gain payment within five days. You might be familiar with the concept of factoring, which got a bad name due to the steep 15 percent commission. This is a tech-enabled and more affordable way to get paid faster.

Beyond the crowdfunding and inventory financing platforms, many Makers do pursue good old-fashioned lines of credit or loans to fund inventory.

Capital Equipment

When it comes to capital equipment, there is a whole capital marketplace built around getting businesses the funds to acquire equipment. Leasing is one solid option, and often the dealers or manufacturers themselves will offer this route. If you are unsure of your long-term equipment needs, a lease may be advisable.

Loans are another traditional option with possible tax deduction advantages. Beyond the tax implications, comparing this decision of buy (with a loan) versus a lease is similar to a personal car decision. If you take a loan and pay down the debt, the equipment becomes an asset to the business. That is not the case with a lease.

The hurdle to capital equipment debt is a little lower than straight business loans because the debt is secured by a physical asset. You can finance all or part of the purchase, you can finance used equipment, and interest rates vary tremendously but are generally lower than other business loans. The core theory is that the revenue produced by the investment will more than cover the annual debt service.

The sources for these loans can be big banks, which have a 23 percent approval rating, or credit unions, which finance 42 percent of all small business loans. The highest loan approval rating occurs with more specialized and online lending sources, at 60 percent. Whichever route you consider, you will need to have these ducks in order:

1. **Credit history.** You can get a free report to see your business credit history. You will get everything but the actual credit score. You can also pay a small fee to access the score that lenders will see. Make sure the report is accurate, and clean up any issues that reduce your creditworthiness. Places to get a business credit report are: CreditSignal, Nav Credit Monitoring, Credit.net, Creditsafe, and Scorely.

2. **Financials.** Get your past profit and loss financial history, future projections, and cash flow projections in presentable order.

3. **Business plan.** This can be a written narrative or a presentation that helps the lender understand your vision for the business and how this capital equipment will help you build the business.

Of all of these financing options, Fundera is a good place to dive deeper into the various options outlined. See: https://www.fundera .com/business-loans/guides/small-business-financing#equipment financing.

On the general topic of small business financing, the Small Business Administration is also a treasure trove of trustworthy information on this topic. See "Financing Options for Small Businesses" at https://www.sba.gov/tools/sba-learning-center/training /financing-options-small-businesses.

Money makes the world go round, and that trite statement is doubly true when it comes to building your business. This area is more creatively addressed by Grommet Makers than I ever expected. Yet their decisions always depend on two things: the viability of the business and their personal resources and financial preferences.

CASE STUDIES

Tactile Craftworks

Sarah Kirkham and Anna Warren of Tactile Craftworks, a leather crafting company in Milwaukee, were working with very little capital. They were using a spare bedroom in each of their homes as work space, and in September 2014 they did a Kickstarter to buy their own laser cutter. Until that point, they had been using one at a local discovery museum. Their goal was $12,500. They raised $15,000, which enabled them to buy a bigger bed for the cutter to rest on as well.

"It allowed us to do as much product as we wanted," says Kirkham. It revolutionized the business for them. It was a small campaign, but sometimes that's all you need to launch yourself to the next major step. They now have three laser cutters and are self-funded.

Warren says they mapped out the entire Kickstarter plan and didn't leave anything to chance. They had a backup plan in case it didn't work. And they had a few people lined up who were willing to pitch in funds on the last day if the goal hadn't been met, in order to push the campaign to the top. (Otherwise, as is standard with Kickstarter, they wouldn't have received the funds.) Warren says they planned for nearly a year before and leading up to the start of the campaign. They also opted for a 30-day campaign rather than a 60-day one, because they felt that after 30 days, the urgency can disappear. "It takes a lot of gumption to ask for money," says Warren. "We decided we'd rather do so for 30 days."

Warren and Kirkham say they were pretty confident going into the campaign. "We had high hopes," adds Kirkham. But what they didn't expect was to feel the emotional support of strangers, friends, and family so deeply. They planned to quit their jobs "and put all of our eggs in one basket," so when they started seeing the numbers climb on Kickstarter, they were relieved but also grateful. They remember getting a $500 donation from someone in San Francisco and a $3 donation from someone in Japan. Total strangers. "We were equally excited about both of those," says Anna.

The cofounders were able to quit their jobs, while continuing to make their product in that spare bedroom they set aside. The company has since moved into an artist's studio space with 2,000 square feet. "Tactile Craftworks is 80/20 certified, meaning all of the labor for our products is done in the United States, and 80 percent of the material is made domestically as well," explains Kirkham. Some pieces are imported, namely the metal flask that the company sells wrapped in etched leather, while half of the leather they use is tanned just four miles from their studio. The rest comes from a facility in Pennsylvania.

Since launching in 2014, the company has grown from offering etchings of 11 cities on their goods to about 200. They started in 15 stores in the Midwest and are now in more than 150 stores around the country plus catalogs including Sundance, Orvis, and BBC Catalog. The founders go to four trade shows a year and are always looking to add more products, but Kirkham says, "Right now, we can't expand faster. We can only work so many hours."

YoYo Mats

Aaron Thornton started his company with a seed round from friends and family. "They're investing in you because they care about you," says Thornton, who designed a self-rolling yoga mat. He partnered with his father Jack Thornton and Yu Tsai. "But it can be a little awkward," Thornton says, noting that entrepreneurs often have to rely on friends and especially family, particularly if the resources are there. "I don't advise taking your grandma's last $10,000," he quips.

But for Thornton, he had family with enough of a cushion to help him jump-start the business. "They were willing to invest."

YoYo Mats did an initial Kickstarter campaign with a goal of $50,000 in 60 days; they earned $165,000. When that money ran out, they went to Indiegogo. All in all, YoYo Mats has taken in more than $200,000 in crowdfunding.

Thornton realized early on that he wasn't just targeting yogis but rather gadget and gizmo fanatics. These were people who would buy the mats as gifts for friends because they were intrigued. On Kickstarter, 80 percent of the buyers were buying gifts.

But Thornton warns that you can't just rely on these crowdfunding campaigns. "You'll top out," he says of sales. After the campaign, Thornton hired a PR firm to help with some of the marketing. *The Today Show* did a segment on the mats about 20 days into the Kickstarter campaign. That day $20,000 came in through Kickstarter. From there, they got mentions in *Time* magazine, *Sports Illustrated*, *Shape*, and others. "That was the snowball we rode through the campaign instead of paying for PR," says Thornton.

The mats have won product awards as well. There are accompanying videos online to demonstrate the ease with which the mat rolls up, featuring the founder and others demonstrating. They are sold on Amazon, The Grommet, HSN, and through Anthropologie's website.

Back to the Roots

Alejandro Velez, cofounder of Back to the Roots, maker of organic indoor gardening kits, says his company worked with CircleUp. "It's a great company," he says. "The funding is decentralized, and CircleUp lets angel investors act as a fund."

"If you get a backer, it gives you that snowball effect," explains Velez. "You need that first person." Velez describes CircleUp as being "almost like a Facebook page of investors." It's a great way to connect with investors and funders, and you can, over time—and if you work at it—form relationships with some of them, he says. Velez adds that he's been fortunate enough to have been mentored by CircleUp investors.

Back to the Roots initially raised $250,000 on Kickstarter in 2013 and a few years later as part of their Series A (their first round of significant investments), Back to the Roots used CircleUp and raised $2 million.

On Kickstarter, Velez says people are "buying a product that doesn't yet exist. CircleUp is geared more toward a tangible goal."

As Velez explains, there are some investors on CircleUp who "have a lot of net worth and others are doing it just for the social investment." An added bonus is that it gave the company a lot of exposure, says Velez.

Zubits

While living in China with three little boys, Ryan Wiens and his wife, Valerie, knew too well the frustration of having to take shoes on and off multiple times a day with a family of five. "We had to find a better, faster way to get shoes on," says Wiens. It was around the time that Crocs, the popular slip-on shoes, were everywhere. At first, the couple thought about creating an entirely new shoe, but they quickly realized they didn't want to get into manufacturing footwear.

After tinkering around, Wiens settled on magnets as a way of shortcutting the tedious process of lacing up a pair of shoes. Although he tried out his new gadget on his own kids, his parents, his sister and her children, and some other family members, Wiens says the best market research came from Kickstarter.

"Kickstarter is a market research platform," he says. "It tells you everything you want to know about your product."

The couple conceived of Zubits in 2013 and went on Kickstarter by the end of 2014. They had done their research, made a very polished video, and sent an e-mail blast to 1,000 people at the start of the crowdfunding campaign.

Once the campaign went live, Zubits was immediately in the top five most popular products on the site. In the first week, the company was in the number one and two slots. That was out of 6,000 products! "It's a great place for gadget-y, convenience items," says Wiens. That first Kickstarter campaign raised $362,000, and a subsequent one brought in $450,000. An Indiegogo campaign, which was completed at the end of 2017, brought in $90,000. For Wiens, Kickstarter opened the door to the international markets as well. "You get noticed by a lot of people," he says of the site.

The company now has 36 different color and size combinations of the Zubits. Wiens says they consistently grew the first few years, and they now bring in $1 million in revenue. They're not looking to grow much beyond this though. "We haven't really tried real ad spending," adds Wiens. And they haven't tried pushing into major retailers. "We are happy where we are," he says. The gadget is popular among the special needs community, and sells well in occupational therapy offices and medical supply stores. "The business is kind of running itself, and I'm happy with where it is." Wiens says that instead of trying to grow Zubits he's been considering launching something new.

Nomad

Noah Dentzel launched a Kickstarter campaign for Nomad in the summer of 2012. They raised $161,000 in just 40 days. The day the campaign ended, Nomad started selling to the public, although Dentzel admits they weren't in production quite yet. "We didn't really know what we were doing," he adds. Nomad's first product was a USB charger the size and shape of a credit card; they started shipping many months later.

Nomad operated by continuing to sell, using that money to manufacture, and keeping that cycle going. "We kept selling as much as possible while shipping," explains Dentzel. "We had a shipment delay time that was slowly getting smaller." But they were also continually trying to catch up, and in order to catch up, they had to build more sales. "That's what bankrolls production, shipping, and buying stamps," says Dentzel.

About a year after the Kickstarter campaign, Nomad launched an Indiegogo campaign. The Nomad team had met with management from Indiegogo and liked that it could serve as a marketing platform as well. "It was awesome," says Dentzel, of the Indiegogo experience. They raised a little more than $170,000 and sold 8,000 units to nearly 6,000 backers. This gave the company the funds necessary for production. It enabled them to close the gap between orders and delivery.

Yet another year later, Nomad, which had since expanded into offering a multitude of charging and technical accessories, decided to use CircleUp. The idea of crowdfunded equity was very new at the time (summer of 2014). Dentzel and his team had heard about CircleUp and started asking friends and colleagues what they thought about Nomad doing a campaign with them. "People said 'nah,'" recalls Dentzel. But they had said the same about Kickstarter.

At the time CircleUp was largely an unknown entity. "They were very professional, very clean cut," recalls Dentzel. He says that as a small, unstable business, they wanted to feel like they were with an established, reliable entity, and they found that in CircleUp. The goal was to raise $1 million, but once they hit $500,000, Noah said he and the team knew they could start accessing the money. They ended up raising $1.26 million. At that point, Dentzel said, "I went from being a hands-on key player to being someone who was chasing down money." While he says he's grateful for everything Nomad has raised, he's hoping not to have to do any more fundraising for now. "I'd do it again if we need to," says Dentzel. "But I want to be self-reliant and self-sufficient."

By the end of 2018, Dentzel said he was still so much in the thick of growing a new business that "we have the cart in front of the horse, trying to hold on and stay alive and get in front of that horse." When Nomad launched they had one product, and they now have more than 50. One-third of the business comes from retail sales, including REI and Best Buy, and one-third is from international distribution. The remainder is direct to consumer. With 13 employees Dentzel says they are finally at the place of planning for quarterly projections rather than taking it day by day.

11

MANUFACTURING

When you are an entrepreneur, most of the time you feel like you are trying to *will* something into reality: an investment, a partner, a new hire, a prototype. That dynamic changes dramatically when it comes to manufacturing. Why? Because your fundamental position has a little more power and objectivity—you become a *customer*. When you set out to manufacture something, you are most likely dealing with an established set of companies— you are unlikely to be cajoling people to do something radically new or outside their experience. As a customer, you have leverage and power. You are not begging, borrowing, or stealing to get a job done. OK, you won't be stealing no matter what, but if you have been banging away at your business, you know exactly what I mean. You are always trying to make something from nothing. Manufacturing is the opposite. You are simply trading *cash* for *something*.

In addition, searching for manufacturing resources has a degree of objectivity. You can review past work by potential producers, talk to their customers, and ask people who make relatively similar products for guidance on sourcing. It's a research project with a clear, expected outcome: a quality product produced to your specification at a cost you can absorb and be successful. You are going to be the world's best expert on whether the job is being done to the standard you envisioned. So many of the inherent insecurities of being a company founder are alleviated during this part of your company's formation.

In some cases, your manufacturing will be in-house, so your sourcing will be for both equipment and expertise to realize your vision. But this is also objective investigative work as opposed to the more amorphous stuff of startups.

That's the good news.

The bad news is that (1) you still will very likely be capital constrained—whether it comes to sourcing your first production units or buying or leasing equipment to begin your own production; and (2) you will have to use powers of persuasion to get skeptical equipment manufacturers or banks to extend you financing if you are self-producing. If you are contracting for production, you will most definitely be convincing manufacturers to lower their minimum volume requirements on the hope and prayer you will bring them meaningful quantity orders in the future. So alas, poor entrepreneur, you are still going to be tap dancing. But at least the goals are clear, and the outcomes are immediately measurable in terms of saleable units of your product.

Over the decade of building The Grommet we have observed a strong push from both consumers and Makers to make products in the United States. When we first started working with Makers, they often did not have a domestic manufacturing emphasis, and when we asked about their sourcing they usually just talked about the costs of American factory production. Over the last five years we find that many more Makers start with a firm goal of producing domestically, and if they end up going overseas they have very thoughtful reasons and close factory relationships.

On the customer side, we find a sharp division. A large, possibly majority, segment of The Grommet's U.S.-based supporters are committed to supporting American-made products, and they show up consistently with their purchases. But U.S.-made goods run the full spectrum of being sharply priced to carrying a 10 to 50 percent premium for domestic manufacturing costs. And especially with new products, it can take months or years for Makers to get their supply chain fully optimized and to achieve the volumes to compete with Asian manufacturers. The full truth is that even within the very engaged Grommet community, sometimes the additional costs of U.S. goods are not tenable. For a great number of people, the commitment to "American made" is not deeply seated, and they spread their budget over less expensive and, often, more cheaply made purchases.

Producing in the United States has distinct sourcing and transport cost advantages. It is safer from an intellectual property perspective as well. Some Makers believe that having their product made in a Chinese factory doubles or triples the risk of being attacked by counterfeit products, so they refuse to take the chance.

Kettle Pizza is a grill-top pizza oven entirely made in the U.S.A. Cofounder George Peters explains, "Sometimes you have to come up with your own items as you invent the product. So we had to find people all around the U.S. to cut the steel, produce the nuts and bolts, form the pizza stones, and make our boxes. So it's been a constant evolving of trying to find the best partners we can. It has been a joy when you deal with other companies—and a lot of family-owned companies—that are still committed, for decades, to making things in the U.S." George's partner Al Contarino adds, "You want to be able to make jobs in your own community or your own country."

The rise of international manufacturing and Amazon's ambition to sell "everything" has opened a tidal wave of cheap international goods flooding the U.S. markets. But the Internet has changed how this works as well. Consumer product companies don't have to rely on printed catalogs such as *Thomas Register* directories anymore when they can source from overseas manufacturers.

The number one factor pushing American companies to produce offshore is the cost of tooling. Tools are essentially the extremely durable molds in which product parts are made. This is high-precision work that straddles both craft and technology. Many plastic products are injection molded—which works exactly as it sounds. Tools have to withstand the rigors of high-volume production, and the parts must have very narrow tolerances (variations from the specification) in order to work. Joelle Mertzel of Butterie says, "Just when I had successfully researched and chosen a domestic manufacturer to produce my butter dishes, I learned that they do not produce the necessary tooling, and they referred me to a variety of partner companies that could produce my tooling. All the quotes came in at six figures."

Mertzel was in a bind. She wanted to produce in the United States, but the tooling bill was a nonstarter. Fortunately, she was part of a peer group of entrepreneurs, and she noticed that several members were using the same factory in China. She ended up happily and fruitfully contracting with that firm for her manufacturing. With blazing success on The Grommet, Butterie maxed out the firm's production capability. Mertzel is now looking to source a second factory to provide her with more capacity but also more leverage on pricing. She says, "I love my first factory, but my costs just went up and I have no recourse. I don't want all my eggs in one basket."

Most Grommet Makers who source overseas work with an agent to help them navigate the complexities inherent in such an endeavor. Organizations and services like Maker's Row, Dragon Innovation, and Timroon are changing this, too, because they are experts in helping small companies source offshore production.

A great number of successful Grommet Makers work with Platform 88, which is a respected group of four factories in China focused on hydration, grill accessories, and outdoor products. They work closely with new companies just off successful crowdfunding campaigns and offer end-to-end design, build, and scaling services. Examples of their Grommet clients include Stojo, The Grate Scrape, Rumpl, Cold Bruer, and Ooni grill accessories.

Our best Makers never fully outsource their manufacturing partner choices, even if they work with a trusted agent. They visit factories before awarding any contracts. They get plenty of references. They establish relationships with the owners and managers of their production partners, whether the factory is across the globe or down the street.

This closeness to production sources is doubly important in a world where consumers increasingly extend the idea of "traceability" from the food world (where did this egg come from?) to the products they buy. Consumer products are rarely fully manufactured in one location. They depend on a full supply chain of materials and component experts. At Grommet we have launched products that come embossed or printed with individualized codes that one can search to discover the composition of each product component, where it was made, and how many people work in that location.

But ultimately, whether manufacturing domestic or offshore, Makers have more options than ever before. Generally, when you are just getting started in sourcing manufacturing, the best way to start is to ask founders of companies who make a product of similar materials or complexity as yours. The needs of a luxury towel Maker are vastly different from those of a portable security alarm company or a board game Maker.

As long as your product is not competitive to theirs, most Makers have great willingness to talk about their experiences. In fact, I would argue this is often their highest learning curve and body of knowledge. Getting in touch with the founders of Maker businesses is not the daunting task that it would be in penetrating a global multinational to find the SVP of manufacturing. Makers are usually justifiably proud of the gauntlet they ran to get their product made, and they enjoy talking about the journey, even to strangers. A Maker might be skimming by on managing her finances, or packaging design, or marketing, but no one gets to market successfully with half-baked manufacturing. The learning curve tends to include many facets of this area, from assessing a factory's capabilities, negotiating contracts, and analyzing costs to managing manufacturing logistics and the supply chain. This is most definitely an area where there is no need to reinvent the wheel when you have fellow Makers who have already learned the ropes.

Here are questions to have at the ready for this kind of manufacturing research call:

- What was your process for securing manufacturing?

- (If they outsource) Are you considering bringing manufacturing in-house?

- How did you vet your current factory or factories?

- (If offshore) Did you find any agents you trust?

- Did you visit your offshore factory before selecting it?

- How do you communicate with your factory?

- Were there any other factories you seriously considered contracting?

- How did your factory bid for your work? What specifications did you provide to them before the bid?

- What were the setup costs to begin production? (Either straight dollars or a percentage breakdown of where the initial investments went—dies, setup costs, tooling, etc.)

- Does the manufacturer provide packaging? (Common for offshore factories)

- What negative or positive surprises occurred with this factory?

- How did you get to the quality level you need from the factory?

- What is the prototyping process you go through to start producing a new product with this factory?

- What kind of minimum order quantities have they required?

- What payment terms do they expect?

- Have they met delivery deadlines?

- Were there any hidden costs (from your manufacturer) in your path to getting your products produced?

- What happens if they produce defective products?

- What contract terms are most important? Are you willing to share any of your manufacturing contracts with me?

- What are the big things I should look for in contracting out my manufacturing?

- What do you know now that you wish you knew back when you were just getting started?

When all of this work is said and done, the bone-deep satisfaction of receiving a well-made batch of products that you conceived is a priceless experience. It's not an event the average person will ever have, and for many Makers this is a pinnacle point of their business journey.

CASE STUDIES

Zkano

"It's tough manufacturing on your own," says Gina Locklear, owner of Zkano socks. Locklear manufacturers all of her socks in her family's facility in Fort Payne, Alabama. From a family of sock makers, Locklear was able to manufacture her own organic, made-in-America socks in her parents' sock making plant. Her family had purchased the manufacturing facility in 1991, and she started make Zkano socks in 2009.

"It adds a whole business to your business," says Locklear of manufacturing on your own rather than contracting with manufacturers. Because the infrastructure already existed for sock making, Locklear didn't have to jump through quite as many hoops as she might have otherwise. But the technology had changed quite a bit since her family moved into the sock business, so much of the equipment was starting to become outdated.

Locklear, for whom eating organic and being healthy were important, incorporating organic fibers into her clothing was a natural next step. And she was committed to keeping the manufacturing and the materials that go into her socks, including the cotton and low-impact dyes, local. "The cost is high to manufacture here," she says, and the competition is with those companies that are manufacturing overseas for significantly less, which means they sell to consumers for significantly less.

But one of the best parts of manufacturing on your own and being right there in the facility is that you can make changes without having to deal with contracts and overseas timing or communications. Locklear can reproduce socks in a day, and she can increase or decrease production depending on sales. It's easy to make small batches, there is less waste, and she can test designs simply as well.

When Locklear launched her sock line she had one color of yarn, natural. Now she works with more than 50 colors and adds new ones every season. "Our color range has been growing since 2011," she says, adding that they needed to find the right dye house to take care of locally sourced, organic material. At first Locklear offered a crew sock and a basic athletic sock. Now they have more than 150 active styles at any given time.

Initially Locklear didn't have the machinery or technology to expand beyond the simple socks but has since added the capability to produce a variety of patterns and styles, including seamless toes. Locklear is now focused on building a sales team. "We know big box isn't our sweet spot," she says, adding that small boutiques are where their socks do best sales-wise.

American Bench Craft

After his wallet fell apart, Jason Angelini just figured he should try to make his own. It was the third one in five years that had worn out, and he found that they just weren't made that well. He wanted a seamless wallet that was high quality and wouldn't fall apart. With a background in design and engineering and his brother Chris Angelini's background in marketing and advertising, the duo decided to start their own company. Enter American Bench Craft. The brothers decided they would do this only as an American-made company. "Personally, it's something I'm passionate about," says Jason Angelini.

American Bench Craft manufactures almost everything in-house. There are a few pieces that they use along with their products—canvas, for example—which they source, but all of the leatherwork is done in their Reading, Massachusetts, facility.

When designing their products, the brothers were particular about making sure they could produce each item with minimal skilled labor, with minimal parts, and on machines and equipment available to them in the United States. Most of their products are fastened with simple rivets, something people can be easily trained to do. It wasn't an advanced skill that would require overseas labor. During the holiday season or peak seasons, American Bench Craft adds several workers to the mix to fulfill orders, but Angelini says the company is set up so that he can quickly train people to get up to speed on manufacturing the quality products they are proud to sell.

Although Angelini says being American made is something he is passionate about, he also believes it's the easiest way to start out. As he says, you don't have to travel overseas to find a manufacturer or set up arrangements with people you've never met at facilities you've never visited. "It's scary how much of the industry has moved overseas."

"When you are doing your own manufacturing, you won't be good at everything," says Angelini. "Figure out what you can make the best. And team up with others when needed." American Bench Craft tried making their own canvas bags but knew someone else could do it better, so they figured, "Why not just go to the place that's been doing this for 60 years?" says Angelini. "Know what you're good at, and seek to work and team up with others."

American Bench Craft launched with one wallet and now has more than 50 products that are selling well, including small leather goods, belts, bracelets, and dog collars. "At first, it was, 'I want a good belt, I want a good knife case.' Now it's about which markets we break into." Angelini says they constantly think about creative ways to position the company, including new products and new markets that fit with their current success.

The company has been making coasters and key fobs for Sam Adams and other major companies, although they can't discuss all of them. Angelini says the company cleared a 10 percent profit in 2017, and having launched in 2014, that makes him quite proud.

Bite Helper

When it came to creating a prototype for Bite Helper, a small device that relieves itching from insect bites thanks to a heat component, Eugene Zabolotsky knew he needed to find a manufacturer he could trust. The first one he found was in China. The prototype came out to Zabolotsky's liking, and he was confident in moving forward. But after that initial prototype creation, the first order of the Bite Helper did not pass muster. "The thermostat wasn't what we agreed on; the plastic wasn't up to standard," he explains, adding that the factory had swapped in substandard parts and materials. "They were trying to manufacture in a cheaper way."

At that point, Zabolotsky says he knew he needed to find a new manufacturer. While at the Consumer Electronics Show, Zabolotsky got to know Heatact, a company that manufactures in Taiwan and had an outstanding heat element. Bite Helper partnered with Heatact and began manufacturing there as well. But first, Zabolotsky visited the factory, inspected everything, and was cautious about standards. Because the factory was accustomed to creating many heat-retaining products and heating elements, Zabolotsky says he was confident he had found the right place. Bite Helper has been manufacturing there happily. Zabolotsky says the plant also has the capability to do all of the packaging of Bite Helper as well.

"It's very important to make sure quality control is implemented at all stages of production." For anyone starting out with finding a manufacturer, Zabolotsky says, "Pay less attention to cost and more to quality." At first, "I liked the idea of the cheapest possible option," but in the end it wasn't worth it.

Since Bite Helper launched, Zabolotsky says sales have been steadily increasing and the company has expanded into Europe, Asia, South America, and Australia. It primarily sells online through The Grommet and in more than 5,000 Ace Hardware stores. The device has been given consumer electronics awards and featured on major news channels and shows in the United Kingdom.

Zabolotsky decided not to go into stores like Home Depot because he envisioned the products, which need some explaining, getting lost on the shelves. Instead, the online platform allows for videos, explanations, and a greater opportunity to reach the customer. He and his partners are working on new products that use technology to improve health through drug-free solutions, and they have a PMS relief product and a musculoskeletal-related one in the works.

Axiski

A butcher in England, Darren Mather was simply looking for a way to have fun with his two daughters when he created the Axiski. With just two laminate floorboards connected by some rope—voila!—he had the most popular sled on the hill. "Everyone wanted to try it," says Mather. The adults could stand, while the kids could sit on this sled/ski hybrid. It became a fun and versatile way to enjoy the sledding hill "instead of parents standing at the top of the hill, getting cold and bored," he says.

Although Mather was excited about "being on to something," he knew nothing about manufacturing or taking a product to market. He spent a long time researching online how to manufacture products, how to sell and source, and more. "I watched a lot of *Dragons' Den*," he says of the U.K. version of *Shark Tank*.

After much research and contemplation, Mather contacted the U.K.'s most popular sled maker to ask for some advice. The company was just 10 miles from where Mather lived, and he had a conversation with the CEO. The soon-to-be-competitor even pointed Mather toward its manufacturer. Axiski spent a while manufacturing at that facility, but once that factory couldn't keep up with demand, Mather found another one, though that one was also unable to meet demand after some time. Currently, he is searching for his third factory and hasn't decided whether production will stay within the United Kingdom.

Mather says it's likely that he will outsource to somewhere in Slovenia or Slovakia. His goal, no matter what, is "to ensure that I get the quality and the price I want." He adds, "Being a brand-new product, I need to get the best possible price in order to make retailers go for it." For Mather, "Price rules over origin of products." Based on the feedback he's gotten from the industry and customers, whether the Axiski is made in the United Kingdom or in another country won't tip the scale on sales in any notable way.

"The order I've gotten from The Grommet has given me the confidence to go out and get more business," says Mather. He's been working on selling through Facebook in Europe, which has been successful, and he's looking at any markets where there's a likelihood of snow.

In 2018 Axiski opened up Ace Hardware stores, which Mather says provides "a humungous potential for sales." He adds that it was his dream to get into the U.S. market but he didn't think it was possible. That alone has been inspiring. When the company launched it had five products, and now there are four and one less color. Mather says the changes were "all to make it more simplistic."

12

PACKAGING

undamentally, there are two primary kinds of packaging: retail-ready (what you see in stores) and shipping packaging (what gets delivered to your door when you buy online). I will mainly concentrate on retail packaging, as it is particularly challenging. But first I want to address the poor stepchild that is shipping packaging.

SHIPPING PACKAGING

The shipping package rarely gets sufficient attention. Think of an Amazon shipping box. Yes, it is branded with a logo and/or printed shipping tape. But it's utilitarian and uninspired. It costs no more money to print a clever graphic or copy on a box than a horrible one. If you are selling online, the way you ship becomes an area of focus, especially for an unproven new business. You are not Amazon. People will scrutinize your work and be a little skeptical. Do you pack efficiently to avoid waste but also effectively to protect the product? Is your shipping insert material consistent with your brand and website? Do you use environmentally responsible materials, and do you brand your shipping boxes?

That last point came to life for me back in 2007 when I opened my first package from the newly launched fashion flash sale site Gilt Groupe. It was a novel concept, and the young company needed to build a reputation for quality and trustworthiness. Due to the high risk of theft, Gilt Groupe shipped in a plain corrugated box, but the entire inside of that package was branded. Opening that beautiful box on my dining room table was a *wow* moment for me, and it reinforced my perception of having made a smart purchase. In fact, the jacket I bought remains one of my favorites—worn for special pitches or day trips to New York. I later met one of the cofounders of Gilt, and I mentioned the happy experience and suggested that they also include a thank you card. Lo and behold, my next shipment had a thick cardstock thank you card signed by Alexis Maybank and Alexandra Wilkis Wilson, the cofounders. Even before the thank you card inclusion, this emergent company had shown me that they were concerned about their customers simply through their care and handling of my package. You must do the same.

When you are shipping low volumes you have the competitive advantage of going above and beyond. Before we launched our business I described Grommet to a friend who is a big car nut. He gave me some good advice. "I buy a lot of car parts. They are a commodity. I could buy them from anywhere, but I always order from this little company that throws a bag of M&M's in every shipment. I can buy my own candy, but I like that little human touch. You should do something like that to connect with your early customers." If AutoZone did the math on throwing in a chocolate treat in every shipment, their accountants would surely squash that idea. But you? If you have an idea for distinguishing your business and its shipments, you just have to look in the mirror and have a management meeting with yourself to decide a go/no go. If your hunch is that you can stand out with some aspect of your shipping, make it a go.

RETAIL PACKAGING

When it comes to retail-ready packaging, here's one of the predictable patterns we see at The Grommet. When a company is first starting out, it often treats packaging as an afterthought. And indeed if it is only shipping online orders, the exterior box usually matters more than the product packaging. When we request samples for testing, we see countless products arrive in plain poly bags, off-the-shelf generic boxes festooned with home-printed labels, and simple hand-done ribbon and tags or bubble wrap. While not optimal, that is certainly acceptable if you don't have any physical retail distribution. The one exception: if your product is primarily intended as a gift, then your packaging should be gift-ready or easy to wrap. For instance, jewelry in a poly bag is totally unacceptable.

Showing Why Your Product Matters

The minute you get your first retail purchase order, the packaging expectations enter a higher plane. In fact, it is difficult to get your first order from any store if you *don't* have appropriate packaging. Here's why: even in the smallest and most lovingly managed boutique, the staff may not fully understand your product and be able to explain it. Or a customer may prefer to browse in private, or the associates simply can't get to everyone. So think of your packaging as the remote version of *you*. If you had a mere three seconds to explain why your product matters, what would you do? Let's say you are in a competition to convince a panel of consumers to pick the very best product based on a three-second pitch. And oh, you cannot speak, use a video or any digital media, or show a physical sample of the product. What would you do? You'd have just a few words or pictures, almost like giant flash cards, and you'd make sure they are clear. That is the essence of good packaging: fast and clear.

There are other layers that matter, of course. They include:

Consistency and Quality of Branding

I recently met with a Harvard startup team that had a novel idea for a pack of recipe cards. The exterior box had a dramatic vintage-inspired design, using elaborate typefaces with decorative elements in a black and gold palette. It evoked a certain mood, but it had no relationship to the actual cards inside, which were a mash-up of different fonts and illustrations of varying colors. This is a dramatic example of inconsistency, but we see a huge range of quality and discordance in startup packaging components. One reason is that offshore factories often provide packaging design services as part of the manufacturing contract. I can guarantee you will get what you pay for: a package that looks like it was rapidly designed by a distant foreign designer with no connection to your business. Invest in a clear visual identity for your company, including your packaging. Vet the printing, surface quality, and thickness of the packaging material from the factory. Take control of any interior materials and inserts. Don't assume anything or take what is offered without many proofs and prototypes.

Format of the Package

If your product is small and likely to be stocked by big-box retailers, you will likely need it to be hangable on pegs. There are plenty of exceptions to the land of pegs: food, apparel, and home goods, for example. But the larger the retailer, the more likely your product will live on a slat wall. In general, study the type and size of packages at retail and try to conform to the standards you see. Target which existing products you want to bump off the shelf and imagine how you can make that easy for a retail buyer to visualize, too.

(Fundamental to succeeding at retail is to understand that if you win shelf space, someone else loses it.)

There are exceptions: times when a radical change in packaging can create a whole new market. Back when more women wore panty hose, L'eggs were a monster product launch simply because the hose, which was quite ordinary, came in a white plastic "egg." It was fun and intriguing and implied a new level or quality or fashion. It also came on its own freestanding display, making it easier to adopt in a store. Similarly, Method cleaning products were introduced in fresh form factors and colors that created intrigue and energized a tired category that had seen very little innovation. These are instances where breaking the rules was essential to success. Just don't break them without having a very solid strategic reason to do so. Getting a product into retail is hard enough—don't build in unnecessary obstacles with an overly novel package that is hard to stock or does not stand up to retail wear and tear.

Functional Information

This is important on two levels: there may be legal constraints on what you could or should say on your package, so this requires research. All packaging designs should start with the essential functional and legal information, and this info should not be crammed around the "marketing stuff." Consumers have a whole other level of needs relating to understanding how a product works and what the box contains—the "marketing stuff." It's a fine balance between achieving speedy understanding and fully explaining a product. In many cases it seems like you can never get it quite right. Part of the reason for this is that when you are an unknown brand, you cannot draft on the goodwill and openness of the population to ascribe some known attributes to your product. You have to get a lot of information and intangible qualities communicated through this package. Yet a package that is densely packed with information on features and benefits will likely overwhelm casual browsers and never encourage them to continue to read. Here are a few more functional tips:

- If your product comes in multiple colors and is not visible from the package, don't show it in just one color.

- If your product is expandable, collapsible, or turns into something cool and/or unexpected, do your best to explain it all on the packaging with pictures.

Visibility of Product Versus Defending Against Shoplifting

In my days at Playskool I worked on packaging for global distribution. While displaying multiple languages was a design nightmare, I anticipated that challenge. What I did not expect at the outset were the various packaging constraints posed by the bane of retailers: light-fingered customers. For our shipments to France, we actually had to wrap packages in those nasty plastic ties that cinch into a permanent death grip around a box. (Those bands that are sometimes used by law enforcement as handcuffs.) It hurt my eyes to see our beautiful packages treated like common criminals heading to a hearing. For the United States, where customers really want to touch a product, we had to balance the size of the open packaging windows with the risk of theft.

Durability

Packages get beat up. Anticipate them being dropped in warehouses, pawed by customers, and their surfaces abraded during shipping. There are tried and true materials and printing techniques used in packaging for a reason—take your risks in other places. If your product is being consistently damaged (or stolen), you will see retailers hesitant to reorder.

Displays

Retailers are highly variable when it comes to interest in displays. Compare your experience going into a department store versus a discount store. The higher-end store has a certain architectural and graphic style that it will be loath to override with your display, no matter how beautiful. A discount store operates with limited staff, so displays can become the hardest working "associate" on the floor. Thus, whether you invest in displays has a lot to do with the size and complexity of your product and your intended distribution. When the Swedish floor cleaning company Bona was looking to break into the U.S. market, it proposed a very instructive endcap display, including a demonstration video integrated into the fixture, to its launch partner, Ace Hardware. Bona knew it had to create product understanding, and Ace was willing to get behind the novel, quality product because Bona was giving the 5,000-store co-op major point of purchase support (and sales exclusivity). Some further thoughts on displays:

- "Pop the top" point of purchase displays are really popular. This means the product ships in the display, often made of printed corrugated cardboard. The retailer just opens it up, puts it on the counter or floor, and lets it sell. Even upscale gift stores will use displays if they are made of quality materials like wood (not corrugated). Our Maker PocketMonkey (a credit card–sized multitool) has penetrated museum stores and high-end boutiques with a spinning wooden display that holds its full range of tools.

- Demonstrable products may want to invest in video displays. Video can be expensive, but for products customers need to see in action, it really increases sales. Grommet Makers' Negg (a hardboiled egg peeler tool) and Chateau Spill (stain removers) are small enterprises that made this investment due to the "gee whiz" demonstrations possible in video.

- If your product is scent driven, you may need to figure out a program to help retailers with testers (e.g., free with a minimum purchase or discounted price for testers). In addition to helping with sell through, it will help protect your retailers' inventory from being destroyed. Customers will want to smell a product whether it says "tester" or not. People have no problem opening up fresh units and making them unsellable, so get in front of that risk.

Functional and Operational Requirements of Retailers

Retail-ready packaging must be designed according to the functional and operational requirements of retailers' warehouse processes and equipment, as well as their store staff. These needs are separate and distinct from consumer-facing shipping packages or retail-ready packages. I am talking about the boxes that get your products to warehouses. The minimal considerations should be:

- **Packing in multiples for shipping.** Design as compactly as you can for shipping purposes. No one wants to pay for shipping or storing space.

- **UPC codes.** Our VP of wholesale, Jason McCarthy, says, "The number one thing I see Makers neglect when it comes to packaging is not getting in front of proper UPC codes. They should make sure to get this right from the start, so they don't have larger problems down the road with retailers or even their own future warehouse." This means:

  o Make sure everything is barcoded—from individual units, to inner cartons, to master cases.

  o Don't purchase an unassigned UPC from another company. If you properly register with GS1 (the UPC governing body that makes this whole system hum), you get a company prefix that identifies your enterprise. Then you have the ability to assign UPCs using that prefix. This allows you to set up consistent case and carton barcodes so when a warehouse receives the product workers can scan it and know that it is, for example, a master case of 24 units with 4 inner cases of 6 each inside.

- We have seen Makers cut corners and use one UPC to cover multiple colors of a SKU. This becomes a nightmare for any retailer with a warehouse and usually leads to stickering the unique products—at the Maker's expense.

- When you set up case packs for an SKU, make sure to have nonmixed case packs for retailers and warehouses. In other words, don't set up a case pack of 12 red items and 12 yellow ones in a case of 24. Retailers can sometimes work around this condition, but it's generally easier if not done that way.

AN IMPORTANT INVESTMENT

At the end of the day, retail-ready packaging is going to be one of your most important investments. One of the biggest challenges to the founder of LÄRABAR as she was launching her nutrition bars was funding a minimal packaging run. It cost $100,000 for packaging for just her first five flavors. There is no point in spending that kind of money on a half-baked concept. Refer to Chapter 8, and apply the same prototyping practices to your packaging as you do to your product. Some professional resources for packaging include services and sites such as Packable, Packaging World, and Assemblies Unlimited.

With the exceptional effort required to bring a product to market, it can be hard to apply that same level of focus to packaging. But your success at retail depends as much on the box as what is in it, so give it the same level of care and attention as the product.

CASE STUDIES

Cord Buddy

As an IT specialist, Steve Kwak was used to getting work calls at all hours of the day and night. He was basically always on call, which meant he was always somewhere near his phone. Whenever Kwak went to unplug his phone from where it was charging, the cord would inevitably drop to the floor, and he'd later have to fish it out from behind a dresser or night table or end table. "There has to be something on the market to hold these in place," Steve thought one night, exasperated. Even his kids, who had phones, had their cords on the floor. One evening, he took a stuffed animal from his daughter's bedroom and plunked it down on top of his phone cord to use that as a weight.

For a few weeks Kwak researched what was on the market when it came to keeping cords in one place and found that there wasn't anything yet. He went to his local hardware and sewing stores, picked up various materials, and tried to make something that worked. At first, Kwak mostly relied on beanbag material and fabric, piecing together a weighted object that kept cords from slipping. But the fabric didn't hold the cords in place in exactly the way Kwak wanted. He was envisioning a boxlike product that had the perfect sized opening for a cord so it wouldn't slip out, could stay in place, but also could be pulled through fairly easily.

Kwak sketched out his ideas on paper and then translated those into Microsoft Paint, where he says it was easy to change the shapes and the colors. Those drawings went straight to the manufacturer. Kwak relied on Microsoft Paint to design his packaging as well.

From the beginning, he has been constantly reinventing the style and shape of his packaging. At first, while introducing Cord

Buddy to the market, Kwak knew he needed to have room on the packaging to explain the product. There had to be an interesting design, and he wanted color. He started with a heat-sealed clamshell-style plastic package. He then heard from retailers that they wanted a package that could stand up on a shelf or hang from a rod. So he went with a snap-closed plastic package that was easier to open and close to demonstrate the product.

At one point, Kwak says he even tried a small cylinder-shaped package, but there wasn't enough space on it for marketing. As the product became more well known—and needed less explanation—he moved to the current box, which is smaller. Early on, Kwak says he was counting on people to pick up the box and read the instructions.

Over the years, while the product has stayed relatively the same, it's the packaging that's needed constant updating. As his business has grown in eastern Canada, Kwak has even had requests to add instructions in French, for French-speaking Canadian customers. And when Kwak was promoting Cord Buddy at a golf conference he had the package redesigned yet again, so that it was small enough for attendees to carry around all day.

There are have been many iterations of the Cord Buddy over the years. The latest model has a motion sensor night-light to further reduce the need for fumbling around for power cords and devices in the dark.

CouchCoaster

When it comes to packaging, there are so many pieces that you have to factor in to how you're going to box up or wrap up your product, says Barry Freeder. As the founder of CouchCoaster, he knew he wanted to showcase how well his product was made. A firm, aesthetically attractive, silicone holder for drinks that rests on either side of a couch arm, the CouchCoaster wasn't easy to explain to buyers without them being able to see it. The first packaging for CouchCoaster was a transparent box without an image on the front. It was on the back, and the bands that hold the coaster steady were tucked under themselves. "It was packaged so beautifully," says Freeder. But no one knew what it was. "It wasn't the best-selling packaging."

The second version had a photo of the product on the front of the package, but Freeder insisted on keeping the coaster in a transparent box because he wanted consumers to be able to see the quality. He kept hearing from retailers, "This looks great, but it's getting scratched up on the shelves." By the third edition Freeder had scrapped the plastic box and instead went with a cardboard one. He says, "We're not quite there yet." Freeder still wants people to be able to have a sneak peek inside so they can have a better sense of what they're buying. "This evolution is just a case of learning and learning and learning."

Freeder says there are so many factors that go into packaging. For example, he sells to Bed Bath & Beyond, which "loves to peg everything," meaning he needs a tab for the box to hang. He'd like to see the "As Seen on TV" label on the box as well. Some retailers have told him he doesn't need that. The product needs packaging that works for both retail stores and shipping purposes. "I want the packaging to be 100 percent right."

The product has certainly taken off even if the packaging will need further refinement. When CouchCoaster was featured on the *Today Show*, Freeder sold 750 units in 24 hours. U.K.-based, the company has brought in £2 million in sales and has manufactured nearly 100,000 CouchCoasters. It mainly sells in the United Kingdom, Europe, the United States, Japan, and the Middle East. Most of its sales are online, and most of those sales come from Amazon, says Freeder. As the company has grown and as people buy online, Freeder realizes he may not need to stick with the content-filled package he designed for in-store use. At some point, the packaging becomes irrelevant if you're selling online, and Freeder imagines the day will come when the CouchCoaster goes right into a poly bag and gets popped in the mail.

Joco

The reusable glass coffee cup, created to help eliminate paper cup waste, Joco is committed to environmentally sound practices as a company. Hopeful that more people will opt for the reusable coffee cup, the company also wants to be sure it's doing the right thing in other aspects of its business. Which is why the packaging for the cup is streamlined, contains no waste, and can be both recycled and upcycled, meaning it can be repurposed. The sturdy brown cardboard cylindrical Joco tube has won a few design awards along the way.

"Joco is all about being plastic free as a company and all about reusables," says James Forte, sales director for the United States. "We had to look at the packaging side as well." The glass Joco cups are designed with a silicone sleeve around them to protect against breaks. The silicone, says Forte, is something that won't leach even if it did end up in the ocean.

Inside the lid of the Joco tube are many suggestions of what to do with the packaging. "Don't throw me away!" it reads. Recommended uses include taping the tube to a bike as a cupholder and using the box as a piggy bank or pencil cup. When Joco first started selling coffee glasses inside the tubes, customers would regularly post photos of their repurposed plans for the tube. Since it's been about seven years since Joco launched, Forte says fewer people do that now, but the company still gets great feedback on the packaging. "People think it's cool looking."

Forte says it's been a balancing act between creating packaging that effectively explains what the product is and is also environmentally friendly. Without a plastic window to see in the box, Joco relies on retailers to display the coffee glasses. Since Joco is primarily sold in coffee shops, people are more apt to know what it is. That, or the intriguing tube leads them to investigate.

By the fall of 2018, Joco had done another redesign on its packaging to reduce the manufacturing required. The box is now square and a bit lighter than the previous one. It saves on transportation fuel and costs, says Forte. Joco is sold in 21 countries and more than 1,000 stores. Its biggest footprint is in Asia and the United States.

Invisibelt

Kathy Kramer invented Invisibelt because she wanted a belt that would lie flat, without a bulging buckle. When she and her business partner got to the point of thinking about packaging, Kathy knew she wanted it to be stackable. As she looked through various catalogs, she came across a candy catalog. Instead of a traditional box, Kathy opted for a round candy container with a clear top. "It had room for fun," she says. There is a silhouette of a girl with a ponytail (and no bulging belt buckle) on the packaging, and the logo is on each of Invisibelt's products.

"It's gift-able," says Kathy. "I wanted it to be a girlfriend product," she adds. "Fun and lighthearted." Plus, she says, the box is creative and sturdy enough because "we intended for you to keep the belt in the packaging." Thin and clear, the Invisibelt could easily become lost among clothes piles, which makes the packaging an essential part of the product.

"We never imagined it would be in a thousand stores," says Kathy. But now that it is, Invisibelt's stackable, clean packaging allows the customer to see in. It's intriguing enough that customers reach for it out of curiosity, and the real estate on the box allows for both a visual of the product and an explanation. Invisibelt also offers display cases for retail shops to showcase its product more efficiently.

Kramer says the company has a nice online presence, through Amazon, Invisibelt's website, and The Grommet. About 40 percent of sales are through Amazon, 30 percent through other online retailers, and the rest is wholesale. "The landscape has changed since I started," says Kramer. "There was no Amazon. And for me, personally, I go to Amazon for everything." Kramer says the company does about $1 million in sales each year. Since they launched, the partners have added many belts in different styles, colors, and materials. There's an elastic belt, a denim one, and more than 25 different styles. They've also added some additional products such as small bags and add-on cuffs that can be attached to a shirt to change a look. But the belts are the core of the business.

13

MARKETING

Marketing is a tale of two cities. First there is business-to-consumer (B2C) marketing—the stuff that builds awareness and drives sales for your company, especially directed at the target user of your product. Second, there is business-to-business (B2B) marketing aimed at attracting wholesale orders from retailers or resellers. They are two very different disciplines with vastly different channels and opportunities, but they can (and should) work together to improve the overall effectiveness of your marketing efforts. The more successful you are at building a favorable and well-known consumer brand and product awareness, the easier it will be to attract wholesale orders. And the inverse is true as well. The more successful you are at attracting wholesale orders, the more consumers will be exposed to your products, which will help build your brand and increase consumer demand. The focus of this chapter is solely on consumer-facing marketing. I will address the topic of wholesale marketing in the next chapter, as part of the larger topic of gaining retail distribution.

First, I need to get a bias out of the way. I started The Grommet largely because I thought that marketing a new product was too difficult and expensive for most young companies. The most fundamental thing we do at The Grommet is build awareness and credibility for a previously unknown product and company. So to a certain extent, we *are* the marketing engine for many companies. I still believe marketing is the single hardest challenge for the aspiring Maker.

But we can't work with all worthy companies and products, so The Grommet cannot be the answer for 99 percent of organizations.

Fortunately, there are marketing activities that are totally within reach and even better done by a small company than a large one. To begin, you can have a credible presence online very quickly—via a website, Facebook, or Instagram. You don't have all the processes and approvals of a big company—you just get it done. You feel out platforms and pick the ones that you believe you can manage most effectively. Whichever platforms you use, be sure to express a coherent brand and visual identity (discussed later in the chapter). It is impossible to be credible without at least a basic online presence.

A small company's advantages are largely related to the ability to create an authentic and responsive presence on social media, gain press coverage, and provide a personal customer experience. But because these competitive advantages depend more on human capital (blood, sweat, and tears), they are hard to scale. For some companies, these activities will prove to be enough to meet their ambitions or financial needs. For a company with large capital costs (such as tooling) or a product that depends on gaining national shelf space (like a personal care product or a food) or with big growth ambitions, these guerilla activities will not be enough. I will address these scaling activities later in the chapter.

When I think of Marketing with a capital *M*—this is the stuff that delivers brand awareness and leads to true scale and growth. To give you a benchmark, at The Grommet we only did low/no-cost marketing for our first four years. Ten years since inception (six of which included actual marketing investments), we now have 11 percent awareness among the general U.S. population. A company like Etsy would be at 60 percent, and the Coca-Cola brand would be at 100 percent. Building awareness takes time and money. A *lot* of it.

The complexities lie in a few areas:

- **It's expensive.** Advertising comes in many flavors, and we all intuitively know that most national print, radio, or TV ads are costly and out of reach for a small company. The production expenses alone can require a large investment. But many people don't realize that advertising on digital platforms such as Google, Facebook, YouTube, Pinterest, and Instagram can require significant budgets to make serious headway on acquiring customers. (I am distinguishing paid placements from the guerrilla/no-cost activities I suggest above.) Additionally, costs and performance will vary as a direct reaction to supply and demand, a lot like what happens in traditional media. Super Bowl ads cost more than late night cable reality shows. During the 2016 election, our media costs skyrocketed when the election coverage sucked up all the attention. Between the overwhelmingly negative furor dampening consumer attention to ads or anything outside of the election, as well as the massive amount of political content and advertising, our normally successful ads became really expensive and were less effective. It was devastating to our budget and expected results because we got only 50 percent of the sales returns that we had planned.

- **Digital media is a fast-moving and sophisticated game.** A slight change in a Facebook policy or Google search algorithms can challenge your previously successful campaign overnight. Further complicating matters, the big advertisers (think Ford and Procter & Gamble) have attentive account managers and digital agencies that help them skillfully navigate the platforms. The little guy has none of those advantages. At The Grommet, we have found that the only time we have any cost advantage over the big advertisers is when we pilot a new program released by one of the digital platforms. Larger advertisers can be slow to adopt these sometimes buggy and little-known programs, even though they do tend to get early exposure to them. But if you pay attention to blogs and the industry press, as well as the announcements from these companies, you can keep up with platform changes and even beta programs that are low-priced while they are trying to gain adoption.

- **It's high stakes.** Few Makers start their business with marketing expertise. In fact, you will likely lack experience in many areas such as finance, legal, and logistics. Whereas you can patch through those other areas with elbow grease or smart hires and consultants, if you don't have sufficient marketing to drive sales, you don't get the opportunity to patch through anything and the business suffers or dies.

Enough with all the doom and gloom. What *can* a young company do to build awareness? Let me give you a bit of a playbook.

CONSIDER COMPANY DNA

Take the time to think about what you want to stand for. A simple, useful exercise is to brainstorm three words to encompass your vision. For Disney that is "family, fun, entertainment." Three words can go a long way to give you guidance on logos, product extensions, packaging design, and the tone of your communications. A food company depends on communicating health, taste, or novelty at the right degree of quality. A firm that uses luxury materials is going to need a name and packaging that conveys indulgence. Refer back to the chapters on design and packaging to dive deeper here. The bottom line: it will be a lot easier to market a product that consistently communicates both your vision and the appropriate quality and value for your price point. Do not cut corners at the very beginning because as you increasingly invest in marketing you want to be proud and excited to share your products and not have a lot of expensive cleanup work to rename or reposition your company or packaging. Come out of the gate strong. Get professional help where you need it.

NAME YOUR COMPANY WELL

It's worth diving in on this. Assume your company will produce more than one product. Even if it is a distant possibility, envision the line of products you want to create and what they stand for. Name the company after *that*, not after one product. Leah Busque, the founder of TaskRabbit, was inspired to create a company that would solve basic life errands such as picking up dog food. Being an engineer, she named the company something very literal: RunMy-Errand. She raised venture capital and did a lot of marketing with that name. It proved to be a too-limited descriptor when the company quickly expanded to offer services including administrative tasks, common home projects such as assembling IKEA furniture, and manual business chores. TaskRabbit was a more comprehensive name. Fitbit is another example of a name that embraced future products, rather than something like StepCounter.

I believe great names are either descriptive or emotive (International Business Machines versus Apple; Peet's Coffee & Tea versus Starbucks; Facebook versus Google.) Both strategies work. The initial name of our company was a reluctant hybrid. I wanted to call the company The Grommet, but we initially went out as Daily Grommet. This was because the idea of launching something every day was highly unusual, and we needed to train people to expect us to show up with something newsworthy. Once we got there, we happily dropped "Daily." Another emotive name is Carol's Daughter, which Lisa Price gave to her personal care company because her mother encouraged her to pursue the business at a time when she was just selling body butters to friends. She had no plan to expand the product line. Neither did she expect that darker-skinned people would become prime customers, so it was fortuitous that "Carol's Daughter" provided a big tent for growth.

Another tactic is to give your company a clever name. Squatty Potty, a toilet stool, comes to mind—though it is limiting in product expansion scope. You can design your packaging and communications to be humorous or attention-getting like Duke Cannon did in creating its line of "military grade" men's personal care products. Each package is a tongue-in-cheek execution with bold "manly" graphics and witty copy. Using overt humor will build in attention-getting "flypaper." How you do this, and whether you use humor, is dependent on your vision. If you are using humor, it should be on display at all customer touch points.

Finally, make sure you can get the URL (own the website name) for your company. It's ideal if you do not have to add words. TaskRabbit.com is better than GetTaskRabbit.com. Sometimes there is a totally noncompetitive business using a similar name, so adding another word clarifies—but it is not ideal.

BUILD A COMMUNITY

This is an area where you can use your David vs. Goliath advantage. Facebook, YouTube, Instagram, and Twitter can become your business growth friends. Whereas larger companies often are cautious about letting employees loose on these platforms—for fear of offense or legal issues—who is going to stop you? Exactly. No one. Pick the platform (or two, or three) where you feel the most affinity between your skill set and products and the type of content on the platform. Think about where your future customers are likely to spend time.

Do you rock videos or have a great sense of humor? YouTube is your destination. Do you love to shoot photos or is your product easy to showcase visually? Head to Instagram. Do you have the opportunity to be a subject matter expert for the benefits of, say, coconut oil? Twitter, or a blog, will be your friend because you can build up a history of contributing to this topic. The key is to be consistent in posting—don't disappear for weeks on end and expect results. One of the Grommet Makers that constantly surprises me on Instagram is Möbi. It has a single product: it is like Scrabble with numbers. The range of settings and occasions in which the creators highlight Möbi is truly impressive. Find thought leaders like this—people who inspire your own creativity and get you unstuck when you can't think of a new post or piece of content to create.

In addition to creating content, you have to be lightning fast in responding to comments and community input. Once you get over whatever initial shyness or hesitation you might have, you will enjoy the interaction. These people are *your* people. They want to talk about your baby. What's not to like?

What about getting started, when you have zero followers and all you hear is crickets? Don't be shy. Reach out to everyone you know to help you gain numbers. In the case of the founders of flash sale site Gilt Groupe, they needed to get going with e-mail, and they harassed all their friends to subscribe and scoured New York mom online groups. As one of the first flash sale sites, their product was novel, so there was natural sharing and virality built out of their initial efforts. Such organic growth is unusual, so don't be discouraged that this growth is usually more a product of steady consistency than virality. The turtle can win the race, too.

USE PAID SEARCH

Jill Balis, chief marketing officer of The Grommet, advises, "The first paid advertising you should consider is paid Google search. You want to make sure you are found when people are searching for your product or related searches for which your product would be a strong match. When people are searching for something specific, they have high intent, so paid search should be your most efficient paid advertising channel. You can get a campaign live on Google with very little budget or time, and you can easily control your budget and track performance to make sure you are getting the return on investment you want. It may be worth hiring a consultant to help you get up and running, but Google also has great resources to help you do this yourself. Paid search is also a great way to do research on which marketing messages are most effective. You can create ads with different copy to see which ones are the most effective."

MASTER SEARCH ENGINE OPTIMIZATION (SEO)

Run, do not walk, to learn about search engine optimization. Simply put, other than social media and press, this is just about the only low/no-cost customer acquisition tactic you will find. And it will be the most effective low/no-cost way to drive immediate sales. The more special and unique your company, the easier it will be to garner SEO-driven traffic and revenue. So sometimes a really little niche player can win over the big guys who have a lot of competing content for Google to crawl. The key is understanding what it takes to show up high in Google search results. Ironically, Googling "SEO" and "SEO best practices" will be your best first step. But I have also found that a modest investment in a credible consultant's time is worth its weight in gold. The consultant will advise you on what content to create, how to structure it online, and all the behind-the-scenes rules and norms that drive Google's search rankings. This work will affect how you use social platforms, how you build and update your website, how and if you start a blog, and how you build relationships with other bloggers and websites.

ROCK PR

At the beginning, rocking PR may seem easy. It is frankly fairly straightforward to get press about a new product. Most media outlets cover products, and fresh products are newsworthy. Journalists vastly prefer hearing directly from a founder than from a PR firm or press release, so there is another point in your favor. Some founders do have an additional advantage here. Lisa Price of Carol's Daughter had left her career as an assistant writer at *The Cosby Show* to start her business. Her network included many makeup artists who gave her access to celebrities, including Oprah Winfrey. Use any routes you have to get a new product in front of an influential journalist.

Running gear Orange Mud founder Josh Sprague says the most effective form of marketing for his company has been the media attention and write-ups that his company has received. Running clubs and running communities have been influential as well. When Orange Mud was featured as Gear of the Year in *Runner's World* magazine in December of 2013, Sprague says that made all the difference for the company. Things changed dramatically after that. And nearly five years later, people still reference that article. For Sprague the blogs and media attention did the most for marketing.

Once a media outlet has covered your product, it is yesterday's news. It is really hard to keep up the attention. It requires continually coming up with timely and relevant themes or new products worth covering. This is infinitely easier said than done. I once had a Grommet Maker who was experiencing this "trough of despair" period after his initial launch. He asked me to introduce him to a prominent reporter—he wanted to share his product, of course. But it was not new, and he was not offering any kind of scoop. The reporter was a friend, and I did not want to waste his time. I asked the Maker to press pause and develop a "long game" approach to journalists. Here is mine:

1. Develop a relationship mindset with journalists, reporters, and bloggers. Dream big, and identify 10 to 20 people you would love to have write about your company or interview you for their program.

2. Start following their work. Comment on it. Share it. Journalists are evaluated and sometimes compensated on the traffic they create. Stand out for the way you amplify them.

3. Send them story ideas. When I was responsible for sales at my first startup, I read a book called *Promote Yourself.* I learned how journalists are always eager for help to do their work—who isn't? I noticed that the business press was totally ignoring the emergence of design as a strategic competency, so I started proposing story ideas to reporters. It worked. I honestly consider that spade work of mine to be the foundation for the emergence of design as a subject covered by the business press, as I was truly onto something important at the right time and place. My firm, Continuum, was a successful pioneer, and I had many client examples to share. Ultimately, my company got on the map because of a couple of key stories in *Businessweek* and the *Wall Street Journal.*

4. Get reporters to see you as a responsive expert source. If you can provide comments or context for a story, they will call you. If you have regularly been commenting or sharing their stories, you will have already gotten yourself on their radar. The trick is to be very fast in answering their requests as they are always on deadline. If you find they extend their interest to your product and they ask for a sample, get it there pronto.

5. Don't pitch your product. Be patient. You will get the story and coverage when the journalist is ready and your story is relevant to him or her.

SHOW UP

Some products are suitable for sampling at retailers or selling at farmers' markets or other local markets. Do it, at least for a while. The sales may or may not be meaningful, but you are also building awareness and doing live market research. Lisa Price initially did all of her sales out of church and street fairs, where every time someone asked for a new product she went home and figured out how to make it, expanding from her initial skin creams to bath salts, body rubs, shampoos, conditioners, and beyond. Just make sure your marketing materials (signage, colors of your booth, display materials) support your vision and desired visual identity. Don't make people work hard to find a diamond in the rough.

TRY TV

Many a Grommet Maker has gone on to a valuable appearance on *Shark Tank*. The show's producers watch what we launch at The Grommet and subsequently reach out to many of our Makers. (In fact, a Grommet launch often leads to a flood of media interest.) As long as you know this is more of a marketing activity than an investor opportunity, use that showcase for all it is worth. Less common but increasingly interesting is that some Makers find success in "branded response" ads. These are not quite infomercials but also not expensively produced brand-heavy ads. They often have a simple format: an actor who poses as a customer of the product or service explains how it works and why he or she likes it. With so many hours of airtime to fill and production costs continually dipping, this rather retro media is proving successful for many startups. As a case in point we are dipping our toes into this medium. Using our internal script and concept, we engaged a professional production house to shoot our first spot for a grand total of $28,000. A media test will cost four times that amount, so this is not something we would have done in our early days. But keep this option in mind as you scale. Further, with the proliferation of cable stations and streaming services, it is easier than ever to target specific audiences most likely to be interested in your product, which will make your investment more efficient. A good way to test the effectiveness of a potential TV ad before making a larger investment is to start on YouTube and see what kind of response you get in terms of video completions and clicks to your website. You can also test different versions of an ad to see which performs better before investing a larger budget on TV. You can get quick results on You-Tube with relatively little investment.

ENGAGE AFFILIATES AND INFLUENCERS

Influencers (people with large followings on a social platform or blog who get paid to try and endorse a product) are helpful for many product categories. Search all the relevant terms on Facebook, Instagram, Pinterest, blogs, and YouTube to find individuals you would like to try and share your product. This is a little hit or miss because it is hard to tell from the outside if these paid endorsements will translate into customers for you. You typically have to pay influencers up front without knowing whether their audience will respond. A word to the wise: results will be much better and more measurable if you can give the influencer a special offer to promote—which also enables effective tracking of the ROI of the influencer's work.

Another similar option to influencers is the established affiliate channel. You know when you see an ad on a blog or content website publisher? Most of the time the blogger or media site gets paid a commission for sales generated. You will see lots of Grommets featured in BuzzFeed stories—those are paid affiliate placements. Same with what you see on Ebates. Rakuten LinkShare is the largest affiliate network—it is essentially a place where advertisers can find publishers willing to promote their product or brand. There are smaller affiliate networks that may offer better terms for smaller companies, such as ShareASale. Do a little research to see which is the best fit for your business. Affiliate networks are a great way to drive sales with no up-front investment, but it will take some work developing relationships with the bloggers and editors to generate more exposure.

HAVE A GREAT PRODUCT AND A GREAT COMPANY

Finally, it sounds basic, but your very best marketing is having a stellar product wrapped in a company that is human, communicative, and transparent. Large companies with established distribution can draft off of their dominant brand awareness and marketing muscle and media budgets. They tend to get conservative about truly innovating new products. Their complacency is your opportunity.

Whereas the marketing muscle of a big company can keep a marginal product humming, no amount of marketing will open the door for an unknown company with a poor product. If you create a truly breakthrough product, surrounded by a compelling and clearly expressed company vision and offering a consistent quality execution at all touch points, you have a great shot.

CASE STUDIES

Squatty Potty

In a rather surprising and comical ad, a unicorn demonstrates the most effective means of using the toilet—not the way most of us do—producing rainbow twist ice cream with ease. The message: magical. And it's all for Squatty Potty, the small stool that fits under any toilet and allows unicorns and people to get into proper elimination position. The demonstration is narrated by a dashing young prince, and the nearly three-minute ad has been watched more than 34 million times.

It all started with Judy Edwards toting around a wooden stool she used when going to the bathroom. She'd take it on vacation, she'd move it around the house, and her family started making fun of her "poop stool." Her son Bobby Edwards says, "It became a family joke." But then one day he decided to actually ask her why she thought it worked.

"It opens me up," his mother said. That's when mother and son started to do some research and found there's quite a lot written on the benefits of the squatting position. Judy thought her stool had some design flaws and asked Bobby, who happened to be taking industrial design classes as a hobby, to see what he could do. Out of plywood and paint the first Squatty Potty was born. That was July 2010.

By Christmas that year Judy had the idea to make another dozen to give to family members as Christmas gifts. Then people started requesting them. "That's when the light went on," says Bobby. "There's a lot of information out there about squatting to poop, but nothing to help you do it."

Bobby had a friend with a CNC machine, and he was able to make a dozen for his mom. And then they started getting requests for more. From there the family bought its URL and continued hand-making each Squatty Potty until they couldn't keep up. At that point, they had the Squatty Potty professionally manufactured. Bobby decided he would send 100 to health writers, vegan bloggers, "anyone in the world talking about health, alternative health." He sent the product along with a letter from Judy. Within a few weeks people started writing about them. And the company quickly took off. That was in 2011. "We bootstrapped the whole thing," says Bobby. They started with $30,000; Bobby put in half and his mom the other half.

It was early influencer marketing, says Bobby. That plus buying a small number of ads on targeted websites was all they needed. In 2013 they started buying Facebook ads as well. Bobby looked at how others were marketing in nontraditional ways and started to think about doing the same for his new company. They put out an animated graphics video about squatting when on the toilet. It went viral. And got the attention of Dr. Oz. Which helped to land them on *Shark Tank*. By 2015 they were working on the unicorn videos. In 2011, the first year on the market, Squatty Potty had $17,000 in sales.

By 2017 sales were at nearly $33 million. They sell through Bed Bath & Beyond, Costco, Target, and Amazon. Most of the business comes from online sales.

Objects with Purpose

"Reaching out to friends and family, asking them to share your products with their circles, is the best way to grow," says Ianthe Mauro, founder of candle company Objects with Purpose. "Doing home trunk shows and flash sales were my best resources in the beginning. The greatest tool to get bigger results is Help a Reporter Out. You sign up for e-mail alerts, which are free, and check the listings as often as three times a day to see inquiries from press and journalists looking to write articles on a wide variety of subjects."

Word of mouth and spreading the word digitally has been very helpful for Mauro. She's become more strategic about marketing on Instagram and Facebook. And she's been working on private label candles. Objects with Purpose does not have a specific marketing budget, but the founder looks at specific niches and audiences as her best targets. Vegan, nontoxic, with wicks that do not give off black smoke, Mauro says her candles are appealing to the people who are concerned about toxins, environmental hazards, and harmful scents.

Her candles are given out as part of gift baskets distributed on the show *Hollywood Medium*, which Mauro says is helpful in getting them into the hands of celebrities and growing awareness of her business.

When Mauro launched the company in 2009 she had four scents and three sizes of candles. At the end of 2017 she had 14 scents and four sizes. As of November 2017, Mauro was able to start giving a portion of her proceeds to charity, something she had always wanted to do from the beginning but hadn't been able to commit to financially until recently.

When Mauro started out she would personally go into stores to sell her products. That first year she got into three shops. Now, she says she adds an average of five new stores a week to the roster of retailers carrying Objects with a Purpose. She was on track to sell 10,000 candles in 2017 (compared to 900 sold her first year).

Articulate Gallery

For Colin Gilchrist the industry access he received early on has been the biggest marketing boost to his company yet. He says the two go hand in hand. Gilchrist and his wife are the creators of practical and classy picture frames to house children's artwork.

When the couple started Articulate Gallery about 10 years ago, they got the word out in the simplest of ways. They stuffed envelopes and passed out a simple flyer and order form at council meetings in their hometown in Scotland. The local government gatherings ended up being a great place to spread the word to community members, many with children or grandchildren. Gilchrist says they got a response from 6 percent of the people and they were quite happy with that.

From there, Gilchrist says their appearance on *Dragons' Den* really helped to catapult the attention they received. Going on other shows did as well. That was the real source of marketing and advertising, he says. Gilchrist continues to go to trade shows to show the product and garner additional attention and interest.

RETAIL DISTRIBUTION

My cofounder, Joanne Domeniconi, and I started The Grommet in 2008 because we could see how difficult it had become for an unproven new product to gain retail shelf space. This was because the historical "ladder" that a new product or company used to climb to retail success was changing. Makers used to introduce their young product at the lower rungs of the ladder: at independent and specialty stores. Once they got their sea legs there (as a company and a new product), they moved up to selling to regional players and small chains. After that, they moved up to national chains, and some might finally land at the larger big-box retailers. As discount mass merchant retailers (and ultimately, Amazon) continually squeezed out the smaller local stores, the places where innovative products got their first chances were disappearing. Think about it— how many luggage, or toy, or stationery stores do you see in your town or neighborhood? People still buy plenty of luggage. But the quality of their retail options has decreased. Luggage is a product you want to lift, open, roll, touch. You want to talk to someone who knows the materials and reputation of each brand, and how well they back their guarantees. You might want to have a bag repaired down the road. For a Maker, if you had the best new luggage product in the world, what specialty retailer could give you the market feedback and credibility required to get a foothold with consumers and other retailers?

Simply put, the retail landscape in every product category has changed dramatically over the last two decades. The United States got overbuilt with chain stores, creating more and more pressure on each existing retailer. In fact, the number of U.S. retail locations quadrupled from 1970 to 2017, while the population did not even double.[1] As stores merged and consolidated (or were bought by private equity firms that put them into unsustainable debtor status), challenged retailers started uniformly adopting the "Walmart strategy" of reducing the number of suppliers.

This was, initially, smart. Fewer suppliers means more leverage with each one, potentially giving the retailer lower prices or longer margins. Competing on efficient sourcing (not on quality or diversity of merchandise) became the top skill for too many retailers. Buyers became far less product-centric and more like accountants, seeking margin improvements and operational efficiencies from their suppliers. As they grew more and more distant from customers and Makers, they became more disconnected from new product opportunities. The huge volumes they had to buy to fill the square footage of their national chains continually increased. This meant that they had to set up demanding operational, legal, and financial contracts for each new vendor to ensure the retailer would not bear the risk of empty shelves, late product deliveries, or weak margins. It became far easier to just carry more products from existing large company suppliers than to take on the risk of an unproven supplier.

Simultaneous to retailers losing access to new product opportunities (and after they had squeezed their suppliers as much as possible), retailers competed increasingly over price—not product innovation, service, or assortment. They started an industry-wide death spiral. It was all very smart—until it wasn't.

Play that out over a decade or two, and you can see how those trends conspired against small companies with innovative products.

This is the problem The Grommet set out to fix.

Retailers still want innovative products. They just can't take the risk of dealing with potentially undercapitalized and unreliable companies with unproven products. Consumers still want to learn about what is new, but they aren't searching online for something they've never heard of or imagined. That is, *your product*. So if Amazon is going to bury your product until you build marketing muscle and demand, and you are too small for the big brick-and-mortar stores, what are your options?

USE CAUTION WITH AMAZON

First, be very careful about Amazon. Your first job as a Maker is to make sure you can eliminate as many risks as possible to get your product on the shelf. Amazon is a risk. E-commerce was just 9 to 13 percent of 2017 retail sales (estimates vary), and while growing rapidly (projected to be 14 percent in 2021), physical stores (and their associated websites) matter.[2]

Still, why not go straight to Amazon? Over 50 percent of online shopping searches start on the giant retailer's platform. Amazon gets $44 of every $100 spent for online sales.[3] It has consumer trust and eyeballs. Some Grommet Makers find Amazon to be their largest wholesale customer, and sometimes their only meaningful one.

Here's why you must be prepared to invest a great deal of effort to protect your company if you sell your product on Amazon. In naming these reasons, I am focusing on fostering the success of your business:

You May Never See Much Volume

Amazon is a place to find what you already know you want—commodity shopping. It does not promote unknown products. It serves up the products people are searching for. It becomes a catch-22.

Your wonderful product can be lost on Amazon, but the costs to your business can be very high for that buried presence.

You Give It Your Data

Let's say you *do* have amazing press and marketing, and perhaps some retailers have given you distribution. Maybe you have been launched by The Grommet or Uncommon Goods, and those businesses have created positive awareness and demand for your products. Given that, you have people searching for your product on Amazon. In fact, Amazon is probably calling you directly to ask you to sell to it based on the search traffic that your existing retailers or press is creating. Amazon has never excelled at merchandising, but when there is external demand, it is the best in class at fulfilling it. From the moment your product starts selling on its site, Amazon has better data about who is buying it, where it sells, its relative growth rate, market pricing, and competition than anyone else on earth. Including you. Since you've probably had nothing but positive personal purchasing experiences with Amazon, you may deeply admire Amazon and even trust it. Why should you care if it has all your data? Read the next point.

You Will Expose Yourself to Counterfeiters and Copycats

Amazon is the fastest route to inviting counterfeiters to destroy your business. We have one Maker who has defended her groundbreaking product against 37 copycats, all of whom sell solely on Amazon and eBay. When your product starts to get traction on Amazon, the underbelly of consumer products—fakers—pay attention. All your positive reviews? All those rankings and listings? They are big neon lights that give great confidence to counterfeiters. Since 2015 Amazon has been recruiting Chinese manufacturers to populate its marketplace, and now fully 25 percent of the listings on Amazon are from China.[4] It's hard to believe, but Amazon did this so it could learn about its biggest competitive threat: the giant Chinese conglomerate Alibaba. Yes, Amazon invited a flood of Chinese manufacturers onto its site to, ultimately, copy U.S. products, all to achieve the goal of learning about a competitor. This travesty is far greater than the 2018 Facebook/Cambridge Analytica scandal, and Amazon is working feverishly to put the genie back in the bottle. Its fraud department went from 7 employees to 150 in just two years. But it's way too late. By the time this book is published, I expect journalists to have discovered the bastardization of Amazon's product offerings, and Amazon's own marketplace will have created a vigorous cancer from within, threatening trust and its current status with consumers.

Before Amazon (and eBay) existed, those copycat and offshore businesses had to do the hard work of building their own brands, of product and packaging development, of marketing, and of gaining retail accounts. Amazon itself did not allow international sellers to sell directly to U.S. customers until three years ago. Now many are there just to steal your hard work, thanks to the exposure of Amazon and eBay. We have had Makers who found their own product photos, brand names, actual verbatim Amazon reviews, product descriptions and graphics, and even their own *faces* on the packages sold by Amazon-listed counterfeiters. This is why many quality brands such as Mercedes-Benz and Trek refuse to sell to Amazon. If you are not present there, you can stay a little more under the radar as a new Maker, but more important, once you are established, you can tell customers that anything on Amazon is not your genuine product.

If and when things do get out of control with your product or similar copycats on the market, you completely box out any other retail opportunities because no one can compete. Grommet VP of discovery Meredith Doherty has been watching this phenomenon play out to the detriment of many terrific Makers. She says, "There is this misconception that putting your product on Amazon is a rite of passage for a new brand with a consumer product, but it's not guaranteed you are even going to see traffic to your page or sales. You are essentially putting all your eggs in one basket, and from there it's just a simple race to the bottom." In one such terrible incident we launched a brilliant Italian kitchen product just entering the U.S. market. We made large inventory commitments and built a plan to help it gain a foothold in the United States. Just before launch, we found rampant Chinese knockoffs on the U.S. Amazon site. When we launched the product, we took the exceptional step of calling those copycats out on our video—trying to protect both customers, the Maker, and our own inventory investment. Alas, it was too late, and the Italian company was never able to recover from the brand damage of the cheap counterfeit products. The company has had to, in turn, lose money on each unit it sells to us to fund discounts so we can sell off the inventory. The product instantly became a one-hit wonder that lasted only one spring/summer season, and we haven't been able to promote it since. It could have been a gigantic hit and a strong entry point to the U.S. market for other product extensions— if only the Maker had stayed off Amazon.

Amazon Uses Its Data to Direct Its Private Label Business

Amazon has become the best of the best in competing directly with the Makers who sell on its marketplace. It has no qualms about seeing a fast-selling product and producing and promoting its copycat private label offering of your idea to its customers. In 2018 Amazon had 125 private label brands. Writing in *Forbes*, David Marino-Nachison asserts, "Amazon's private label business could be worth $25 billion in sales by 2022, according to new estimates, which would make it one of the country's biggest retailers by itself.[5]" Let me pause here. You find the market opportunity. You invent the product, and take tremendous career and financial risk. You build the business. And then you hand over all your market data to Amazon, which did none of the hard work, and it knocks you off and wipes you out. Because you served your business up on a silver platter. It's like blaming a shark for eating a fish that swims into its mouth.

You Give Amazon Control over Your Pricing

Since 50 percent of online shopping searches start on Amazon, it sets market prices for anything it sells. Even if you only sell it one unit, Amazon—not you—determines the market price for your product. The quality retailers who have invested thousands or millions of dollars in your product, and supported your fair market price, will be harmed overnight by the single unit listed on Amazon. And you will be eating a lot of returned inventory with no market value. This risk can be largely avoided if you sell only on its marketplace and manage your own Amazon storefront very tightly.

Chargebacks

A big profit center for Amazon is charges to vendors who do not exactly meet their terms of service. This means meeting delivery dates, packaging standards, and shipping turnaround times. Many Makers find that Amazon issues highly questionable chargebacks and that it is a full-time job to dispute them.[6]

You May Have Just One Customer

Big brands do indeed coexist on Amazon and in quality retail. It's harder for the little guy who does not have established customers to do so. The first thing a retailer will do when you pitch it to buy your unknown product is to search for your presence on Amazon. Imagine: you are in a meeting in which you are asking a retailer to take a chance on you, to pay expensive rent, maintain its physical stores, hire and train its staff to sell your product, invest in holding your inventory, and take some other company's product off the shelf to give you that square footage. And then the retailer searches Amazon and says, "Do you think I just fell off a turnip truck?" Big brands bring customers into their stores. They have done the hard work and made the investment to build demand to protect retailers (somewhat) from Amazon. You have not. Most businesses would not set out to have just one customer. It is too risky. Sell to Amazon for all it's worth, but don't expect retailers to bear the risk of carrying your product if you won't first protect your own business, and theirs.

Considerations If You Do Use Amazon

If you do decide to make Amazon part of your distribution strategy, plan to staff up to support Amazon's ever-expanding policing, listing, advertising, compliance, service, and operational demands. In the beginning this will take five or ten people to cover the platform effectively. After you get to $1 million in sales, a rough rule of thumb for scaling on the platform is to assume you need one full-time employee per each additional $1 million in Amazon sales. A potentially wiser and more effective alternative is to contract a specialist rep agency to manage your Amazon business for you. As you can imagine, the challenges of navigating Amazon have provided fertile ground for a whole ecosystem of savvy marketplace listing businesses. You could sell such a partner just a subset of your best-selling products (at wholesale) and give it strict parameters for your presence on Amazon. As discussed in Chapter 7, these rep services have distinct advantages because of both their expert Amazon know-how and their ability to get Amazon to answer the phone when issues arise with your business. One example of such a service is Indianapolis-based SupplyKick.

Both "going alone" and "getting help" strategies have advantages. If you handle Amazon yourself, you will get a fast education on running a tight ship. Bob Land, vice president of consumer engagement at Dorel Juvenile, a large Amazon seller of car seats, strollers, and other similar products, posits, "Selling on Amazon has made us a better business. Meeting their best-in-class demands is not for the faint of heart. Their quantitative vendor scorecard clearly upped our game." The rub for an emerging business is that this Amazon-driven demand will take your attention away from areas where you really need to be distinctive and create competitive defense: developing great products and a compelling brand and building an effective company in many different competencies.

HEALTHY ROUTES TO RETAIL

So assuming you are in business for the long haul and want to have a healthy book of business spread across many retailers beyond, or instead of, Amazon, what should you do?

First, make sure you have covered all the bases discussed in the previous chapters on marketing and packaging. There is no substitute for a competitive product in an effective package, and you do have some meaningful marketing avenue advantages over bigger companies. Use them.

Beyond that, here are the healthy routes to retail:

Trade Shows

Trade shows are inconvenient. They are expensive. But retailers really do attend them, and some shows are quite vibrant. Makers understandably fear the huge cost with an unknown return. What is often missed is that beyond just the cost of the booth space, most shows offer excellent educational sessions and pitch panels that are opportunities to get feedback from experts in the industry. Chicago International Home and Housewares is a great example of this, with its Inventors Corner and Inventors Revue. The presentations on distribution and retail packaging and pitch panels are incisive and informative. Sometimes this can be just as valuable as sales in your early days.

Make sure to ask other Makers in your general product category which trade shows work for them, as the show dynamics change from year to year.

At The Grommet we attend or show at:

- New York Now
- Atlanta International Gift & Home Furnishings Market
- Toy Fair
- National Hardware Show
- Outdoor Retailer
- Dallas Total Home and Gift Market
- Natural Products Expo
- Consumer Electronics Show
- Ace Hardware Convention
- Global Pet Expo
- SuperZoo
- National Stationery Show
- Beautycon Festival
- Las Vegas Market
- ABC Kids Expo
- Chicago International Home and Housewares
- Maker Faire NY
- Specialty Food Association Fancy Food Show
- International Travel Goods Show

One way we have conquered the trade show investment hurdle for our Makers is that we offer to represent their product at the shows where we have a booth and a substantial presence. Depending on their investment and inclination, Makers can also choose to be personally in our booth. At our last Ace Hardware Convention we had over 100 people from about 60 of our Makers in attendance. It's an efficient way for our Makers to skim the cream off of shows without doing all the investment in booth space (which is usually in a bad location for new or small Makers), beautiful fixtures, and expensive marketing to drive show traffic. They also avoid the extra time and hotel nights required for staff opening and breaking down a show. And most of them otherwise would not attend at all, so they really are getting a lot of the gain, with no pain.

Sales Reps and Distributors

Many product categories have established sales representative organizations that call on retail buyers to place new products. They get the sale and own the retail relationship. You get the order and ship the goods. Distributors also handle sales to retailers, but they go further in that they also stock the inventory. Reps take 10 to 15 percent off of a wholesale invoice. Distributors take 15 to 25 percent. If they do a good job, they are worth every bit of that "toll."

Doing a good job means fulfilling the promises or expectations that they set with you when they signed the contract to be your representative. Reps will not likely make firm commitments, but they do give you guidance on what to expect. Success is, quite simply, delivering sales and quality customers to meet those expectations.

In considering this partnership, you want to make sure the rep or distributor is aligned with your retail strategy. Reps have multiple lines and competing priorities, and in the end, want a commission. So you want to make sure that they aren't going to just place your product wherever they can, but that they are placing it with the right retailers. Meredith Doherty says, "They are working for you—not you for them, which I think is a mistake we see all the time in early days with Makers who are a bit hesitant to challenge a rep's decisions."

Distributors buy inventory, so the simple act of taking possession of the goods makes them motivated. But they will also want to be the distributor for all of your retail accounts, so you have to accept that some of your pavement pounding is dedicated to sending them orders.

Many Grommet Makers avoid reps and distributors. They want direct customer contact with retailers and consumers, at least in the beginning. Once they know the market and reception for their products better, they may sign limited agreements to be represented.

The biggest factor to watch for in signing a rep or distributor agreement is being able to get out of it. Some Makers use reps to build the business and *then* go direct. As long as the contract anticipates that, and the rep organization is paid its due, that is a fair plan. Some Makers quickly become disillusioned with their reps or distributors and want to recover direct control. Your lawyer is your friend in these endeavors because you cannot see around corners in terms of rep or distributor performance. One product may work beautifully in their organization, while another one may just never gain traction.

Here are some things to anticipate in retailer negotiations:

- **Retailers need 50 percent margins,** on average, to fund their buying staff, store operations, marketing, and inventory carrying costs. Some categories such as tech and food have lower margins, and some have higher ones such as apparel and jewelry, where retailers are likely to get stuck with overstock as fashions and seasons change.

- **They like companies with full product lines.** The wider your range of products is, the more interesting you will be to a retailer. It's not that they won't like your brilliant single SKU product. It's just hard for it to compete with its limited physical presence, and it's a pain in the neck for a retailer to onboard you for a single product. It takes the same amount of negotiation, training, systems integration, and paperwork as it does for a company with 10 or 100 products.

- **Know your inventory turns.** Retailers measure success in margins, sales per square foot, and inventory turns. Any data you can share in terms of your success at other retailers will help them evaluate your potential in their store. In fact the first question a retailer will ask you is, "Who carries you, and how does this product do there?" They want to know the success stats.

- **Competitive pricing.** This is now becoming a big topic of conversation because of Amazon as a disruptor of pricing. Retailers are investing in the software to track pricing so that they can be competitive. We encourage our partners to establish a MAP (Minimum Advertised Price) and have all retailers sign a reseller agreement that respects this price. This gives you enforceability, and it will reassure quality retailers about your intent to keep pricing clean. Stop shipping to anyone who is not adhering to it. Even better, have traceability (custom codes) on your production runs that you ship to retailers, so you can accurately shut down the resellers running a backdoor operation and discounting your product.[7] Reputable retailers care about adhering to MAP, and as a brand you should care deeply about it, too.

- **Line reviews.** The bigger the retailer, the less frequently it will change its product assortment. It might only be once or twice a year.

- **Other terms.** They might ask for markdown money (so they can fund end-of-season or closeout discounts), displays, a price discount in lieu of sending you returns, free inbound freight, product samplings or demos in store (usually staffed by you—very common in food, especially at Whole Foods), slotting fees (payment to get your product on the shelf—often charged based on the prominence of placement and by SKU), marketing promotions payments, and media allowances. They might also have chargebacks or penalties similar to Amazon, so read any contracts carefully to make sure you can meet their terms of service, operationally speaking. Many terms are negotiable.

- **Payment terms.** This will matter to you as much as margins because you will be funding your inventory to sit at a retailer long before you get paid. Find out what they promise, and ask anyone you know who sells to them what they actually do. Ninety days can quickly become 120 days at many retailers.

- **Exclusives.** Selling your product exclusively to a quality retailer is a good move in some cases. For example, Williams Sonoma is a premier place for a novel or complex kitchen product to get traction because of its skilled sales staff and demo capability. A retailer who has an exclusive product is highly motivated to support and promote it, so if an exclusive agreement is requested by a retailer, proceed with caution, but consider the deal. Go for it if the retailer is top of class and likely to give you credibility with future retail customers. Go for it if the term is limited to less than a year and tied to a commitment in sales volumes. Go for it if the exclusivity is limited to just a category (like online, or hardware, or pet) and you can pursue other distribution channels. Go for it if the exclusive is limited to only one of your products and the rest of your business will not be impaired. For example, you could offer a single special color or style to that retailer, or a model with a differentiated feature. Ask for successful examples and case study references. Ask for promotional plans and display commitments. Ask what your commitments will be. Ask for a lot because you only have one product, against their many thousands, and once you have signed an agreement, you lose all your leverage.

Wholesale Platforms

A few years after starting The Grommet, we expanded into Grommet Wholesale. It became obvious that we could do more than build credibility and awareness for new products; we could help them gain retail distribution effortlessly. Our offering is unique in that we validate, test, and vet products with a very large (several million strong) consumer audience before we take a Grommet Maker's product to retailers via our Wholesale platform. This market data and operational de-risking from our consumer business is like gold to retailers.

There are other flavors of wholesale platforms: Joor (fashion), RangeMe (grocery and pharmacy), Etsy Wholesale (handcraft), Indigo Fair (gifts and accessories), Hubba (Canada), Wholesale in a Box (more like a boutique finder service), and Fitzroy Toys (obvious). They all recognize the risks and inefficiencies of the traditional routes to retail and are trying to provide an online alternative. If your product fits one of these platforms, it is worth checking out and submitting your product for consideration. The Grommet only accepts submissions to our consumer platform. Grommet Wholesale becomes an opportunity if all goes well on consumer.

As I know all too well, these wholesale platform businesses are capital intensive because you need to assemble two sides of a marketplace (products and retailers) and build a platform that connects the two seamlessly and effectively. As such, I expect that some players will come and go in this space simply because assembling both the capital and tenacity to stick with these businesses is challenging.

Finally, if you want to find a healthy and vibrant retail sector to help your product, you have to do your bit as a citizen and business-person. Shop at local stores. On average, 48 percent of the dollars from each purchase at local independent businesses is recirculated locally, compared to less than 14 percent of purchases at chain stores.[8] You could go as far as only buying online from retailers who have a physical presence as well. Sometimes a local purchase will carry a marginally higher price tag, but the cost of losing a good local retailer is far higher to you and your community than the potential impact on your wallet.

CASE STUDIES

Joco

While the reusable glass coffee cup maker Joco has some sales reps, the company mainly sells through Joco.com, The Grommet, and Amazon. "Amazon is king when it comes to selling directly to the public," says James Forte, the company's U.S. sales director. Plus, he says the Joco cups are visual products, something customers need to see to understand or consider buying. "We do our best when the products are displayed well," he adds.

Forte says Joco attracts interest and has built a loyal following because of the message behind the company—one that is best expressed through its packaging and when the company story can be explained. Founder Matt Colgate was tired of seeing plastic and trash in the ocean whenever he was surfing. He decided to make a reusable glass drinking vessel, one that had a protective silicone sleeve and would help to eliminate single-use cups.

In order for the company's story and message to reach people, Forte says when it comes to distribution, "The gravitation is more toward direct to consumer." Since 80 percent of households in the United States have an Amazon Prime membership, it's hard not to make a big push in that arena. "If you have a consumer product and you're not on Amazon, I feel like, 'What are you doing?'"

Pacific Shaving

Stan Ades and his wife started Pacific Shaving, a shaving products company for men, from their home. It was just a side gig at first. After about seven years, they started selling online before working to move their shaving products into local stores and small chains. Ades was bold enough to go straight to CVS and Walgreens, without an agent or sales rep. Although it didn't work initially, he found other avenues of success. Ades says no matter how unique or interesting your product is, you'll always be asked the same two questions: "Who else carries the product?" and "How long have you been there?"

"Every retailer wants to seem progressive, but they need to mitigate risk," says Ades, explaining that few people want to be the one to take the leap and sign on with a new and unknown company.

Pacific Shaving was started in 2003. It began selling online, and by 2006 the products were in some local retail shops in the San Francisco Bay area. A big breakthrough for the company came when Pacific Shaving was carried by several regional Whole Foods. The store had set up a form on its website to solicit suggestions from customers of products they'd like to see sold at their neighborhood store. Ades decided to start flooding the suggestion form with the suggestion that Pacific Shaving—his own company—be put on the shelves at Whole Foods.

Three weeks after he did this, a Whole Foods buyer called and was furious, because she had learned that he was the one suggesting the store carry Pacific Shaving products. "All you had to do was fill out a form and send me a sample," she said to him. Three months later Pacific Shaving was at Whole Foods, where its products spent many years on the shelves.

"I was trying to be strategic and scrappy," says Ades. "Plus once you have the credibility of Whole Foods, you must be legitimate." Now, years later, they are in 18,000 stores nationwide, including Target, Big Y, CVS, and more.

Although Ades says he likes dealing with direct sales and online sales, about 97 percent of the company's sales are through retail or wholesale channels. Getting into the bigger stores can be very expensive, cautions Ades. There are slotting fees to get a particular place on a shelf, and if you have a product that's not selling, the costs aren't worth it.

"You really need to give thought to the retail process," says Ades. There are upsides and downsides to nearly all situations. Once a large company takes on your product, you have additional work and sometimes expense, but if you don't end up in a big store, you may be hustling for the long haul to get sales.

Over the past 15 years, Ades says much has changed. When he started the company (and had another job), he had only one child. Now he has three. Once he left his job and committed to Pacific Shaving full-time he was able to make his own schedule, although it was still a hectic one. But he hasn't had to miss important games or events in his children's lives. "The most important metrics are least quantifiable in a conventional way," says Ades, when talking about success.

"We've built a sustainable business that has grown," says Ades. The products are in 15,000 retail stores, and they sell into spas and hotels, while their shaving cream is ranked number three on Amazon. They started with one SKU and now have ten. "That's been sustainable growth for us." Ades says they've never wanted to keep piling on the new products but instead carefully choose which ones to add. They are now considering other men's grooming products, but aren't rushing things.

Möbi Games

Before starting a toy company, Toronto-based Vanessa Elling-son was a professional basketball player in Germany, and then a practicing chiropractor. She had the insight for Möbi when on a road trip with her husband. Self-confessed game nerds, they spun through endless rounds of Bananagrams and Boggle, and it struck Vanessa that they owned no similar games based on math and numbers. When she got home she did an exhaustive search and realized there was a big hole in current game offerings. And she got to work.

As soon as she had the game in production, Ellingson sub-mitted the first Möbi Games product to The Grommet and was accepted. She says, "The massive response of that community put us in business. We had to scramble hard to make that first order. I had to figure out how to ship and was Googling really basic stuff like 'logistics.' I had everyone—even my granny—on an assembly line to put together the products for Grommet. The Grommet online presence led to a great deal of inbound interest, and when I tell sales reps or retailers about the success and cus-tomer reviews on The Grommet, we have instant credibility."

Today, Ellingson's business is about 35 percent online between Grommet, Amazon, and Möbi's website, and the rest is brick-and-mortar retail. The product is represented in 20 countries through exclusive distributors and is in about 2,000 U.S. specialty retail stores. Much of that business, including international inqui-ries, got started at Möbi's showing at the 2016 New York Toy Fair. Ellingson was familiar with the various educational game compa-nies coming to the show, and when offered a booth space near a particularly engaging company, Tenzi, she snapped it up. It paid off, because the founders of Tenzi generously sent show traffic straight across the aisle to check out "the cool new math game Möbi."

Ellingson was particularly thoughtful about opening an Amazon presence. Some of her new friends in the toy industry had lost control of their pricing and presence on the marketplace, and she wanted to prevent that, as she knew that a botched Amazon execution would threaten the rest of her retail distribution. She called around to see how toy companies with a clean Amazon business (only one authorized seller) managed to protect their pricing and presence. She got a strong referral to a Utah-based FBA (Fulfillment by Amazon) seller and contracted that firm to manage Möbi's Amazon sales. When issues come up, such as unauthorized sellers, they tag team on the follow-up to get the sellers to cease and desist. Ellingson says she's happy with the FBA seller and acknowledges it takes constant vigilance to keep the Amazon business healthy in terms of pricing.

Ellingson ultimately gave up her chiropractic practice. She explains, "I did two jobs for quite a while. I would be working on a patient and I would see a phone call come in about an international shipment or customs issue. I was hopping back and forth between the two, going a little crazy. One day my husband asked me, 'Which job is more fun? Which job gives you the time you want with the kids?'" She quickly answered "Möbi" and knew she was ready to make it her central focus. She never looked back.

Walton Wood Farm

Leslie Bradford-Scott started making bath salts with her KitchenAid. From there she found herself labeling and packaging everything herself. She had six SKUs when she launched the Ontario-based company in June of 2014. Her distribution method at that point was to load everything into her truck and drive around knocking on doors. She said she really couldn't have afforded to do it any other way at first. By driving around her products, Leslie was able to learn that people were interested in stocking them. It was a great market test for her.

Now an all-encompassing personal product care company, Walton Wood Farm contracts with about 70 sales reps and two in-house sales reps, who cover the territories in the United States and Canada not already covered by the contractors. "The inside sales team can find out where there are gaps," explains Bradford-Scott. The company has 2,200 retail partners, including gift shops (the primary market), aesthetician offices, barber shops, and coffee shops. Walton Wood Farm products are sold through Amazon as well, but Bradford-Scott says she controls the pricing so that online sellers can't drop the prices and undercut retail shops.

"We're a two- to three-million-dollar company, and we've grown 100 percent every year since we started," says Bradford-Scott. That's astounding when you think of where it all started: at her kitchen table. With 80 products, which includes lines for men and women, Walton Wood Farm is in 1,600 brick-and-mortar shops, which makes up about 97 percent of its business. "We decided we could only focus on one customer at a time," explains Bradford-Scott. And to do that she wanted more contact with consumers than online shopping provided, which is why the company focuses on sales into stores and boutiques. Bradford-Scott says the company has been adding 15 to 20 new products each year and intends to keep up that pace.

15

DIRECT TO CONSUMER (DTC)

After absorbing the last chapter about the complexities of selling to retailers, it'd be logical to wonder if selling direct to consumers might be preferable. There are prominent examples of successful direct-to-consumer (DTC) businesses such as Casper mattresses, Away luggage, and Warby Parker eyeglasses. These are companies that build, market, sell, and ship their products right to customers, skipping any middlemen such as retailers.

The advantages of such an approach are compelling. If you can truly craft your business independently, you will have much more control over your expenses because you will retain the 50 percent margin a retailer needs to charge to sell your product. Equally important, you will have direct access to your own customers—which gives you rich data and insights to continue to improve your product and services. These are powerful levers for success. In fact, every month when I go to Harvard Business School to meet with student startup teams, about 50 percent of them tell me their plan for acquiring customers is to go direct to consumer. (They usually say "DTC." It makes them sound savvy.)

Here's the rub. Recently I was at HBS for a different reason. A case study about The Grommet was being taught at an elective course on e-commerce. The professor, Thales Teixiera, kicked off the class with a simple statement: There are two main reasons that explain startup failure. The first: when they create value for their customers but fail to capture a large enough portion of this value. The second: when startups don't acquire enough customers to sustain their business.

If you are going to skip over the retail channel, which exists because it can bring you customers, your core business competencies have to include—if not prioritize—customer acquisition and service (what retailers fundamentally do).

Direct to consumer is not a typical route to true growth for a Grommet Maker, so I will "reverse engineer" some of the more public success stories and share the common threads that helped DTC businesses such as Bonobos (men's apparel) and Glossier (beauty products) defy the odds to go straight to consumers.

SIMPLICITY OF PRODUCT DESIGN

Most of these businesses are aimed squarely at millennials, a population that embraces a consumer-savvy mindset. They (rightly) observe that many product categories have evolved over the decades to become overcomplicated and difficult to purchase. Just think of the painful process of buying a mattress, where a sea of choices immediately confronts you as you enter the shop. It's overwhelming and downright awkward to test out mattresses. But you would feel like an idiot if you did not lie down under the watchful eye of a strange salesperson before making such an important purchase. In addition, many of the mattress styles are exclusive to the store, so you can't easily compare models among competitors, and stores often use different branding for the exact same mattress. Almost before you even begin the process of buying a mattress you feel like a rube at risk of being sold an expensive disappointment.

The founders of Casper recognized that in mattresses (as in life), too much choice can be a bad thing—their core product strategy was to call "bs" on the entire mattress industry and instead offer just a single "perfect" mattress. So it also goes with Harry's and Dollar Shave Club. They attacked shaving products because razor names and features have become as complex as automobile models. In addition, the process of keeping razor blades in stock is mildly inconvenient for the average guy. And finally, razor blades had become a profitable cash cow for large CPG companies—and thus ripe for some disruption. So the upstarts boiled their product positioning down to a retro back-to-basics and "I'm not buying all that marketing hoo-ha" starting point. My oldest son, who is discerning and vaguely anti-consumer, actually gifted a starter Dollar Shave Club subscription to one of his brothers. He would never in a million years have put a Gillette razor and pack of blades under the Christmas tree. Dollar Shave Club made him feel like he was giving the smartest of shaving choices. And like he was the wise older brother giving his sibling an inside tip. He was not alone. The competitor Harry's began in 2013 and sold out its first 10,000 razor handles in a few days. Today they do about $200 million a year in sales.[1]

I am a customer of PillPack, a company founded by a young pharmacist who understood the inconvenient process of filling prescriptions and managing medications. TJ Parker created a digital storefront and service to eliminate calling in refills, picking up meds, vitamins, and supplements, and dispensing them accurately. Every day and evening I just tear open a little package with my own combo of pills and get on with my life.

DTC companies tend to start with a core observation about a painful, inconvenient, or untrustworthy (in their view) convention in a consumer product category. They find a shopping experience that is inefficient and a product category with large built-in margins (such as prescription eyewear) and then take a "back to basics" approach to the product. The core message is "buy the best, don't trust the rest."

COME OUT OF THE GATE WITH A BANG

For most of us, these DTC hit companies seem suddenly to appear out of nowhere. Well, yes and no. In the case of beauty products brand Glossier, the company was based on a wildly successful beauty blog, *Into The Gloss*. Emily Weiss started the blog in 2010 and built it the old-fashioned way, brick by brick and post by post, until she had assembled a massive and engaged following. By 2015, introducing products that were formulated to respond to the blog's built-in audience and powerful market research machine was a natural and smart second act—and one that could go from 0 to 60 because of the inherent cultivated customers.

But one of the less-understood aspects of these businesses is that they tend also to gain attention and customers with a venture capital–funded checkbook. Few breakthrough messages or products actually break through without fuel. Whether right at the beginning or fairly soon after they have proven an ability to execute and create a desirable product, they attract a war chest that enables them to cut through the general media and retail clutter. That is not to say that the investments are not savvy—these founders genuinely offer a radical disruption of a product category and contemporary product positioning. Having a queen size mattress that magically ships stuffed in an attractive branded box is going to lead to automatic PR coverage. So is the revolutionary promise of delivering three eyeglass frame styles for you to try on at home before committing to a purchase.

Thus Glossier turned its 1.5 million blog readers into a $35 million investment. Allbirds, the no-brand, distinctively shaped, minimalist wool sneaker, attracted $27.5 million in capital.[2] There tends to be a lot of inside baseball in these companies and their funding sources. One of the cofounders of Allbirds, Joey Zwillinger, is a good friend of Dave Gilboa, the co-CEO of Warby Parker, who invested in the company. The Honest Company's founder, Jessica Alba, has unparalleled access to celebrity influencers (which translates to massive customer acquisition) and funding sources. The companies are often located in Los Angeles or New York, where founders have exposure and routes to powerful media sources who shower adulation and attention on the telegenic entrepreneurs. Alternately, they are based in San Francisco, where the tech crowd gravitates quickly to trends and disruptors, and then uses its outsized digital media and investor influence to drive awareness for their newest finds.

When we started The Grommet in 2008, I was inspired by what the Bonobos founders had done on Facebook to start the business and drive sales for their single pair of pants. In other words, they had one product. The trousers were indeed designed to fit American men far better than existing offerings, but that was an inherently difficult concept to sell online. So they caught their target customer's attention with ads based on the man's expressed sport allegiances on Facebook. If you lived in Chicago, were the right age and demographic, and posted about your loyalty to one of the two hometown baseball teams, you would very likely see an ad for "Cubby Blue" pants. That was clever and distinctive at the time, and the pants actually delivered on the fit promise. You could order multiple sizes and return the rest for free, and the customers got a great story to tell their friends as well.

PROVIDE A GREAT CUSTOMER EXPERIENCE

As much as these DTC successes trade on the notion of quality and prestige, much of their true innovation happens in the end-to-end customer experience. Regarding The Honest Company, CB Insights postulates, "Make no mistake, sometimes choice is not the virtue it seems to be. If you're an expectant mother looking to stock up on soap for when your new baby arrives and you search the word 'soap' on Amazon, you get 57,325 results. If you're especially ingredient-conscious, then you may have to comb through pages of results to find something sufficiently chemical-free that you actually feel comfortable using."[3] Meanwhile if you head over to The Honest Company site and search "soap," there are five chemical-free choices ready for swift delivery. That is true convenience for a conscious consumer with limited time. While Amazon makes the mom do all the work, The Honest Company goes two steps further in providing convenience and surety in the purchase.

To be sure, some of these companies have come under fire for overhyping their quality and, in the case of The Honest Company, actual product recalls. But their critics fail to understand that their loyal customers are buying the whole experience and may never have assumed that the Bonobos pant, or the Allbirds sneaker, or the Warby Parker glasses are the top of the class. As products, they are "good enough." It is the whole interaction with the company that creates enthusiasm and loyalty and the most valuable asset of all: trust.

Large consumer products companies too often wrap their marginally innovative products with expensive marketing veneers. They confuse people with an excess of hard-to-decipher choices. They make customers go to understaffed stores or navigate the mass of flat product offerings on Amazon, which are both experiences that cede control to someone else and distance the customer from the brand.

As an example of the failings of brick and mortar, I recently set aside time to buy a new pair of hiking boots. My boots are my single most treasured possession because they are associated with my favorite type of activity and vacation: hiking. I had not bought boots in many years, so I was out of touch with the brands and options. As I started to evaluate my choices, this much-anticipated happy project quickly turned into a chore. I don't fundamentally believe I can expertly understand the difference between 50 or 100 online boot choices, and boot fit matters a lot. So I planned a trip to REI. The salesperson in REI was pretty good, but the store was busy and did not stock the styles I had targeted on its site in my at-home research. I ended up getting the REI salesperson's advice on the best-fitting brands for my feet, which was truly valuable. But I also went home empty-handed. Armed with a bit more knowledge and a lot more confusion about the range of choices, I went back to the REI site and quickly fell for the 89-year-old Italian brand Zamberlan, based on the exceptional performance of a pair of waterproof sneakers I had bought from the company several years ago. I was totally open to change and excited to find new choices. In fact, I probably missed out on some meaningful construction or materials advances, but I wanted to trust my purchase more than gain an edge. Neither the REI site nor the store delivered the experience I hoped for in terms of being an efficient and effective navigator.

Whereas consumers may not automatically trust or understand the actual benefits of a DTC product—how can you *really* tell if that mattress is good quality—they tally up the total experience of a purchase: getting social confirmation from seeing their friends post about the product, the ease of using a modern, beautiful website, the clever tone of the marketing that flatters you for your savvy, experiencing great speed of delivery, the appeal of the shipping or product packaging, the ease of returns, and the experience of getting a smart person on the phone if service or information is required. The pants, or the razors, or the soap do not need to be the best in the world if the total experience is a joy. The trust established through the end-to-end experience creates a halo effect for the product, whether it is exceptional or . . . just good enough.

SCALING THROUGH DIGITAL SAVVY

The core reality is that these companies come out with a bang, but they also create huge competitive advantages by using the Internet to their advantage because:

- **The competition is weak on that front.** It is hard for established brands to be effective digital competitors across a wide product line. They tend to spread their efforts against a lot of financial goals. And fundamentally, their relatively high brand awareness removes one of the core reasons a person would share them with others—that sense of discovery and cool factor. There is no "news," and big company executions lack the kind of edge that inspires engagement. At a fundamental level, a big company is both unlikely to disrupt its own industry and profits, and even if it does, it will be met with skepticism by millennials.

   With these DTC companies, the Internet is their native environment. Whether it is creating fantastic Google search results (both paid ads and organic), or working with Instagram influencers, or getting their customers to post photos and videos of their products in use, or producing engrossing viral content like videos and Infograms, these companies tend to dance circles around the incumbents.

- **Their products and messages are hyper-narrow and targeted.** A mattress company like Casper goes hard against every aspect of sleep, convenience, shipping, delivery, and comfort from a digital-first perspective. And in particular, it understands how to win at SEO. Just Google any word that describes an aspect of mattresses and see who pops up. If you live in a city where Casper can offer same-day delivery, the results will be even more powerful. Because the company knows what you want before you even know you want it. It knows what you fear or loathe about mattress shopping, and it stands ready to provide a welcome fresh solution before you even knew it existed.

- **Some do it with money.** You can expect that much of the $240 million Casper raised from venture capitalists has gone straight into Google's bank account. It is preempting the reach of any would-be competitors.

- **Some do it with smart content strategies.** Dollar Shave Club is famous for putting itself on the map with a $4,500 investment in an "Our Blades Are F***ing Great" video that went viral and garnered 25 million views. Or it *appeared* to "just go viral." In reality, a great deal of media savvy went into the production, previewing, pre-seeding, and timing of that video, as well as a sophisticated battle plan to follow up on its success. The content looked organic and unpaid. It was anything but—although it genuinely earned every eyeball by being smart and funny.

  Similarly, one of our early Grommets was an engineering toy for girls called GoldieBlox. The founder's husband had video-marketing savvy, and they produced a brilliant piece showing a girl using their toy in a giant "Mousetrap" kind of setup. That video alone might have done the trick, but I believe their unlicensed use of a sexist (and thus spoofed) Beastie Boys song, "Girls," and the subsequent lawsuit had every bit as much to do with the spread of that video—and with GoldieBlox's outsized brand awareness.

If I have done my job here, you have realized that retailers more than earn their 50 percent margins if they can save you some of the efforts and investments described. DTC is never a "build it and they will come" strategy. It takes more savvy and more funding than the classic middleman route, but the rewards can be prodigious.

Direct to consumer is a fantastic route if you can address all of the following cornerstones of DTC positively:

1. **Big market ripe for disruption.** You have identified a large mainstream consumer purchase and process that is inconvenient or unpleasant, and it is associated with a product that has long margins that will give you plenty of funding for both reducing prices and building a brand.

2. **Unfair advantage.** You have conceived of a company position and customer acquisition strategy that will take the company from 0 to 60 because you have unique insight and ability to execute on that vision, or you have direct access to deep pockets of capital, technologies, influencers, or experts who can make your product a compelling and newsworthy breakthrough.

3. **Total experience.** You have thought out the entire end-to-end consumer experience and can specifically identify how your company will radically improve over the current experience. You are capable of executing that experience from Day One.

4. **Digital savvy to scale.** Your founding team has deep experience in harnessing the Internet for customer acquisition, and you have a clear sense of what digital strategy and channels you will prioritize.

One final observation on DTC businesses from Bain Capital investor Scott Friend, "I am seeing far too much capital going into these businesses. So many of them could be beautiful $40M to $45M businesses because they really do fill an interesting niche. But many of them are having difficulty scaling profitably beyond that level and they are under pressure because of their investors' expectations." So I do expect a reckoning in this space, and the current playbook of taking massive venture capital investments to pursue a market share land grab may implode, with future successful DTC businesses taking the more bootstrapped and slower approach.

CASE STUDIES

SimpliSafe

The pioneering home security company was formed by Chad and Eleanor Laurans as a response to a personal need: in 2006, three of their fellow Harvard Business School student friends experienced traumatic apartment break-ins. Concerned, the Lauranses investigated a solution for their own rental and discovered that all existing security company solutions from companies like ADP required a professional installation as well as multiyear contracts. There was nothing on the market to meet the requirements of renters or of people who moved frequently. The Lauranses got to work on a fresh approach. They hand-built prototypes in their own kitchen over the course of two years, before launching in 2009.

While the Lauranses were upending the security industry, they were also early pioneers of a sophisticated direct-to-consumer approach for building the business. SimpliSafe chief marketing officer Melina Engel was the company's first employee, joining as head of sales and marketing. She offers this window into the early days: "We had no office. I worked from my couch." Their customer acquisition efforts started with a simple bootstrapper mindset. Engel recounts, "We had no money. We just said, how do we get this product in front of the most people possible and maintain a positive cash flow on each sale? Though we *did* have aspirations for a recurring revenue subscription business, that was not yet real, so we expected each early sale to be profitable. We used those gross margins for each product shipped to fund our future marketing budget."

Engel focused on media that was both measurable and very easy to spin up and down. The early successes were with Google search. Engel reveals, "But, critically, before we were able to scale Google, I had to learn how to tell our stories so our budget could be super-efficient. I spent the first year on that effort, running A/B tests on our Google ads and landing pages. A big moment of transformation came during that year. I ran a survey and discovered that 70 percent of our customers were homeowners. These people were super researchers and had somehow found us despite the fact that *all* of our messages on our website, ads, and packaging were geared to renters. We had to rework everything to encompass this new customer base."

So many entrepreneurs back into new opportunities, and Engel reflects, "This outcome was a great example of universal design at work. For example, curb cuts were invented for physically disabled people, but they are great for parents with strollers, travelers with suitcases, homeless people with carts, and the elderly. Curb cuts made sidewalks better for everybody. Similarly, we set out to make security effective and accessible to renters, and in providing a solution for that very hard set of needs, we ended up solving home security for everyone. We switched all of our messaging, and that is when our double-digit growth started."

SimpliSafe has effectively used every digital marketing channel available (Facebook, PLAs, Google, podcasts) except display ads. They also found a profitable opportunity in three fairly old-school media channels: TV, radio (terrestrial radio endorsements, Pandora, and Sirius), and direct mail. "The cool thing about direct mail is that it gets more profitable with scale, as opposed to many digital channels."

The company has experimented with partnerships with big-box stores such as Best Buy because their customers have expressed interest in seeing the product in person. Engel says, "Retail is getting better as the category gains more awareness, but until then, it was problematic. I had a Babson professor who said, 'Retail is great if you have a broom with a rubber handle.

It works when you are selling an improved version of something people are looking for. It's hard to do it for a brand-new category.'" Retail expansion is rigorously tested as with all channels, but Engel says she still focuses primarily on D2C because there is plenty of growth still to be had.

One of the core competencies at SimpliSafe is its ability to test out its modes of communication (phone, chat, e-mail) and specific messaging to home in on the customer needs. They also need to have an extreme degree of availability both before and after a purchase. This commitment to a positive end-to-end customer experience is reflected in the fact that the majority of SimpliSafe's 600 employees work in customer service. Engel enthuses that "we learn every day from quantitative customer feedback."

After many years of bootstrapping and self-funding, SimpliSafe took a Sequoia Capital investment of $57 million in 2014, followed by a private equity investment in 2018 that valued the company at over $1 billion. Engel says proudly, "Being a 'no contract' company, our customers have the upper hand, and we take our jobs seriously. We are taking care of their families. Forty percent of our customers say they were nervous about the purchase before they made it. My favorite customer review said, 'OMG the installation was so easy. You made my husband a hero.' We now protect 2.5 million souls."

Knixwear

Having had many conversations with her mother, a doctor and mom of four, about "what happens with women's bodies and how complicated that is," Joanna Griffiths decided to start Knixwear. The underwear company touts itself as "reinventing intimates for real life." After talking with many women who weren't satisfied with the sort of intimate apparel already on the market (think too many wires, too fussy, and too "sex dominated") Griffiths knew she was on to something and launched a line of underwear for women of all shapes and sizes.

In its early days, Knixwear was a wholesale and online company. The products were also sold at Saks Fifth Avenue and Lord & Taylor. For the first three years Knixwear did trade shows and trunk shows, and its people were on the road pitching to buyers. They were in several hundred retail stores. The company received lots of press initially. But then, says Griffiths, things became more complicated. "We underestimated the time and energy it took to service wholesale partners."

It turns out many stores weren't tracking inventory carefully, and sales associates weren't familiar enough with Knixwear to speak to its benefits or sell it effectively. Customers were complaining that they couldn't find their sizes in the department stores, making multiple stops at various stores and still coming up empty.

"We decided the customer experience would be better if we took control of it," says Griffiths. So they did just that, going entirely direct to consumer by the end of 2016. They even bought back inventory that was already out there. "We ate a lot of money," says Griffiths, adding that it was completely worth it. They also grew from 5 to 35 employees in 12 months.

The benefits of controlling the customer experience and the inventory are many, says Griffiths. "We're bringing products to market faster because we're not adhering to the traditional fashion calendar." Knixwear uses Shopify, Facebook, and Instagram to get out the word. And Griffiths says another benefit is the opportunities to interact with consumers. "We can build a real relationship with customers now." At this point, 97 percent of Knixwear's sales are through the website. They do the occasional pop-up, and Knixwear is still in about 70 small retail stores, most of which have been loyal to the company from the beginning. "We're controlling the messaging and the relationship," adds Griffiths. "It's really exciting."

In 2017 Griffiths said the company had grown its online sales by 2,000 percent over the previous year and the company was on track to do $20 million in sales for that year.

iFixit

When iFixit started as a parts seller on eBay, few people knew how to fix their phones, computers, and other devices. iFixit began providing manuals online because people didn't know how to install the parts they were buying. "People loved the basic paper manuals," says Eric Essen, the company's chief tool officer. From there, the company grew. iFixit sells repair kits as well as publishes free online repair guides—more than 44,000 by the fall of 2018.

The repair manuals alone started to drive traffic to the iFixit site. They were selling 40,000 of them, and users were flocking to the site. "Customers would come to the site to find content on how to fix something," explains Essen. "They'd see the whole solution is right there in front of them." Ultimately iFixit leveraged what it had online to set up a brick-and-mortar presence.

Being able to sell direct to consumer provided the company with many advantages, including being able to tap into its customer base, understand them, and talk to them. iFixit has since started selling to wholesalers, retails, and major electronics centers. Today direct to consumer accounts for approximately half of its business.

When it comes to getting into retailers, Essen says, "Retailers will ignore you until you get into a competitor." He adds that most buyers are simply too hesitant to buy something brand-new, something they haven't yet heard of. But once your product gets picked up elsewhere, suddenly the interest is high. "They trust the competitors more than your sales pitch," says Essen, laughing.

"We are a social and political company," says Essen. "We're forcing manufacturers to put in replaceable batteries." And iFixit has been a leader in getting the Fair Repair Act passed in nearly 20 states, which requires manufacturers to offer repair information. The tool kits are sold through Amazon, Fry's Electronics, Ace Hardware, and Micro Center.

16

LOGISTICS

The most classic image of a technology startup is of two people in a garage (Google, Apple, and Hewlett-Packard all share that origin story). The most classic image of a Maker startup is of two people in a dining room, packing boxes. That is where most Grommet Makers begin, when it comes to shipping their first product. Even our own business did self-fulfilling—for about a year too long.

There is a satisfying degree of control and positive feedback to be derived from seeing the fruits of your own labor stacked for shipping. For us, during the holiday season, it was a bonding experience. There was no way we could effectively staff up and train to handle the crush of demand for the peak six weeks. So each person on our small team did their normal day job and then signed up for weekly shipping shifts (nights and weekends). It sounds terrible to do such double duty, but honestly it was a beautiful thing to see the helpful enthusiasm of the team and to experience the results of our hard-won growth together. We'd share a few pizzas, compete for "fastest packer" cred, and talk about the orders we saw flowing through our hands.

But we also shipped more than a few empty boxes. I'm sure those customers on the receiving end were not amused if they got a stale piece of pepperoni instead of their brother's Christmas gift in a Grommet box.

Before a big office move, when we knew we could no longer stock our own inventory, we pulled the trigger on outsourcing our warehousing and fulfillment. It was a good thing we did. When that 2013 holiday season was over, we did a look-back on the results of that decision. There were two stark realizations:

1. We did not ship one empty box via our new logistics partner.

2. If we had self-shipped the volume of Black Friday orders that they handled, it would have taken us 37 days to get the orders out the door. The packages would have arrived sometime in January.

The Internet has made logistics services more readily available, with vendors such as Shipwire (the company we hired), ShipStation, Shyp, Barrett Distribution, and Fulfillment by Amazon (FBA). In addition, most of the major carriers (UPS, FedEx, DHL) also offer fulfillment services. The beauty of these newer offerings is that they can deliver enterprise-levels of service when you have only very low volumes. Which means you can ship like a pro from the very earliest days of your business. With the explosion of new e-commerce sites, crowdfunding campaigns that promise products to be delivered as perks, and direct-to-consumer brands, a whole new layer of demand for logistics services emerged, and this is only growing.

A word of clarification on Amazon: you can sell from any site you like and still use Fulfillment By Amazon. It's a bit expensive and you have to rigorously abide by their operational guidelines, but you can be assured of efficient logistics for your shipments.[1] FBA still exposes you to the broader risk of Amazon noticing your volumes and setting out to copy your product with its private label, so it's a buyer beware decision. (See Chapter 14 on retail distribution.)

Here are services a third-party logistics (3PL) company can provide:

- Picking and packing your orders

- Shipping and handling your orders

- Providing shipping pricing/rating on your website (unless you only provide flat rate or free shipping)

- Right-sizing your orders for the standard box sizes in the warehouse, before packing, to avoid waste

- Customer service (some do this; some do not)

- Product returns

- Storage per cubic foot per month

Don't hesitate to go with self-shipping to get yourself started. It can be a family operation, and when you have very small volumes it will not be taxing. But think ahead. It is better to save your resources and energy for where you excel in your business and outsource this work as soon as possible. You will learn a lot about logistics during your onboarding, and you will be prepared to meet the lovely customer demand you will be freer to create *if* you are not distracted by shipping. You will also have many logistics activities to support your 3PL partner, so it's never going to be totally out of your control or, on the converse, a "set and forget" operation.

The things you have to address no matter how you approach logistics are vast. Be sure to read Chapter 12 on packaging because retailers have the same requirements as 3PL warehouses in terms of routing information and labeling. Shipping boxes and packing materials are also marketing vehicles, so logistics decisions impact your brand presence very directly. Your boxes are the closest thing to you personally delivering your products—make them work hard.

Beyond that, a 3PL warehouse staff will need something called an ASN (advance shipping notice) so they are alerted to an incoming delivery of your product. It is often transmitted via an EDI (electronic data integration) system. At its most basic level, EDI just means having an electronic communication bridge between two systems, so e-mail is a very rudimentary form of EDI. But e-mail won't cut it with large retailers, so formal EDI systems can become essential to doing business with them. Working out the kinks of an EDI implementation with your 3PL is a good first step before risking mis-shipments or miscommunication with a wholesale customer over a large order.

If you are currently shipping from your garage or basement, and you just read all that EDI hoo-ha, you probably wanted to scuttle back to business as usual and pretend you never heard of EDI. Here's the good news: it can wait. Most of our Makers delay or never implement an EDI system if they do not take on the largest of retailers. In the case of working with The Grommet, we assign ASNs alongside our purchase orders, so a Maker grabs both at the same time when getting an order from us. If Makers have an EDI system, we hook directly to that, but most do not, and they just log in directly, as they do with their other wholesale accounts.

Other logistics questions you will tackle:

- **When to add another warehouse** if your volumes justify cross-stocking your inventory in two places to make your shipping times faster. It adds a level of complexity to your inventory management, but it might be justifiable for customer service benefits.

- **What shipping options will you offer your customers?** You should evaluate the shipping choices that similar businesses offer to get a benchmark for your own customer expectations. Then get to work matching those expectations. With shipping services, your business is purchasing a commodity. So the two key factors to nail down are which carrier(s) makes sense for you, and how fast will you need to ship? A box of chocolates needs different terms of service than a pair of flip-flops. Pricing for shipping small items tends to work out better with the U.S. Postal Service. Larger items tend to ship by UPS or

FedEx. Basically, shop around and renegotiate your contracts frequently. There is a lot of variability in these contracts, and as your volumes go up, you will gain automatic leverage for better pricing.

- **Will you offer gift wrapping?** Some products can be warehoused already wrapped, but most 3PLs do that as an on-demand service because already-wrapped gifts are hard to handle and prone to damage and labeling issues. Another option is to simply offer gift boxes for self-assembly by customers.

- **What will you charge for shipping?** This alone is the biggest question you will face. At The Grommet we have found that objections to shipping charges (in principle) are the single biggest obstacle to a potential purchase. At the time of this writing, we offer free shipping for orders over $50, and free shipping on all orders for our Perks members (our loyalty program). In the 10 years we have been operating, the pressure to offer free shipping on everything has risen tremendously—it was not even a factor in 2008, and today 60 percent of e-commerce goods are shipped "for free." In building your product's price you would do well to assume that you will have to cover its shipping costs for your customers. Even though people know better (rationally), as consumers we forget that there is no such thing as free shipping. And if you offer it, you will be eating the costs.

- **What delivery promises will you make?** Because of the increasing speed of e-commerce deliveries, I tend to believe online customers subconsciously start expecting *any* package to arrive within three or four days, no matter who is shipping it. But I have been pleasantly surprised to learn that our Grommet customers are more concerned about the accuracy of our tracking information than speed alone. So depending on your customer, this may be where you can save a bit of expense as long as you set clear expectations for delivery time frames.

- **How will you handle returns?** One of my favorite stories about this came from meeting Alexis Maybank, the cofounder of Gilt Groupe. She told me that when they launched their business, they had no systems—either online or off—for taking customer returns. They knew returns would be a big factor in their business model, given the nature of their merchandise. She said, "We estimated that we could not possibly get hit with our first return any sooner than three days from launch, so we knew we had three days to figure it out." While that worked out well for their well-resourced and ambitious technology company, get in front of that reality. The dirty underbelly of these decisions is what the pros call "reverse logistics," which means you can walk into any warehouse that ships to consumers, and you will see a very unlovely pile of returned boxes. They may be pristine and unopened, or crushed beyond recognition. Whatever their state, they all have to be opened and assessed, both for refunding your customer and for determining the outcome of the goods. Are they resaleable, or do they need to be sold in a secondary market? Which ones are good enough for donating to a charity, and which ones have to be discarded?

- **How many returns can you expect?** Return policies matter a great deal to converting a potential customer to a real one, so lean toward being generous. If your product does what you promise, you will not go broke taking in returns. If you are selling shoes and competing with Zappos, which makes a public virtue of sending out multiple sizes, you can expect returns of over 25 percent of your sales—I've heard figures as high as 40 percent for shoes. If you are selling something very precise and inexpensive, like replacement parts for specialist gear, you will have single digit return rates. On average, expect 10 to 15 percent. Again, it all depends on what you sell. Because we are so rigorous about product quality, and we provide extensive and accurate information about our Grommets, our return rates are always under 3 percent. I never expected that when we started, but it is a leading indicator I watch carefully to make sure we are maintaining the trust of our customers.

For some Makers, nailing international logistics becomes a core competency. It's something we had to navigate, and I recommend getting help from a knowledgeable service provider. We work with Angela Czajkowski at Shapiro Freight Forwarder and Customs Broker and have learned the ropes through trial and error and through their guidance. Czajkowski advises:

- **Know your terms of sale** (international commercial terms—Incoterms) and the benefits and risks of each. Don't be fooled by low-cost merchandise or materials without considering these terms of sale. You could find yourself holding an unexpected yet hefty bill in the end, prior to receiving your cargo.

- **Deeply evaluate a quote,** and ensure you are comparing apples to apples if you shop your freight. There is still service differentiation in this space. This is not yet a commoditized business, and shippers must remember that.

- **Reasonable care.** Importing is considered a privilege, and there are significant responsibilities for reasonable care expected of the importer. Even if you hire a broker (who will have responsibilities of their own as well), you (the importer) are also responsible for regulatory compliance. Know your responsibilities and create best practices around each. This includes, but is not limited to, classification, timely filing, bond maintenance, and document retention.

- **Valuation, classification, duties, and tariffs.** Learn about your products' HTS classifications. Proper in-depth classification by a licensed customs house broker can help you maintain compliance and avoid unfortunate surprises later. Analyze your commercial documents and know your product valuation. Understand the implications of any special programs you may utilize and consider the long-term impact of these programs. Trade agreements are a common discussion point here. A shifting trade program, or unexpected tariff assessment, can dramatically impact your overall product cost and duty responsibility. This is especially important if you single-source your materials.

- **PGAs (partner government agencies).** Familiarize yourself with the applicable PGAs and their requirements for compliant importing. This includes entities such as USDA, FDA, Fish and Wildlife, FCC, etc. Each entity expects and may request additional information or inspection of your goods. Some items would obviously be associated with a specific PGA, but others can be more surprising.

- **Consider trade programs** such as C-TPAT and how your participation could positively impact your supply chain. Participating in this program provides specific benefits but also requires commitment from the participant. This is not an initiative to be undertaken lightly. It requires significant time investment to both initiate and maintain.

- **Accept the potential of an exam** or other unforeseen expense. With the privilege of importing comes the potential of exam fees and involved enforcement agencies do their due diligence. The cost of these exams will be the responsibility of the importer.

The bottom line of nailing logistics—both domestic and international—is that this aspect of your business is one of the most central ways you either delight or disappoint customers. Think about your own experiences in purchasing from new sites. You impute a lot of characteristics onto that business based on the only things you can see and touch: their communications around your shipment, the state of the packaging, and the speed and accuracy of the service. A fantastic product can help you get past minor logistics shortfalls, but no product can easily make up for a botched delivery. In today's day and age of high service expectations and the existence of many credible vendors who are prepared to make your business logistics shine, this is not a place to skim by on good will or amateur practices.

CASE STUDIES

Quickloader

"You have to convert dollars into inventory," says Ulrick Westergaard, who handles inventory for Quickloader, the popular ratchet-style tie-down. "Once you've turned $10,000 into a product sitting in your garage, you need to reconvert it back to money. Without inventory you have nothing to convert, but before you make your first dollar you have to stock up." The cycle is endless and a bit dizzying at times. "Without a clear plan of how to convert it back to dollars you will fail."

When considering how much inventory to make and stock, Westergaard says it's imperative to calculate the amount you're selling to retail, wholesale, and direct to consumer. "Inventory management is tied directly to the channel through which you are distributing," says Westergaard. "Inventory management for startup companies is incredibly difficult."

Westergaard says another challenge is when larger wholesale orders come in unexpectedly; if you don't have the inventory you may have to pass on those, but if you aren't established it's hard to have much excess inventory.

Quickloader has a warehouse in Yonkers, New York, as well as in Ontario, at the manufacturer. Produced in China, Quickloader buys a full container of components each time, and everything waits on pallets in Yonkers.

When inventory demand spikes, Quickloader has to request a quick turnaround from the manufacturer. Westergaard says it can be a tricky decision whether to fulfill a large order from a big new customer or take care of the tried-and-true ones. "You have to support the businesses that have supported you," he says. In other words, fulfill your current promises before getting swept away by a big new offer.

Selling widely since 2011, the patented Quickloader is sold through Home Depot, Amazon, Ace Hardware, hardware stores, and ToolBarn.com. The company continues to expand into new markets and has also added additional products such as rope that can also be used for hauling and tying down.

Neighborwoods

Born as a design studio, Brooklyn-based Hyperakt typically does client work in the social impact space. In 2012 the group had bartered for a laser engraver, and a designer at the studio came up with the idea for Neighborwoods, laser-engraved wooden coasters, wall hangings, and more of various cities. Deroy Peraza, principal and creative director at Hyperakt, says he and his team hadn't thought through the logistics of the whole production side of things, the labor required for customer service, and the profit margins of using expensive wood before launching.

Peraza was fortunate enough to have options. His parents own and run a signage and rubber stamp factory in Miami.

Neighborwoods decided to move all production there, where there were several laser engraving machines and more space. All prototyping happens in Brooklyn, but everything else comes out of Miami. Generally speaking, Neighborwoods is an on-demand product, with only the most popular items made ahead of time and stored as inventory. As Neighborwoods has grown, so too has Peraza's parents' business. "It's a unique arrangement," says Peraza. "We all know each other very well."

Peraza says there is an operations manager in Brooklyn as well as one in Miami. They each handle the logistics of orders coming in and production. When it comes to shipping, all of that is handled by the facility in Miami, says Peraza. "All of the sites have different requirements with labels," he says of various retailer specifications. Neighborwoods tends to ship via USPS because it's the least expensive. On occasion they use UPS, says Peraza. And they rarely ship internationally, but when they do it's through DHL.

Neighborwoods has been featured as a great gift option in *Real Simple*, on the FoodNetwork.com, and Men's Health. They sell through boutiques, Uncommon Goods, their own site, and The Grommet.

Patent Prints

Already in the printing business, Cole Borders was looking to make a bit more money. "They're very unique, very cool," he says of Patent Prints, recreated, unusual patent drawings that he prints on canvas and other material.

Patent Borders owns its own warehouse where it produces everything on demand. Once an order comes in, they print. "We don't inventory anything," says Borders.

Everything is produced and shipped from the company's Bowling Green, Kentucky, location. "It's a good spot to be," says

Borders, explaining that they have two-day shipping to 27 states from there. Most orders go out first class through USPS, while some go via UPS.

Borders uses a logistics company, as well as ShipStation to manage and track all shipping. "They have the technology to integrate this," says Borders of the shipping contractor. He says he doesn't have to individually log into and check on Amazon orders and deal with shipping. That all happens automatically. When it comes to The Grommet, Borders says he has to track those orders manually.

Java Sok

"I'm the shipper," says David Laks, founder of Java Sok. All of the coffee koozies are shipped directly to Laks from the manufacturer. Laks distributes them according to orders from his website, Amazon, and The Grommet. He says that while The Grommet produces the shipping labels, he generates his own invoices and paperwork for the other sources.

Everything Java Sok ships goes out through the post office in Roseland, New Jersey. Laks says it's the most economical since the product is a lightweight neoprene coffee koozie. When it comes to getting the outgoing orders to the post office, Laks says it's a simple operation. "We strategically located our office a block from the post office." He'll walk them over. When the order is too large to carry, he'll drive. "It's been a big learning curve," says Laks of figuring out when the best time of day is to arrive at the post office with 300 or 400 packages at a time. "Two or three years later it's a very, very smooth operation." Laks says he's been incredibly pleased with the post office so far. Having shipped nearly 15,000 orders, Laks estimates that only five have been lost. "It's a remarkably efficient machine."

17

E-COMMERCE AND PAYMENTS

At the very start of your company's launch you most likely will have created a website, Facebook page, Instagram account, or blog for your business. This online presence is mainly informational and/or a place to interact with potential and existing customers. You will likely extend that to enable direct sales to consumers. Ultimately, you may even decide to take wholesale orders on a specialized extension of your e-commerce site. There is a multiplicity of off-the-shelf e-commerce platform options, ranging from quick and easy to modify and get going, to more complex customization platforms that require advanced software coding skills.

CHOOSING A WEBSITE PLATFORM

In the vast majority of cases, you will not need to build a custom e-commerce website. This is because there are great standard options available. If you are super intimidated about creating your site, you can work with an engineer, a designer, or a tech-inclined colleague to customize your platform, but with a bit of focus, you can also tackle this work on most e-commerce platform options without any technical background. That is the core mindset for this project: you are customizing, not *building* an e-commerce site. When you need transportation, you don't build a car, but you do put an enormous amount of thought into what car will best serve your needs. You read reviews, study the costs of operating the car, and its service reputation. You do test drives, and you labor over the customization packages and features and ultimate, all-in purchase pricing. Think of your website like a similar tool—it will get your customers from A to B, in terms of learning about your product and company, sharing it with friends, offering customer service options, and letting them buy what you have to offer. Put effort into assuring it is the right tool for you, and don't just go for the first platform you encounter.

There are a few cases where a product may need a robust custom website, especially for Internet of Things and app-centric products, and those Makers may use their custom sites also for selling.

If you are just getting going, you will want to focus on the platforms geared toward small-to-medium-volume businesses. Here are the most prominent:

- Shopify (start here, as it is the most likely to suit your needs)

- BigCommerce

- WooCommerce (extension of WordPress)

- Wix

- Squarespace

Beyond evaluating this list of options, I refer you to www .HowWeMakeStuffNow.com, an online resource that I am maintaining to give you up-to-date information on any new platform choices that emerge. This is a very dynamic space, so expect to make Google your friend in getting up to speed, and talk to a few small business customers for any platform you are considering adopting.

When we started The Grommet we had to build a custom e-commerce website because few of the current user-friendly options existed. In 2008 e-commerce was still more of a big enterprise endeavor, and not a lot of new startups or investments were emerging. Even more relevant to The Grommet, there was no concept of a "daily" offering within the standard platforms, as flash sale sites like Groupon and Rue La La were just forming. Further, we evenly straddle behaving like a media site and community as much as an e-commerce site. Until very recently we had a live conversation board that kicked off with each product launch, so that you could speak directly with the Maker of a product right at the moment of discovery. That was a special condition, as well as our need to put videos front and center with each product launch. No one was doing videos in any form in retail or e-commerce. Hence the custom site. We ultimately moved to the more robust and complex Magento platform (not for beginners—it requires heavy customization) once it caught up with our needs.

I can tell you I did not actually fully anticipate many of the needs we would have for our first e-commerce site. The most prominent mistakes I made in specifying it (remember it was built from the ground up, so we had to give direction to our engineer on every aspect) were:

- **No catalog.** This is one of the most boneheaded things I have done, but since we were so into the idea of presenting one new product a day (we were even called Daily Grommet), I had no notion of having an easily shoppable "back catalog" customers could peruse. That was hilariously silly. Of course people wanted to go back to prior Grommet launches, and we quickly fixed that with a kludgy update. It took us a few more cycles to make a truly accessible catalog.

- **Reporting.** I did not understand the importance of capturing all the data we were creating: things like customer behavior on the site and specific qualities of the products that were most popular. Our software developer alerted me to this gap in the spec, but we barreled forward and painfully had to retrofit in reporting.

- **Content management system.** Since we are first and foremost a media site, managing content effectively is critical. Suffice it to say we did not.

This is my tale of woe. You will not have this level of challenge because the standard platforms these days have done much of the thinking and anticipating for you. Having said that, you still should do your internal thinking and external diligence. And when you do commit to a platform, think of it more like renting an apartment than buying a house. Your needs may change, or new, better options may arise. It is honestly fairly difficult to fully test drive an e-commerce platform, so you may become dissatisfied with your choice despite your best due diligence efforts. Be prepared to switch platforms if that occurs.

Here are the factors to consider when choosing your platform:

- **What kind of products do you sell?** These platforms all have a variety of standard templates that you should peruse to see which comes closest to accommodating your merchandise. Some of the templates are free, while others come with an upcharge over the basic software cost. Selling apparel is vastly different from selling terrariums or power tools. Do you anticipate a relatively complex and unrelated group of products that need to be separately navigated, or are you creating a single coherent product line? What is your SKU count likely to be? (Be bold and ambitious, not conservative in this thinking.) How often do you plan to add new products or styles?

- **What kind of media do you need to present?** Related to the merchandise, how can you best present your products? Will you rely heavily on videos, or are zoomed-in photos of your product details and materials going to be your go-to sales, education, and conversion tool?

- **How stable and established is the platform?** You are taking a lot of risk in starting a business. Picking an e-commerce platform is not a place to pile on more exposure. No matter what the claims of an upstart platform, stick with the more established companies because they will have the resources to continue to update their offerings and they will not go dark on you like a fragile startup could.

- **Volume of sales/fees.** Carefully study the way the platforms get paid. Do they take a percentage of your sales? Do they have monthly fees? What are the upcharges for hosting your site or other necessary functionality? Depending on your volume ambitions, this may not be your biggest decision, but you should still know what you are getting into.

- **Mobile.** Your visitors from mobile phones and tablets will likely be your top traffic source, so make sure the platform has responsive (flexible) technology to ensure that no matter what screen size, your site is presented in the correct proportions and content will adjust accordingly. You are not likely to have your own mobile app anytime soon, so this is the next best thing. However, some platforms have out of the box mobile apps as part of their offering.

- **Shipping platform integrations.** It's essential that the order functionality on your e-commerce site can talk to your warehouse or 3PL. (See Chapter 16: Logistics.) Investigate how the platform you are considering communicates orders to that crucial partner. Dave Swift, vice president of engineering at The Grommet, says, "I think the main things to look for are: What is the cost of shipping out your product? For example, does the platform provide shipping labels? What do they cost? Do they use the right shipping carrier for you? Do they provide packing slips? Beyond that, try to study the customer experience around tracking and delivery dates—how well does the platform handle those key communications?"

- **Marketplace integrations.** If you mainly anticipate selling on other platforms like Etsy, Amazon, or eBay, you will want an e-commerce site that is biased for that capability, like YoKart.

- **Payments.** How do they handle this? All the platforms offer a multiplicity of third-party payment options. Some (like Shopify) vary their fee structures depending on whether you use their payment system or a third party.

Doing online research and calls with the salespeople at the platforms will get you part of the way to a decision. Talking to their current customers will complete the work most effectively. Here are some handy questions to ask when you are checking customer references for a particular e-commerce platform:

1. Were you able to find and customize a template to suit your needs?

2. What is the process to create new product offerings and SKUs?

3. How do you pay the platform? Did you encounter any hidden charges or unexpected costs for additional needed functionality?

4. Who do you use for your 3PL, and how well does it interact with your e-commerce site?

5. What functionality do you wish you had that is missing?

6. What happens when you have a problem with your site, either in customizing, updating, or troubleshooting it? What do you do? How responsive is the company when you contact them?

HANDLING PAYMENTS

Handling payments from consumers—whether selling your product at a street fair, on your website, or in your own store—is another animal entirely. In contrast to wholesale accounts, for which you are required to conform to your customer's systems, B2C payments systems choices are entirely in your hands, so there are more decisions to be made. You likely will be navigating two choices: how to handle your online payments and how to handle in-person transactions at a store or market if you plan to do offline sales.

If you take consumer orders on your website, you have probably found that all of the relatively simple/accessible e-commerce platforms like Shopify, Wix, Squarespace, BigCommerce, and WooCommerce/WordPress have built-in third-party payment processors. You will be up and running and accepting payments without navigating the complex world of online payments directly.

But let's assume you do some in-person sales at markets or even trade shows. You will need a point of sale (POS) system. Here is a range of payment processors that you will likely consider, depending on your needs.

- **Stripe:** A great start if you are a new digital-only startup.

- **PayPal:** A customer-facing payment option that also offers payment processing. Since 12 percent of Americans prefer to pay with PayPal, it is smart to have it on your site, whether or not it is your payment processor.

- **Square:** If you're anticipating both online and offline sales, Square is the choice for you. Just beware of high transaction costs when your revenue increases (you can always switch to a different provider by then).

- **Braintree:** Large/enterprise customers should consider this provider. It offers the payment services of Stripe while also delivering PayPal and low currency-conversion rates. But it's not for non-techies, implementation-wise.

If you Google "POS systems," you will be quickly overwhelmed. It is one of the most fragmented technology areas you can find. This is partly because POS itself is nothing new. A cash register is a POS system. The old credit card devices with multipart carbon paper forms that you used to capture the credit card number (like a tombstone rubbing) were POS systems. The newer ones just do more, faster, and can eliminate bulky cash registers and paper, relying on simple tablets and touch screens. If you've bought something at an Apple store you know what I mean. A sale can be made anywhere there is Wi-Fi.

So what to choose? When we were doing research to determine what POS system we wanted for our own Grommet retail store, we reached out to 47 of our small retailer customers from our wholesale platform. They were using over 25 different systems! There were no trends or commonalities except that most of them were unhappy with their choice, saying things like, "And it sucks. Hopefully, we will change in the next year or so."

We ultimately went with Square.

As with keeping abreast of e-commerce options, we will be periodically updating www.HowWeMakeStuffNow.com with information on payment providers and POS systems.

Figuring out your e-commerce and payment platforms will probably not be the most exciting part of building your business, but it is fundamental. Beyond addressing your business needs, these choices become part of your overall customer experience, so try to treat these implementations as thoughtfully as you would your company name or packaging design.

CASE STUDIES

Vermont Rolling Pins

Cyndi Freeman and her husband Ken do most of the work behind Vermont Rolling Pins, started in 2009. Ken hand-carves almost every single rolling pin (they occasionally bring in additional wood turners during busy seasons), while Cyndi handles the other aspects of the business.

Vermont Rolling Pins are sold at numerous boutiques and kitchen shops as well as through trade shows. "We've gotten some press," says Cyndi Freeman. "We're not unknown." That always helps. "It's hard if you haven't gotten press," she adds. As Cyndi points out, it's a tough cycle because in order to get press you often need press. That said, the press is what gives your product some sort of legitimacy, adds Cyndi. "It says that you've come on to a product that might work."

The small company works with PayPal for both online and in-person orders. When at shows, Freeman says she prefers PayPal over other payment options. Compared to Square, Freeman finds PayPal faster and "it seems easier to me. And it seemed more intuitive." Most of the company's sales are done online and through stores, both retail and wholesale.

P-Mate

P-Mate, billed as "a reliable stand and pee device" for women, is a small operation that has been run out of Karen Diamond's home since 2005. "I have a huge basement," she quips. That's where all of the inventory lives. Although Diamond has considered contracting out for drop shipping, she also handles all of that herself.

Diamond handles payments for her business in a variety of ways. "I almost always request prepayment" when it comes to retailers. Some larger companies won't agree to that, but Diamond says she's gotten burned in the past, so she tends to require it. For wholesale Diamond uses Inspire Pay, which allows you to create professional invoices with links to payments. Diamond says she sends these out via e-mail and most customers tend to pay through the link. A few still send checks. And she accepts PayPal as well.

Diamond says she doesn't track finances through Quicken or another program, but rather with pen and paper, the old-fashioned way. "I have a handwritten list of accounts on my desk," she laughs. P-Mate is sold through Amazon as well as online camping gear sites and through the company's website.

18

CUSTOMER EXPERIENCE

The title of this chapter probably evokes an image of a company that answers the phone promptly and treats people courteously. That is true and certainly an aspect of customer service, but it's too narrow. The better place to begin dissecting best customer service practices starts at a higher level. Customer service excellence starts well before anyone calls you on the phone. It is embedded in all of your policies and practices, your overall orientation as an organization, and the total customer experience you craft and nurture.

I like the way Juhi Gupta Gulati, the founder and CEO of food storage company Frego, thinks: "A successful company should first and foremost be a responsible company. It should be responsible toward its customers, its employees, its environment, and people with whom it has relationships."

Let's begin with your products themselves. It might seem a stretch to claim inanimate objects could be dynamic customer service agents, but then imagine building products that come with a lifetime guarantee. The minute you see the words "lifetime guarantee," you ascribe a level of trustworthiness and customer focus to a company. Those two words on a product's packaging or within its marketing messages have a positive halo effect on the general business practices of a company. Imagine what you'd expect from that company's people if you did telephone them. You'd expect a smart and knowledgeable person on the other end of the line— just because they backed their product's performance so forcefully. Further, such a product responds to the growing "buy it once" movement. Google those words to see what is happening on that front. People have always preferred companies that sell their products with a lifetime warranty. This also implies a level of responsibility to the environment, per Juhi Gupta Gulati's philosophy.

So first and foremost, true customer service orientation depends on producing a product that delivers on its promises, whether or not it is suitable for a lifetime guarantee. That is the most fundamental building block of your customer experience and the first place you should start. Doing anything less puts your entire company on shaky ground and no amount of traditional customer service will get you beyond an irresponsible foundation.

Caring about customers starts at the top. One of the reasons I asked Joanne Domeniconi to join me in forming The Grommet is that I had seen her stellar work as a vice president of product development when we worked together at the footwear company Keds. She was responsible for the design, engineering, sourcing, and manufacturing of the entire product line at this $350 million revenue company. I watched how she carefully scrutinized every production sample. Were the materials and manufacturing as intended? Was this shoe—even one that sold for only $24.99, good enough to carry the blue Keds label? Would the department stores that carried it be proud of it, and would it be durable and comfortable for customers?

But her commitment to service went beyond her immediate purview. I will never forget the time when a few of us on the team (including me) were slow to respond to a difficult request from another business. It was a restaurant chain—I think it was Chuck

E. Cheese—that wanted us to make a custom line of giant shoes for its costumed employees to wear. The company was willing to pay, whatever the cost. However, it was a project we could not execute at any price—we were only geared toward making high volumes. I, and the other people who passed off the request, knew that this was a nonstarter. When Joanne saw the unanswered letter kicking around, she chided the unfortunate last person sitting on the request with something like, "You represent Keds in the way you respond to someone. Even if our answer needs to be a no, they should have heard from us by now. Please take care of this." That is excellent customer service, especially considering the effort was expended for a distant entity that was never, ever going to be a customer.

Start there. At every point of contact with a potential employee, customer, supplier, or partner, you are representing your vision and brand. In the beginning those practices and behaviors might only come from you, as a sole proprietor. You might feel like an overly stretched jack-of-all-trades for the early months and years. But when you are small, you are in a prime position to have personal and direct contact with customers, and that is like gold. You set an example, you learn about your business's opportunities faster, and you build loyalty. In those fatigued moments when you don't feel like answering another e-mail or tweet, remember that there are very real costs to acquiring each customer. So open the e-mail to protect your investment! Retention of customers is vastly more cost effective than losing them and paying for new ones.

Here's a sterling example from our senior director of operations, Bobby McLaughlin. "I was doing customer service tickets and reviewing stale (overdue) shipments when I came across an order for Formfire Glassworks. It had been sitting in the Maker's queue for a few days, and the customer had reached out for a timeline. The handmade necklace was needed for the upcoming weekend as it was a special birthday gift for his wife. He had ordered with plenty of time, but the Maker had not shipped (now Thursday night).

"I called him and found out exactly when he needed it. Then I called the Maker. She had been sick, causing the delay. The shipment would be dropped off at the local UPS store with overnighted service. Phew . . . birthday saved. Closed my computer. Put it in my bag. Hand on the light switch in the office . . . my phone rings. The Maker sneezed . . . and she *dropped* the *glass* jewelry . . . apparently from the highest building in town so it was not fixable. It also was the last one she had ready-made.

"In a whirlwind of creative problem solving, I was able to work out a solution. The (horrified, apologetic, and extremely congested) Maker had a slightly different version ready to roll. That one would be sent overnight as a placeholder. She would then make a replacement over the weekend to be sent ASAP. I called the customer back. He was surprised but extremely grateful."

This story sounds heroic, but versions of this happen every day at The Grommet. At the last trade show I attended, a loyal retail customer admired the custom Grommet shirt I was wearing. Another employee overheard and literally offered the one on her back, knowing she had a spare back in her hotel room. Just today I reminded our hiring managers that I expect all job applicants to hear back from us when we fill a role. Even though the bad news is hard to deliver, it is far better to have a human touch than to leave the potential employee in the dark.

Grommet director of customer experience Doug Murphy admits, "In my experience at The Grommet, few Makers are really good at customer service. It's not their discipline; they're experts in their Grommets. Partnering at an early stage with someone who is good at it (like us, or a quality retailer) before they develop the competency seems lifesaving to me."

Sometimes we have to play cleanup after Makers have badly botched an earlier crowdfunding campaign. They may have not delivered effectively on the promised rewards, and they create unhappy and even irate crowdfunding backers. These Makers damage their own brand because they don't understand that digital breadcrumbs left by unhappy backers are permanent. Kickstarter and Indiegogo are a great source for the first capital into your business, but you must embrace the fact that a crowdfunding campaign is not easy money. It is like a mini-business. Your backers give you a loan against a promised reward, and they expect frequent communication and effective delivery against your commitments. They expect service.

In contrast to the uncommitted, some Makers have "above and beyond" DNA. Over the holidays last year when Grommet Maker Candle by the Hour couldn't fulfill on its shorter burning product, it did not want to disappoint anyone. It fulfilled the orders with the longer burning, more expensive candle for no additional charge.

The bottom line is that mistakes will happen, you will be stretched to deliver best-in-class business operations, and the real test of your commitment to a solid customer experience is how you handle those missteps. At The Grommet we are often exposed to the weaknesses and foibles of our Makers. They run out of inventory. They are severely capital-constrained and understaffed. They are not always technically savvy. They have awkward transitions to new packaging or products that affect our customers, and they forget to tell us.

But there is a world of difference between a company that is committed to success and consistently responds promptly to us, and one that does not. I am still shocked to find that during the crucial December holiday period we will still occasionally get a "Gone skiing" type of message from a Maker. We immediately realize this company is not committed to its own success. (Go skiing in late January, after all the returns are processed!) Similarly, many companies will have to deal with a botched production run. The committed ones will proactively issue a recall and refund or replace the defective units. They go out of their way to protect their reputations and that of their retailers. Mostly they simply don't want a customer to experience anything less than their best product. The uncommitted Makers sweep issues under the rug, not realizing they are sweeping their own future away, too.

Committed Makers can have terrible misfortunes and yet still power through. I will never forget an experience with Back to the Roots, a young San Francisco company whose first product was at-home mushroom growing kits. The "soil" was used coffee grounds. BTR started slipping on its normally prompt deliveries during the 2011 holiday season. I was doing a lot of peak season customer service personally, so I saw its emerging problems. I investigated and learned that we were sending the company more volume than it could handle. Specifically, it was running out of the coffee grounds that it still individually collected from the back door of coffee shops. In a stroke of luck, I was able to connect the founders to my sister, who worked in operations at Peet's Coffee & Tea. She was in a position to get them a reliable source of grounds, delivered to their plant. If they had not already proven to be a "can-do" pair of founders who fully owned their opportunities and problems, I would never have made that valuable connection. In cases of weak customer service, we have to walk away from brilliant products because the company founders do not understand that running strong operations is part of the total customer experience.

These days, with social media and so much happening online and publicly, Invisibelt founder Kathy Kramer says when it comes to customer service, "It's out there for everyone to see. I always try to be on top of it. Negative goes a long way." Kramer says if a customer has a problem, she always tries to fix it. "Whatever their issue, I'm always trying to resolve it." Kramer says if a customer lets the company know that a belt broke, Invisibelt won't just send one replacement, it'll send two. It just doesn't pay to do it any other way, says Kramer.

Beyond our Maker experiences, we've had a firsthand view on providing a great customer experience through our partner Ace Hardware (it became a wholesale customer and made a subsequent investment in The Grommet). Doug Murphy says, "I believe Ace and The Grommet will thrive even against Amazon because we're not just selling products, we're providing experiences. People are loyal to The Helpful Place because more than likely they are greeted at the door, escorted to the item they need, and given some advice on how to best use it. At Grommet, they'll be presented an innovative item that is assured to work as described, told why it's an important discovery, and will easily be able to talk to a human being about it if they have questions. Amazon is happy to serve a customer that would rather save $0.50 than engage with their community and a Maker to optimize their experience."

Having a vision for a company extends to having a point of view on all your policies and communications. Some opportunities to address are:

- **Website information.** Everyone is time starved, so self-service can be the best kind of service. If people can answer all their own questions about your products, return policies, shipping standards, or employment practices because your site is well ordered and easy to navigate, go you.

- **Tone.** Beyond that, scrutinize not just the availability of the content but also the tone. It's boring and difficult to write up terms of service, return policies, accurate product details, and to prepare the copy for "frequently asked questions" before you launch your company. I know. I personally wrote much of that copy for our first website. I wanted to make sure our site spoke to people the way we would behave in person, and not be loaded with harsh or legal language. Over time some of that copy can get inconsistent when other people start adding content, so it's worth reviewing all your communications with a fresh eye regularly. If and when you can afford a real copywriter, hire one.

- **Policies.** When our director of customer experience Doug Murphy joined Grommet, he took a figurative red pen to all of our customer-facing policies and communications to make sure they accurately represented the company we try to be.

These are living, breathing aspects that need to evolve and advance as much as the rest of the company. The world (and customer expectations) will change around you. You don't want to lose ground by keeping your head in the sand.

- **Points of contact.** The days of publicizing a phone number and a generic customer service e-mail address and calling that "customer service" are over. Yes, you need to be extremely responsive to those communication conventions. But customers are going to reach out to you in whatever mode suits them. It is as likely to be Facebook, Twitter, or Yelp as it is your formal contact methods. Ideally, you are using a variety of social channels as a core part of your marketing. Even if you are not, carefully monitor these social channels at a minimum. At The Grommet, we answer all social postings within the day, and usually much more quickly.

- **Customer service platforms.** There are many tools available to help small Makers run effective customer service operations. Software as a service (SaaS) platforms are often a good choice because they require little up-front investment and can scale with the operation. Here are some useful tools to consider integrating into your business to up your game:

  - **Ticketing systems.** A ticketing system can help efficiently manage customer contacts. Platforms like Zendesk make sure nothing gets lost and allow Makers to monitor response times closely. One of the most powerful features is the ability to put customer requests on hold and resurface them later to make sure issues are resolved completely. In recent years these tools have been optimized for omnichannel customer service; tickets can be created from e-mails, web forms, online chats, phone calls, and even social media.

○ **CRM (customer relationship management).** The more you know about your customers, the more you can optimize their experience. Making this information easily available to customer service reps is key. CRM platforms like Salesforce.com, HubSpot, and Marketo can capture everything you know about your customers, their contacts with you, and their order history. They're particularly useful for B2B models and can be very effective in unifying the sales and service disciplines.

○ **Customer experience monitoring.** Understanding customer sentiments and acting on them is key. Providers like Delighted and Medallia can make it easy for customers to provide feedback on their experience, while surfacing automated analysis and opportunity identification. At The Grommet we use a popular tool called "Net Promoter Score." This involves asking each customer a single question: "How likely are you to recommend The Grommet to a friend?" The collective responses give us an honest and clear numerical picture of how we are doing. Customers can also write anything they like, and I personally read every comment, every day. We also follow up on any comments that indicate a failure on our part. Sometimes I call people to ask more about their comment, if it could help us improve our website or overall experience.

○ **Social media monitoring.** You might wonder how a small team can effectively monitor a variety of social platforms. This is the answer: a social media marketing and monitoring platform. We use Zendesk for monitoring Facebook, and TweetDeck and Hootsuite for Twitter and Instagram. These are low-cost options. Mike Lovett, marketing specialist at The Grommet says, "None does everything I want them to, so I often resort to just using the platforms natively. There are paid solutions out there that are more comprehensive in their functionality, but you really have to shell out for them. The pros of Hootsuite and TweetDeck are that you can schedule posts, which is a huge timesaver. You can see your timeline and notifications in one place, and you can monitor topics and hashtags. The last one is incredibly useful if you are announcing something big like our Ace Partnership, and you want to keep tabs on the public's reaction and respond quickly."

○ **Call center platforms.** Allowing customers to talk to you directly is becoming a differentiator, and the tools to do it are less expensive than ever. You no longer need your telephone company to set up a call center. Just an Internet connection and IP telephony provider like Talkdesk or Grasshopper can get the job done. They have features like call recording, voice mail, and voice response menus built in.

This is a very competitive space, and while many of these providers span all the verticals, they also integrate well with each other.

You might be thinking, "This is all too much." While I believe it is critical for you to stay close to customer communications, you do not have to cover it all. A jujitsu hiring move to cover this area could be employing a mom who is returning to the work force to own this area. Women are, statistically, the most proficient personal users of social media, and you can give someone a good career boost by having her extend her media competency into the professional realm. Relaunch moms usually represent a degree of maturity, resourcefulness, efficiency, and good judgment that makes them skillful at social media and written communications. They are easy to screen: you just have to look at their personal accounts and give them a writing test to ensure they are competent in that arena.

Tools are helpful for being efficient. Hiring the right team is essential. Solid customer-friendly policies will go a long way to build trust and goodwill. But even with the best of efforts, you will disappoint some people. Their concerns will usually be legitimate: a late delivery, a botched order, a defective product, a failing in your marketing communications. And sometimes their expectations will be positively insane. Whatever end of the spectrum they fall on, your general playbook for communicating needs to be:

- Acknowledge and restate their question or concern objectively without being defensive.

- Express your positive intent to help them.

- Do the work—whether it is processing a return, placing an order, or providing information. Give them time to cool down or relax by experiencing you working on their behalf.

- Go beyond solving the customer issue and invest in their long-term satisfaction. Train your customer service reps to determine the customer's *true need*, provide advice on how to use the product, and perhaps offer recommendations on other ways customers can employ your company's products more completely to serve their needs. For example, at The Grommet, if customers call us for help on how to use their Garlic Twister, we have a conversation with them. We might find out that their knives are too dull to safely and effectively chop garlic. First, we'd make sure they know Garlic Twister is great for chopping herbs and nuts, too. Then we might also suggest they consider Liquidiamond knives that stay sharp longer and provide complimentary lifetime sharpening, which could help them with related culinary challenges. Customer contacts are expensive, so while you're at it, you should take the opportunity to deepen your relationships with customers.

- Be human and allow anyone with customer contact to do the same. This means using rich adjectives and natural language—not parroting company rhetoric or bland policies.

It's really hard to do this right when you are swamped with other work or your customer support team is understaffed. You have to remind yourself that your investments in your product development, team, marketing, and customer acquisition are considerable, and are at risk if a single touch point with a customer is flawed. In the case of social media postings, a single person can have a massive megaphone. One mishandled complaint can inform a whole host of strangers that your company stumbled. So whenever I found myself answering customer e-mails or tweets at home late at night after a long day in the office, I would remind myself of what my Irish friends say to me when I don't want to hang out for another round in a pub: "You can sleep when you're dead."

CASE STUDIES

Frego

As a mother, Juhi Gupta Gulati was looking for a food container that wasn't plastic, wouldn't break easily, could go right into the dishwasher, and would be useful for packed lunches as well as storing leftovers in the fridge. It didn't seem like a tall order, but there wasn't anything on the market that covered all of those bases. So, Frego was born. Gupta Gulati created a durable, multifunctional glass container with a super protective silicone sleeve.

Frego comes with a lifetime warranty. If the glass breaks, the company replaces it for free, says the founder. Having sold more than 40,000 units, Gupta Gulati says the company has replaced maybe 25 bowls. The company ships for free as well, and "we get so many compliments," she says. "Everybody who buys it is happy."

When it comes to the future of Frego, Gupta Gulati says, "We need to scale in a way to be able to bring costs down, especially when it comes to shipping." Gupta Gulati is currently hoping to add additional dish sizes and rotate color themes depending on the time of year.

Frego launched with one size in four colors. It now has two sizes and multiple colors; colors change seasonally as well. It's working on a dish that contains compartments, and the founder is constantly considering the many request she receives for new products.

Gupta Gulati says that as Frego has grown, the company has received continuous validation. It gets routine requests from Europe for additional products, and it is looking to expand into other markets as well, including the United Kingdom and Australia, where demand has been increasing. It sells on Amazon, HSN online, Home Depot online, and has been in Crate & Barrel. The company mostly sells online, and Gupta Gulati says this allows her company to feature videos and tutorials on the products.

Clear My Head

Brenda Stansfield has a 3,000-square-foot production facility in West Carrollton, Ohio, for manufacturing her essential oils, soap, lip balm, and related products. "When we get orders, we manufacture that day," says Stansfield, founder of Clear My Head. She wants everything to be made to order and fresh, and that's just how it is. She has one full-time production person, is often on the floor herself, and hires others temporarily during busy ordering seasons. "If someone orders something from you, their first impression of the company is when they receive their package," says Stansfield. "If something goes wrong, the best thing you can do is make it right."

She's had some angry customers give her a hard time, too. One man e-mailed about a broken product, and when Stansfield promised a quick replacement, he continued to write back and tell her, "It shouldn't have happened." By the time his replacement item arrived, however, expedited and with a personal note, he wrote back to say, "I'll be a customer forever."

Stansfield admits customer service is a tough part of running a business, but something that companies have to take seriously. "If we failed them the first time, we try to make it better than right the second time."

As someone who ships glass, it makes Stansfield cringe when she sees packages being tossed or dropped by carriers. But she knows breaks happen, even with proper padding and packaging. Stansfield never askes a customer for a photo of a damaged product and never asks people to send back the product in question. "Anyone can send you something. It's what happens when something goes wrong that counts." Often Stansfield includes a personal note and expedites shipping on an order that needs to be replaced.

Stansfield launched with two products in 2004 and now has more than 30. Clear My Head sells around the country to spas and hotels, pharmacies, boutiques, and Ace Hardware. Stansfield deliberately does not sell on Amazon.

Bee's Wrap

When Sarah Kaeck started Bee's Wrap nearly seven years ago, it was just a small operation, but the business grew very quickly. The company, which makes an alternative to plastic wrap out of organic cotton and beeswax (which can be reused over and over again), got a large bump in sales from a BuzzFeed piece that had 87 million views.

After the BuzzFeed attention, Bee's Wrap completely sold out in a few hours. "We've continued to grow at a steady rate from there," says Kaeck. The wrapping has sold through Amazon, Anthropologie, The Grommet, Uncommon Goods, the NPR gift shop, and has been the subject of many a blog post and write-ups on useful kitchen tools.

The company is looking to move into a new facility—it started in Kaeck's house, moved into a workshop in her home, and then into a production facility in Vermont. It's outgrown that and is looking for new space. "It's exciting," says Kaeck.

When it comes to continued growth, Kaeck says all waxing used to be done by hand, and then the company had a machine manufactured to do the same. It's improving on its cloth-cutting system and increasing its waxing capacity. Kaeck says the company is currently exploring expansion of its product line as well as bringing in new prints for the designs on the wraps.

"Customer service is really important to us," says Kaeck. "We believe we have excellent customer service." Kaeck says the company has more direct engagement with its wholesale customers than the ones who come through the Bee's Wrap website. Because the company started in small brick-and-mortar stores, that's where its best and strongest relationships are. It doesn't have as much interaction with the web customers. But Kaeck says as a company she always wants customers to feel as though they are accessible.

Having just put in a new phone system, Kaeck said it was important to her that an actual person answer the phone. And employees try to have a quick response time on social media. Kaeck says Bee's Wrap employees don't work on the weekends or outside of normal working hours, but they do work to get back to everyone within 24 to 48 hours.

For Kaeck it comes down to the old rule that "the customer is always right." Which means if someone isn't satisfied with a purchase, the customer gets a refund. Kaeck says she often prints e-mails that include concerns, questions, or compliments. "It's something we bring to our weekly meeting," says Kaeck, adding that it's one way to keep the folks at Bee's Wrap connected to their customers.

19

FINANCIAL
MANAGEMENT

Our accounting team has seen it all, so I asked them for a new company playbook regarding financial management. As opposed to so many aspects of starting a business, it is refreshingly simple:

- **Use QuickBooks Online.** It's extremely user-friendly and affordable. It makes it easy to integrate with your bank accounts. It has all the financial statement templates you will need. Virtually all of our Makers use QuickBooks. So do we. The reason to use the online version is security. Our CFO, Jon Conelias, said, "The cloud keeps your data safe and allows you to work from anywhere. This is the digital age, so why tie yourself to the office when you can access your information from anywhere and in real time?"

- **Hire an accountant to set it up.** Unless you are fascinated with this project and have a generally strong quantitative bent, it's a better use of your company resources to have a pro do it. You can network to find a local consultant. If you have a personal tax accountant or attorney, he or she can probably make a referral to a colleague. Target the midsize firms in your area. Solo bookkeeper/accountants are rarely sophisticated enough to handle the full range of your needs, and the national firms are too expensive for a young company.

- **Take a basic managerial accounting class.** You can do this online or at your local community college. Like most professions, finance has its own vocabulary, and there are many basic standards of reporting and analyzing that you can easily learn to become a responsible steward of your company's finances. It is also a confidence builder to know you cannot be bamboozled with fancy language.

- **Keep on it.** Nick DeSisto, our staff accountant said, "Too many Makers only hire a bookkeeper for the end of year. Then they have a nightmare project to reconcile invoices and payments, and it ends up costing them more than if they had that same person come once a week or even once a month."

CASH MANAGEMENT

The fundamental financial competency you will need to develop is a strong, abiding affection for managing your cash. This is not a "nice to have"—a fact that is already dead obvious to you if you manage a household budget. And if you have been in business for any time at all, no one needs to convince you of the importance of getting paid. You have likely already been navigating this territory quite well, or you would not be around.

At The Grommet we do a cash flow forecast with great regularity. In our early days it felt like a daily activity. I will never forget a sleepless night when our bookkeeper told me our cash balance, and it was vastly smaller than I had thought. I could not imagine how I could be so out of touch with this key fact, and I was sweating bullets about meeting payroll and other operational costs. The next morning she said, "Oh I forgot about the $25,000 in a different account." I had to fire her—she did not understand the core importance of her own work in our business.

Years into the business we can easily foresee that we will end the year with our strongest cash balances because of the heavy proportion of holiday sales in November and December. We ride on that cash balance until we hit a negative point between August and October, when we are stocking up on holiday inventory. At this point we heavily tap our credit lines to get us through the pinch. Many Maker businesses have a similar annual cycle that is arranged around whatever seasonality is inherent in the business.

Generally speaking, though, getting paid on your e-commerce website is a simple and beautiful thing: immediate credit card deposits to your bank account. I will focus on the cash management aspect of wholesale payments and what we have learned, from our early days.

First, imagine the nature of The Grommet's business. Every single day we take on a new Maker with a fresh set of contracts, operational agreements, and financial integrations (invoices and payments). We need our Makers' products to arrive as promised, and they need to get paid in a timely fashion. This is not a trivial volume of relationships; whereas Walmart buys the vast majority of its merchandise from just 75 suppliers, we have around 2,000 Makers live on our site. For many of them, we have a two-pronged wholesale relationship: we are buying inventory for The Grommet's consumer-facing site, and we are placing drop-ship orders for shipment to the retailers who are our own wholesale customers. It's complicated on many levels. Walmart must employ hundreds if not thousands of people in its accounting team. We employ five. So we are constantly evolving to find areas of improvement.

In the early days of The Grommet we managed with two part-time accounting and finance people. These two women each worked one or two days a week. Our systems were basic: QuickBooks and cutting manual checks to our Makers. We did not focus on automating anything: our goal was accuracy and timeliness of payments and reporting. As the number of Grommet Makers grew (remember, a new one every day), our accounts payable work alone was becoming a ridiculous mountain of manual work. Our chief financial officer, Jon Conelias, recalls, "I will never forget starting work at The Grommet, and seeing our bookkeeper Gerry haul huge binders of ledgers to keep track of our accounts payable. After a day of work she looked like she was sitting in a patch of fresh snow from all the paper hole punches she'd put into the tower of weekly invoices so she could clip them in the books." I myself will never forget the weeks when Jon was on vacation, and I had to manually sign a couple inches–high tower of paper checks. I used to think, "What decade are we in? This has to change."

And it did. We've done about 50 percent of the automation we would like to have on hand to eliminate reconciling invoices—it is still a painful manual activity, albeit at lower volume than before. But worse than that is seeing how slow and inaccurate many Makers are with invoicing us. We truly want to pay them, but they can make it impossible to do so in a timely and accurate fashion. We find invoices showing up months and sometimes more than a year after they shipped us their goods. They often contain inaccurate quantities and the wrong negotiated discounts. That is no way to run a business—for us, but especially for them.

Related to cash management, we converted 90 percent of our Makers from paper checks to ACH (electronic) payments. It still shocks me that there are a handful of our Makers who prefer paper checks. Why? Every day counts when it comes to cash management—if I were a Maker, I would choose fast payments over slow. I would choose seeing funds in my bank account over opening envelopes. Maybe that laggard 10 percent of check-payment Makers like the certainty of a check. Maybe they trust themselves more with dealing physically with payments. Come to think of it, I asked McGraw-Hill to send me checks for the advance on this book, so I am in no place to judge. But I am only getting two checks—one to kick off the book and one when I deliver this manuscript. It was such a treat and bucket list thing for me to write a book that I wanted to be able to hold a check and maybe take a picture of it. But our Makers are getting up to 52 checks a year from us—not to mention all their other wholesale customers. That paper check thrill would wear off in a few weeks for most people.

Every large retail account you open will bring special new systems and requirements. Call that original consulting accountant (see bullet two at the top of this chapter) back in as needed. Convert the position to full-time as soon as you can. The Grommet's business provokes a new learning curve for each of our Makers, too. Today, nine years into the business, we still hit many accounting issues whenever we introduce a new activity such as selling display programs and products to Ace Hardware (which has a special proprietary payments platform for its stores and vendors). Opening our own physical store and providing marketing services to our Makers, such as mailing catalogs and representing them at trade shows, are recent complications, too. Sometimes we introduce a new and seemingly benign contract term into our Maker agreements that becomes a major tracking headache for our accountants. So if this area is painful, I feel you. Just farm out the pain to the pros early and often, and keep your accountant close to head off problems that you may never see coming.

BUDGETING AND FORECASTING

Budgeting and forecasting are the second financial competency (after cash management) that you will need to foster in your company. This becomes especially important when you are committing to buying or leasing capital equipment, taking out loans, contracting inventory runs, and making team hires. QuickBooks will give you the tools to build a great forecast and budget. (Though we ourselves do those activities on Excel, and we are looking to upgrade to NetSuite soon for all of our financial management. This is not a viable startup option, but we are overdue for an upgrade.) Your accountant can skillfully walk you through the steps to build a budget. But the actual brainpower to predict the business's revenue and costs resides more with you and your leadership team. There is a necessary degree of educated guessing required for any revenue forecasting, especially when you are at the beginning and really just inventing a business plan. Though admittedly uncomfortable, doing this work is essential to making commitments, raising capital, and keeping yourself honest about the prospects for the company.

The bottom-line good news about the financial management of your company is that the tools and professionals to provide best practices are accessible and affordable. This is the last place where you should skimp, nor would you want to.

CASE STUDIES

CHART Metalworks

Although continually experiencing growth, Maine-based CHART Metalworks operates its finances like a small business. The company, which features map-themed jewelry, keychains, and personal items, was recently acquired by Sea Bags, another Maine-based, locally owned company that produces hugely popular tote bags from recycled sailcloth.

CHART Metalworks relies on QuickBooks for payment-related tracking. Most vendors seem to be moving toward QuickBooks, says Mike Nicholas, operations manager for the company, and so it made the most sense to align with them. When it comes to wholesale sales, CHART Metalworks accepts credit cards through the back end of its website. The company often receives payments via direct deposit.

Nicholas still manually enters everything through Quick-Books, and that works for the company right now. Nicholas says even though Sea Bags is so much larger, it, too, uses QuickBooks and manually enters everything. It's given Nicholas the confidence that CHART Metalworks can stick with this system for the foreseeable future.

Nicholas says the company has made a big effort to improve its website and increase retails sales. "We've simplified everything, and because of that, we've seen more ordering." Launched in 2008, the wholesale side of things has always been strong, says Nicholas. The founder primarily sold on Etsy until things started to pick up. There were initially 12 products, and now there are closer to 100. The company tries to add three or four products to every trade show, and representatives go to about six each year. "It's our way to stay relevant," says Nicholas.

Happy Mat (ezpz)

For Lindsey Laurain, the creator of Happy Mat, an all-in-one silicone plate and placemat that reduces kid messes at meals, QuickBooks has long been her go-to. She says it's "automated and easy." The whole philosophy behind her company ezpz was just that: things were supposed to be easy. Easy for customers and easy for the people running the business.

She finds QuickBooks fits the bill and says the interface is simple and the ordering process is easy. "Everything is automatic," she adds. According to Laurain, ezpz has more in sales than the typical small business using QuickBooks, but she has no reason to switch. Plus, it's relatively inexpensive—$50 a month for her company—and some of the larger financial management systems get quite costly.

Since Laurain launched ezpz, the company has sold more than 2 million Happy Mats, and it's extended its product line to include cups and utensils. There are mini mats and mini bowls. The company has partnered with Care Bears to put out a special line, and Laurain says she is exploring other licensing deals. Happy Mat is sold in Buy Buy Baby, Nordstrom, Target, Pottery Barn Kids, Crate & Barrel Kids, and more than 1,000 retailers in the United States.

Laurain says ezpz is launching a revamped website in early 2019 and will be pushing for more direct-to-consumer sales. The founder is constantly looking to add sales channels, and the company is looking into more formal PR and marketing strategies. The founders have also added a sister company, Ono, makers of a silicone pet bowl and mat.

Patent Prints

When it comes to payments, Patent Prints founder Cole Borders says he doesn't even have to think about getting paid by Etsy or Amazon. "You don't have to worry about it." "The third party collects and deposits it on a schedule you can rely on." Occasionally there is a vendor he has to invoice, and often those payments come through PayPal.

Borders spends much of his time on the artistic side of things, recreating patent drawings from various inventions, from household gadgets to electronics and machinery. He had been working for a company doing printing when he realized he could have his own business, make better money, and be more creative. Borders started his company in March 2013. It has its own warehouse, where it produces everything on demand.

Borders uses QuickBooks to manage everything. "Once you reach a few hundred thousand in sales, I'd recommend it," he says of choosing an online financial management system. Someone else at Patent Prints handles QuickBooks for him. "A very important part of your business is understanding your numbers," says Borders. "If you don't want to do it, you have to hire someone to do it. You have to know if you are making money and where."

As Borders points out, you don't even have to hire a full-time employee: there are plenty of freelancers out there who can handle this aspect for you. Borders says he knows many Makers are simply focused on the creative side of things but urges anyone starting a business to be sure to focus on financial management and tracking as well.

Patent Prints has approximately 20 boutique stores that order from the company on a regular basis, but otherwise most of its business is online. It uses online advertising and optimization of search engines to help with marketing. The company has tried catalogs and trade shows but finds that those avenues aren't as profitable for it. "You always have to be pushing your business forward," says Borders. "As soon as you stop, you will see your business go the other way."

Zubits

Zubits has an interesting take on financial management. The more the company grew, the less founder Ryan Weins wanted to outsource this aspect of his business. "All of that scared me," says Weins, when he originally thought about the financial management aspect of his magnetic shoe-closing gadget business. "You don't know what you don't know."

Initially Weins outsourced the financial management, paying accountants to take care of everything. But over time there were too many mistakes, and since he was already the one collecting data and info from clients and retailers, he decided to do it himself. The mistakes were costing him time and money as well. Now, through QuickBooks, Weins handles the invoicing and bookkeeping.

20

INVENTORY MANAGEMENT

If cash management is one of the two critical financial competencies in a Maker company, inventory is going to be the friend—or foe—of that activity. More likely, foe. Skillful inventory management is the biggest place where your operations can make a positive or negative difference in your cash balances. Why? When you have inventory in storage, you can think of it as the magic carpet to generating cash. You have already prepaid for the goods, and as soon as you can get them sold, you can recover all of that cash plus your profit margin. In the early days of a Maker business, it is usually the biggest drain on cash resources.

BENEFITS OF INVENTORY MANAGEMENT

Beyond the conservation of cash, good inventory management:

- **Prevents dead inventory.** This is inventory that is obsolete, out of season, or overstocked. If you are not on this like white on rice, you risk having dead inventory to sell or dump.

- **Avoids spoilage.** This is only relevant to perishable goods like cleaning, beauty, health, and food products.

- **Prevents overpaying for storage.** Warehousing costs fluctuate directly with your product volumes. This is a tension that counterbalances an opposite pressure: you can get scale economies by producing bigger inventories.

- **Enables planning.** By knowing exactly how much product you have and your projected sales, you can figure out when you will run out and make sure you replace it on time. Any gap in inventory balances kills customer goodwill and is really hard on your cash flow.

E-commerce platforms have integrated, albeit basic, inventory software management systems, so you don't need to build the tools, but you do need to apply skill and knowledge of your business to use the tools to your benefit. Your goal will be a balance between removing manual error from the day-to-day operations and applying skilled human judgment to your decisions and processes.

Other than paying for the goods, forecasting inventory is the single hardest aspect of dealing with inventory. It is job 1, 2, and 3. We practice it as an extreme sport at The Grommet, where every day we are forecasting demand for a groundbreaking, fresh product that is innovative and for which we have no direct sales history.

Sean Fitzpatrick manages our inventory forecasts at The Grommet. He says that because we issue POs in big lumpy chunks, our newer Makers often get a happy surprise when a PO exceeds their expectations. They do not have visibility into The Grommet's sales velocity week by week. Also they may have no experience to predict seasonality or the impact of our marketing. It thus becomes incumbent on us to start to train them on what to expect. We are quite often the largest customer for a Grommet Maker, and the earlier-stage companies essentially depend on us to teach them how to do inventory forecasting. For our fastest, highest-selling Makers, we provide a 12- to 14-week forecast model that gives them the ability to extrapolate their full inventory needs, based on what percentage of their demand The Grommet represents.

WHAT TO INCLUDE IN INVENTORY FORECASTING

Assuming you do not have the benefit of Sean Fitzpatrick directly, but you have some sales history under your belt, here is his forecasting playbook of what to factor into your inventory forecasting:

- Last year's sales during the same week or month

- Seasonal factors (if you do not have a full year of sales history)

- This year's growth rate

- Market trends

- Any guaranteed sales from existing contracts from large retailers

- Upcoming promotions, PR, or new trade shows where you plan to introduce your product

- Planned ad spend

- Any other relevant factors. In our case, weak reviews cause us to retire a product. In addition, periods being out of stock on any given product shake our confidence in the company and cloud our ability to forecast.

Any retailer's marketing and promotional efforts add further complexity to forecasting as demand is always fueled by marketing—whether it be including your product in a catalog, a sweepstakes, or a Facebook ad. Quite often you will see a retailer tie the size of an upcoming PO directly to your funding of a promotion. This "pay to play" is a normal convention in retail and has the benefit of giving Makers more control over their sales growth. It also offers the opportunity to draft off the expensive and sophisticated marketing of a larger organization.

TIPS FOR INVENTORY MANAGEMENT

Here are a few tips to get in front of many of the common inventory management problems we encounter with our Makers:

Use FIFO (First In, First Out)

This means always sell your oldest inventory first. Just like milk is stocked from the back in grocery store refrigerators, make sure your warehouse or 3PL is stocking your product in this way, so that the oldest product is in front to be picked and shipped first. The need to do this is obvious for perishables, but it's also relevant for other products. Having packages sit around too long leads to damage, and you are likely to update your product or packages at some point, so you want to sell out the older models.

Set Minimum (Par) Levels

Your inventory system can seamlessly trigger you to place a PO, but you have to determine the set point for that alert. That decision is based on two primary factors: the velocity of sales for that item and the difficulty or delays in sourcing it. These par levels shift with seasons, marketing campaigns, and overall customer demand, so periodically reassess all your par levels to make sure they reflect the current conditions of your business.

Keep Suppliers Close

Envision your inventory needs as having a domino effect on every business in your supply chain. Whether you are ordering materials and self-manufacturing or contracting for finished goods, those materials and components have to come from somewhere, as does the labor and the warehouse storage. Regularly discuss your sales forecasts with key suppliers and partners. Quickly communicate any unexpected shifts in demand, whether up or down. Your warehouse and your manufacturing and packaging suppliers will be far more flexible if you are communicative and they trust you to be shooting straight.

There is a second aspect to this relationship management: you have to balance loyalty and leverage. Giving your suppliers steady business and riding through some of their bumps with them will make them more willing to do the same for you, whether it is producing a rush order or a forecast reduction that leaves them with expensive unused capacity. But don't be blindly loyal: periodically put your business out to contract with competitors, so you have alternatives if your supplier drives up prices too quickly, becomes unreliable, or cannot meet your demand.

Do a Regular Reconciliation

Your inventory software and sales reporting will give you regular updates on your inventory balances, but that only goes so far. Inventory gets damaged. It goes missing. You need to do a regular reconciliation to make sure your inventory system counts are accurate. This means doing a physical inventory count. If you've ever worked in a retail store, you know exactly what I mean. The options for doing this are:

1. **One big annual count.** It's tedious and disruptive. But it works for us to do this around April. At that point, we are far past the holiday rush, we've processed all January returns,

271

and we have restocked to par levels. This count gives us a very solid base for planning the rest of the year. We carefully coordinate this count for a time when our warehouses can stop all receiving and shipping to do the count. We also do it in the beginning of April when we have no major holidays or marketing pushes that require all hands on deck. It takes two to three intense weekend days, and our customers never experience a visible disruption.

2. **Cycle counts.** We also periodically do a rolling test of our inventory counts, working through our A, B, and C products on a regular rotation. (As are our 100 biggest volume sellers, Cs are the slowest sellers, and Bs are in the middle.)

3. **Spot counts.** These are very granular counts that are usually the result of a Maker mistake: either because they had a mis-ship or sent a mixed case (what is on the shipping carton's exterior bar code does not square with the contents). We don't charge for those mistakes, but big retailers will definitely hit you with big chargebacks, so avoid this like the plague. The Grommet is kinder and gentler than the rest of the retail world.

Even if you follow all the best practices for inventory management, there will be breakdowns where contingency planning can save your bacon. Our senior director of maker operations, Bobby McLaughlin, says the most typical issues arise when Makers increase production volumes without realizing that their manufacturing or warehousing processes are not scalable. It's usually not an issue with simple and small products, like the credit card–sized wallet tool PocketMonkey. But a complex electronic device, large piece of furniture, or multicomponent cooler may take several manufacturing runs to get the product, packaging, or warehousing right. No amount of careful planning can fully alleviate these conditions. Just expect the worst and have Plans B and C ready.

Allocate Inventory to Your Committed Stores

I have a final word of advanced advice on inventory management, specifically inventory *allocation*. God willing, you will have times when because of a press event, a fresh marketing campaign, or an order from a new large retailer, there won't be enough inventory to go around. We see Makers make the mistake of chasing the bright shiny object of a new account and leave the retailers who helped build their business high and dry. This is an amateur mistake. My advice is to *remember who brought you to the dance*. It's good advice for life, and for succeeding as a Maker.

As long as you are not selling to its direct competitor, a large retailer can wait for your inventory. The fact that you are represented at The Grommet, a museum store, or a chain of specialty boutiques only makes your product more desirable. These are the committed stores that will build your customer awareness and will take risks to help you. Never leave their shelves empty in favor of a new guy on the block.

It used to happen to us fairly frequently: we would build demand and awareness for a product that attracted The Container Store's or Amazon's attention, and that new account would vacuum up the Maker's limited inventory. We would stop promoting it, and the big retailer's demand would also dry right up. Those retailers depend on high inventory turns, and they will quickly send back that inventory if it does not meet their financial goals. So you can piss off or lose your healthy base of existing customers for a brief phantom of an opportunity.

Similarly, never have plentiful inventory on your own site and cause out of stocks for your retailers. Bobby says, "I don't mind if Makers keep a handful of units on their site, so they don't go out of stock. But when it's the reverse—when they hoard inventory— that's when I want to go through the phone and shake a Maker." He says a responsible Maker will understand that The Grommet has customer reach and credibility that far exceeds the buzz Makers can generate on their own, and it's a better bet to get product into our customers' hands where reviews and additional promotion can really build a big business. Bobby confides, "The more savvy Makers understand that we're in it to help them win it. If quantities are tight, they will send us virtually all their inventory and even put a link on their site for their customers to buy on The Grommet. The greedy ones will sit on it, burning cash."

There's a reason why investors love businesses like software that have no inventory issues. Why? Managing inventory is expensive and difficult—especially with offshore production lead times and communication issues, or simply due to successfully achieving high growth rates. After managing cash, staying close on your inventory flows is going to be your most frequent analytical activity.

CASE STUDIES

Java Sok

When it comes to managing his company's inventory of neoprene sleeves for coffee cups, David Laks, the founder of Java Sok, does it all in-house—at least for now. The company works with several channels, including Amazon, The Grommet, and its own website. But because Java Sok is manufactured in China, all orders arrive packaged in plastic sleeves not meant for retail or distribution. Laks wants to be able to control the quality, so he or someone else from Java Sok inspects every single item, cuts lose threads from the seams, reshapes the drink koozies, and generally has his hands and eyes on every item that goes out to the customers.

Laks works out of a small professional office and has a warehouse for the Java Sok sleeves. The items don't stay boxed once they arrive at the warehouse, so that they can be reshaped and breathe once they're in the United States.

Laks says he hasn't found a good multichannel inventory tool that works for him, so he keeps track of inventory himself. He allots a certain number to Amazon and The Grommet but maintains the physical products in his warehouse. He then receives low inventory warnings from both, whenever appropriate. He tries to maintain 5,000 to 7,000 pieces at any given time and has gotten his manufacturing down to a 13- to 20-day turnaround, so when he needs orders fast he knows he won't be waiting three or four months. Over the past few years, Laks says he's gotten a sense of how many koozies he will need on hand at any given time, so that he isn't warehousing too many and isn't running out if he gets an unexpected order or two.

When he founded the company in the summer of 2014, it was purely a hobby for Laks. He was hoping to make a little extra money to help put his three children through college. Although things had been plugging along at a steady pace, they've picked up to the point where Laks expected to quit his consulting work and only work on Java Sok by the beginning of 2019.

Laks says moving into traditional retails (once Java Sok has an appealing package set) and working on the custom business side of things are the ways in which he is looking to grow. He says at this point he isn't looking to add products, just markets. He's started to partner with other businesses; for example, a recent order for 150,000 sleeves came from a smoothie franchise.

Pacific Shaving

Pacific Shaving, a popular men's grooming products company, has bootstrapped in many ways to become the success it is today.

The company has an amazing story about inventory management that proves you never have to take no for an answer.

The company had just received a large order—only it was out of inventory. The order was from a new account that Pacific Shaving had fought really hard to win and didn't want to let down, says cofounder Stan Ades. Ades called Amazon, which happened to have "a whole lot of inventory" to see if he could get some of the product that way. But Amazon doesn't send back product to its sellers on a whim. Ades realized that since he controls the price on his own products on Amazon—and he and his wife had an Amazon Prime account—they could drop the price of the product to 1 cent and ship it all out of Amazon and back to their warehouse for next to nothing. Ades says he tried going through the back door at Amazon, and instead "walked it out the front door for free."

Pacific Shaving has two warehouses and a shared contract with a distribution facility. It also has two manufacturing centers. "Almost everything we do, we have two of them," says Ades. That way, if there is an error, delay, shortage, weather-related closure, or anything else unforeseen, the company has a backup plan and options.

NEAT Art Glass

A better, more aromatic, and flavorful way to drink alcohol? That's what the founder of NEAT Glass discovered when sipping liquor from a hand-blown glass that looks more like an hourglass than a typical whiskey tumbler. With the company's glasses manufactured in Europe, cofounder Christine Crnek says the owners have to order a 20-foot container—nothing less. "We have to order for the future," she explains.

The company has a European distributor as well as a U.S. one. The Vegas-based company stores some inventory for its direct online sales. NEAT also has pallets sitting in the factory for a period of time, waiting to be shipped out around the globe. NEAT can keep that inventory with the manufacturer for up to four months, and then it starts having to pay rent, explains cofounder George Manska.

NEAT Glass uses a separate fulfillment center in the United States that acts as the broker and importer. It often has as many as 40 pallets on hand at any given time. The center imports, stores, transports, and fulfills orders for NEAT. "It saves us a lot of trouble," says Crnek. "It's worth it."

Crnek and Manska handle some things in-house, though. Any orders that come through The Grommet or through their website they handle directly. They keep inventory at a storage facility and deal with smaller orders on their own.

Currently NEAT sells one style of glass—for liquor—and they're working on developing glassware for wine and beer, specially designed to enhance the flavor and drinking pleasure. The partners explain the improved drinking quality with science: the shape of a glass enhances or stunts aromas. They see similar effects possible for wine and even coffee. "The complexity will go up," explains Manska, if they add products to their line. "We don't believe we could handle another 20 SKUs," he adds, at least not with their current configurations. "At that point we'd need a different setup."

But that setup, say the owners, is a natural progression—if they need a bigger space in the future, perhaps at that point it will be feasible. As the company and the SKUs grow, so too must the supporting infrastructure around that expansion. Manska says they have to be prepared for that before launching any new products. NEAT is selling around the world and uses distribution centers to handle many sales. The owners are looking to grow into chain liquor stores and wine shops.

21

GROWING INTO THE FUTURE

G rommet Makers enter their businesses with wildly different ambitions about growth. Some never intend to leave their day job but want to have an engaging side hustle. Christian Hahn, a Kentucky dentist with a swimming goggle invention, said, "I just want Frogglez to grow enough to pay for my kids' college." Some Makers know from the start that they plan for their first product to be a springboard to a full-time endeavor and sustainable business. Others hedge their bets with a "wait and see" attitude, and work hard to find proof that they can ultimately leave their jobs.

Because the obstacles to growth are unique to every company and the ambitions of the founders are equally diverse, there are few universally true growth hacks. But for the Maker looking to scale, cycling through the following pool of options is a productive place to start.

CREATE NEW PRODUCTS

This scaling option is equal parts necessary, expensive, and fun. It's fun because the joy of creating products is why you get into this business in the first place. It's expensive, in the same way developing the original product was. It's necessary for a host of reasons: to stay ahead of the competition, to command more shelf space and thus open up retailer doors, to create more scale in the business to cover your fixed costs. Twice the products to sell can mean twice the revenue.

Here are a few ways you might think about product line extensions:

- **Good, better, best.** You might consider "knocking yourself off" to preempt competition and to have an appropriate value/price point for various tiers of retailers. A specialty boutique is going to have very different customers and needs from a big-box store. Some Makers anticipate and even occasionally address this tiered offering right from the beginning of releasing a new product. Some do it under separate brand names, and others create slightly different visual identities under their original brand.

- **Adding SKUs.** Often a Maker starts with just a single color or feature set and then enriches the original product offering to meet demand for new "flavors" of the product. For some products adding additional SKUs is the fastest way to create an engaging display at retail. This is particularly true of adding additional colors that can extend the visual pop of your product as well as command a larger share of real estate on a shelf or display.

- **Adding related products.** Ideally you will have anticipated a full line of products right from the start so that your company name and visual identity can easily accommodate line extensions. This is harder said than done, as so many Makers start with one genius problem solver and do not foresee "what's next." In those cases they often have to go through the rather expensive effort of either renaming their company or creating separate brands for a variety of unrelated products.

- **Building exclusive SKUs.** Retail is a fiercely competitive industry, and one of the most powerful tools to increase a retailer's purchase order is to offer an exclusive range of your product. Even just a dedicated color or product bundle can do the trick—it just has to be enough to give the retailers credibility in marketing your product as exclusively theirs.

PURSUE LICENSING

Some Makers take their product to a limited point of development and then license their intellectual property to a larger company. This move is particularly prominent in housewares and kitchen products. Lifetime Brands, Joseph Joseph, and OXO are the big players in those spaces. The toy industry also has credible licensees such as Mattel Inc., Fat Brain Toys, and Melissa & Doug. Beyond these two "license-heavy" categories, in virtually all categories of retail, the large players who have a private label (store brand) business are actively engaged in licensing IP.

Trade shows are the fastest and least expensive way to get a face-to-face meeting with a potential licensee. Secure a meeting with your top prospects before you arrive if possible. Approaching cold might also get you a face-to-face with the person who handles open innovation product licensing. Outside trade shows, identifying the company matches and the right person at the target company will require research. Contact the legal department (it handles the back end of these contracts), and it can refer you to the appropriate person or team.

Beyond these tried-and-true licensing routes, the "As Seen on TV" companies are fierce competitors, and they will often reach out proactively to license IP. As outlined in Chapter 7, they also present the most clear and present U.S.-based danger of knocking off a product if it is easily demonstrable (in a TV ad) and has mainstream appeal as a problem solver or novelty. The major companies in that space are Guthy-Renker, Telebrands, and Allstar Products Group.

Typically Makers who gain a successful license have begun to produce their product and have gained some distribution before a licensing deal will be struck. The licensee will quite often redesign and reengineer the product to take out costs or improve its commercial appeal. It will take over manufacturing and usually give the product a new brand identity. The advantage of this partnership is that the licensee can achieve better margins and distribution due to its supply chain and manufacturing skills as well as its existing broad distribution. The large company also has deeper pockets in the event that litigation is required to defend intellectual property. Makers thus put the future of their product in the hands of the licensee. The likely outcome is that they will have little or no ongoing commitment to the business, other than collecting royalty checks. In some cases Makers negotiate to keep their original brand and product IP (and business) but give the licensee permission to develop the product for other channels, typically big-box.

This path of pursuing dual brands for one product is particularly true in the case of private label. Ace Hardware might redevelop a product to sell under its own name but also expect Makers to continue to develop their brand separately. This route is especially true for the food business. Virtually all the suppliers to grocery private label brands (think Kirkland at Costco and Whole Foods 365) also sell a version of that same product under their independent brand. When they agree to a grocery store licensing deal they just start a separate production line under the new label, tweaking the recipe as needed (or not).

Successfully licensing a product can open doors to similar future licenses, and some Makers happily stay in the realm of "serial inventor" rather than business builder.

Most Makers will be in the position of licensor—selling their own IP to a larger company licensee. A narrow band of Makers may do the reverse move: become a licensee of a property that helps them extend their product line. These properties are licensed to give name brand recognition and implied endorsements to an unknown product. They include celebrities, chefs, experts, authors, TV shows, movies, video games, or cartoon characters. Most licensors with true power and reach will prefer to work with a large brand with established distribution. But a product with exceptional quality or distinctiveness could attract a license that helps elevate awareness and taps the celebrity's community. Think of Jessica Alba's Honest Company line of natural household products or Gwyneth Paltrow's Goop media property. Many celebrities are looking to extend their reach and personal brand through products that express their values. Not all of them will want to develop that business and product line on their own.

HIRE AN INTERNATIONAL DISTRIBUTOR

The idea of hiring a sales rep firm or distributor for the purposes of domestic sales was generally discussed in Chapter 14: Retail Distribution. While Makers are highly variable in their use of reps for sales in their home country, it is the rare Maker who does not engage an international distributor. These distributors are dedicated to one or many countries and have retail reach that Makers would have a hard time accessing on their own. The contracts can be exclusive or nonexclusive on a country-by-country basis.

Robert Valerio, a consultant to creative companies, advises:

> Officially international distributors get 20%–30% off the *wholesale* price charged to retailers, to allow them to sell

to retailers in their own country. In actuality, most international distributors take the discount from the brand, then mark it up 35%–50% as the country-specific wholesale in their distribution territory. This leads to higher retail prices in other countries than the home country retail price point.

Remember, international distributors have to pay for the product (at distributor discount), pay shipping (most brands are FOB factory or HQ), duty and customs, and their own warehousing and sales overhead.[1]

Key questions to ask an international distributor include:

1. Which brands do you represent, and what are the sales volumes by country?

2. Where do you sell these products? (You are vetting the depth of their retail relationships.)

3. What are the minimum sales volumes I can expect in XYZ country? (Get that in writing.)

4. What support do you expect from me?

5. Will I get paid at time of shipping my goods? (You should!)

6. Ask for a sample engagement contract. (And get good counsel on terms and termination.)

In terms of finding an international distributor, a good place to start is with the federal government. In an article for *Entrepreneur*, Randy Myers writes that according to David Archer, president of International Business Trainers:

Like virtually every other country in the world, the U.S. wants to increase the quantity of goods it exports. To facilitate that, the Department of Commerce's

International Trade Administration, through its U.S. Commercial Service, operates a network of 107 Export Assistance Centers in major cities across the country. The export and industry specialists employed there can help you find appropriate distributors in your target markets.

Don't expect the government to do all the work for you, though. Before contacting one of these offices, identify two or three countries that you think would be good targets for your products—and be prepared to explain why. Also think about the type of distributor you'd like to do business with."[2]

USE LOW(ISH) COST MARKETING INITIATIVES

While I discussed the basic building blocks of marketing in Chapter 13, some options for building the business become a bit more viable with growth.

- **Hire a PR firm or consultant.** It's not hard to get press for your first product through your own grassroots efforts, but it is exceedingly difficult to sustain. A public relations firm is an expensive option to solve that problem—expect to pay $5,000 a month. But a part-time independent contractor can take on your PR outreach work for a fraction of the cost. This person will do the activities I described in Chapter 13 but on a much more consistent level than the busy entrepreneur can sustain.

- **Build a content machine.** Whether it is videos, blog posts, expert white papers, or photos, there is real work to be done and rewards to be reaped in creating a steady stream of high-quality content. Similar to the PR effort, you can and must initiate that on your own in the early days. But generally speaking, content pros are affordable, and a great move as soon as you can contract them. Just make sure their content execution is tied to the SEO goals you have established for your business so that the content really does drive inbound traffic to your site or to the retailers who stock your product.

- **Set up an Ambassadors program.** Once you have a bit of bulk in your customer list, there will be fans of your company and products who will be natural candidates to become volunteer spokespeople and amplifiers of your mission. I particularly like the way the lingerie and swimwear company Lively has done this (https://www.wearlively.com/pages/join -the-lively-crew). Its program is unpaid, and it requires a simple application that depends greatly on the reach and quality of an applicant's Instagram feed. Lively promises early access to products and discounts and the all-important possibility of social sharing of an Ambassador's Instagram posts and, most centrally, participation in Lively's mission.

This effort is a cousin to perks/rewards and referral programs. Rewards and referrals are especially effective for a business that expects a frequency of purchase, like a lingerie, food, apparel, toiletries, or beauty brand. Or The Grommet. Because of the unique nature of our products and their general giftability, our most avid customers appreciate our Perks program, which offers free shipping and 10 percent off all purchases. It's a good move for Grommet as these happy customers become even more attached to the company, and their frequency of purchase is simultaneously rewarded and increased.

RAISE CAPITAL

Admittedly this option is a dead obvious choice. If you have a business that is already scaling with a clear path to profitability and an attractive set of options for an exit, taking on equity capital could become a viable choice. The various routes to this are discussed in Chapter 10. However, the most frequent way Grommet Makers do this is with a series of crowdfunding campaigns. With each new major product release or enhancement, they go back to the well to fund the first production run and gain new customers. These campaigns are spaced out in terms of years, not months, and require a level of attention and focus that makes the funds anything but free money. But the Kickstarter and Indiegogo communities have proven to be steady supporters of Maker businesses and can be the gift that keeps on giving.

DOUBLE DOWN ON RETAIL DISTRIBUTION

Beyond building your wholesale business via reps, distributors, exclusive products, and tiered good/better/best product extensions, there are three other routes to building your retail footprint.

Pop-Up Stores

Holiday markets, which first originated in Vienna during the thirteenth century, are one traditional expression of this opportunity. Some of our Makers have found, for example, that the Grand Central Station and Bryant Park holiday markets have excellent ROI for generating both sales and general awareness. On a more year-round basis, Lovepop has created a network of kiosks in train stations and malls where customers can touch and feel its products and be constantly updated with new designs.

There is a whole industry forming to fill the excess retail space across the United States. Businesses such as Storefront are matchmakers between empty mall spaces and young brands. They sometimes offer turnkey pop-up store solutions in terms of managing the build-out, marketing, and staffing of these spaces. At Grommet I am approached at least once a month by a mall leasing company doing this kind of value-added service as well as independent companies who work across many real estate developments.

In addition, real estate companies building and managing mixed-use developments are looking to enliven the streetscape of their projects and local areas. In Boston's Seaport—the newest growth area in the city—there is a permanent village of micro shops created by WS Development called The Current. Every six months a new set of brands occupies the nine 180-square-foot shops, organized under a unifying theme. Operating these shops is a bit like running a trunk show or street fair, albeit with a longer-term presence.

Established Retailers

Large retailers, originating with Best Buy, have started to capitalize on their foot traffic and real estate locations by renting space to brands. Best Buy started it with large established players like Samsung, but Macy's is trying this opportunity out for small brands. The core notion is to give the upstart companies exposure while upping the cool factor for Macy's ground floor shopping experience. A related effort by a young company called b8ta—in which Macy's invested—is building Apple-like pristine stores that rent out display tables to up-and-coming brands to gain customer exposure and the irreplaceable benefits of a touch-and-feel trial.

Your Own Stores

Examples of DTC companies expanding into physical retail are rampant: Casper, The Arrivals, Warby Parker, M.Gemi, Allbirds, Rent the Runway, MM.LaFleur, Miansai, Nic+Zoe, and Outdoor Voices. And even Amazon and Everlane (though the apparel CEO famously declared that they would go into retail over his dead body). Some execute like regular retailers in prominent urban and suburban locations, and largely treat the stores like brand builders. They offer a full range of inventory and some offer special customization, product launch, or event opportunities for their fans. Some, like Bonobos, with its Guideshops, turn traditional retail a little sideways. They may have very small second-floor shops, and the inventory is merely a showroom to allow the trial that leads to an e-commerce purchase and future shipment to the customer's home. While on the one hand I am convinced of the brand-building benefits of these shops, these companies tend to also have deep bank accounts funded by venture capitalists, so the economics of these stores may be quite warped by that unusual condition. The numbers may not make sense for the typical bootstrapped Maker.

A Word on Scaling

Scaling is, by definition, a never-ending activity for the business. In your direct-to-consumer sales arena, customer acquisition costs continually rise as you pick off the lowest hanging fruit customers. Your wholesale customers will have an endless appetite for your marketing support and new products.

My own playbook for figuring out the next moves for The Grommet is largely based on continually asking people in my network what is working for them. The problems of scaling are universal, but the solutions can be quite creative. Sometimes they are transferrable to our business—such as a suggestion for a new marketing technology platform. Sometimes they are best practices, such as upping our SEO game after a period of neglect or stasis. In a fast-moving world of marketing platforms, technologies, and shifting consumer behaviors, we can easily miss trends and opportunities. As a CEO I find myself heading out to events with a general sense of dread and "I am too busy for this," and almost 100 percent of the time I come back with a new idea or important contact. While I still grumble about speaking at an event, or getting on a plane, or taking a call from a stranger, I have learned to trust the universe and the likely benefits of these efforts.

And sometimes—the best times—the real magic happens when you just try something that you haven't seen anywhere, and that novelty or special arbitrage opportunity puts unexpected wind in your sails and you ride that condition as long as you can or until others discover it.

CASE STUDIES

EcoFlow Tech

Four friends started EcoFlow Tech in 2016 while living in China, where they'd been challenged by small power banks and difficulties recharging devices. Hannah Sieber, one of the founders, says the team decided there should and could be a portable system for power, something better than a home charging hub and less bulky and expensive than a home generator. From there EcoFlow Tech was born, with an 11-pound, 500-watt generator replacement. The product was brought to market about a year later, and is sold through Home Depot, HSN, Amazon, The Grommet, and other major retailers.

The company has had some unexpected growth challenges along the way, largely because its first product, the River, contains levels of lithium ion that put the generator into a restricted shipping category. "It's clean, green, silent, and rechargeable," says Sieber, but there are restrictions on how (and who) can ship the devices. That means third-party shipping options have been limited, and EcoFlow has to work with a fully certified hazmat warehouse.

Amazon and HSN are not certified to ship such a product, so while they can sell them, it's EcoFlow Tech's warehouse that does the shipping. In effect, EcoFlow is running its own drop-shipping program. The good news is that Sieber and her partners have a lot of information about their market. They know where their products are going. They're shipping direct to the customer, although they aren't selling direct to the customer.

In order to grow, the EcoFlow team knew they needed to make some adjustments to the lithium ion limits in their products. Enter River Bend, the next power device from EcoFlow. Smaller and more compact, it can be shipped by Amazon and taken on planes.

Looking ahead, Sieber says EcoFlow is hoping to expand into developing countries. The company has started working in Puerto Rico and sees a market in areas where power is unreliable, and where natural disasters routinely create power issues. The founders are launching a campaign "to encourage people about preparedness," says Sieber.

"We want to get into larger systems and take energy on and off the grid," explains Sieber, adding that she and her team want to show the world that they can take power with them, for whatever reason.

The team has continued to grow its markets and products. HSN featured EcoFlow in the fall of 2018 and put in the largest order the company had up until that point. They were expanding into Lowes as well. "That is a huge validation and realization for us," says Sieber. "That's a huge win." Sieber said the company had more than 30 full-time employees, and they expected to double that in six months. "We're seeing great sales," she said. "The product is moving." Sold through Amazon as well, EcoFlow pops up in the top 25 searches for "portable power."

Maria Shireen

Shireen Maria Thor and her husband Arni Thor are both engineers, had been working in the field of medical devices, and were familiar with bringing ideas to fruition. But they never personally had to deal with all of the steps of getting a product to market until they launched Maria Shireen.

Maria Shireen is an attractive and practical solution for dealing with hair elastics that typically tighten around wrists, leaving marks and looking, well, rather sloppy. The original hair tie bracelet was created for Shireen by her husband as a gift, and the bracelets are now in more than 500 boutiques and in Hallmark stores, and one of the lines is being tested in 12 Anthropologie stores around the country. The bracelets are also sold in more than 20 countries.

It's been tricky for the company to figure out exactly in which sector of the market they most belong. Is this an accessory? A gift? Jewelry? For Target, the store wasn't quite sure where to display Maria Shireen, says the founder.

When it comes to future growth, the company is always looking at new avenues for sales. Shireen says one such option is for the company to consider teen and kids lines as well. Being tested in Anthropologie is another huge leap for the company, one that may lead to further growth.

The company has struggled to combat copycats as well—nearly 1,000 in all since launching in 2015, says Shireen. "We believe licensing with bigger companies that already have relationships and infrastructure is the way to go," says Shireen about growth. Shireen says there are larger jewelry stores that have expressed interest. The licensing would allow others to manufacture their products, and Shireen could continue designing while still maintaining control over the new lines and products. The company has several brick-and-mortar stores as well, something Shireen says they would like to maintain control over even if they do branch out into licensing.

Hydaway

Niki Singlaub had worked with product design and launches for almost 20 years. He wanted to do his own, was opposed to single-use plastic, and had an idea for a collapsible water bottle, something that would be convenient for travel and not too bulky. "I figured someone already made it," he says. Alas, they did not. That was in 2012, and Singlaub has been working on Hydaway since. He knew he was on to something when his Kickstarter campaign was funded on the first day and went on to quickly raise $250,000.

Now in more than 600 specialty stores and available through The Grommet, Singlaub says he always thinks about future growth. "I tend not to live enough in the moment," he adds. "Every week we're learning about a new chain of stores." In the short term, growth means expanding his sales force and looking at more gift shops and natural grocers as potential future retail outlets that would carry the Hydaway bottle.

Singlaub says long-term growth has to be about balancing wholesale with direct-to-consumer sales. The latter is better for his company as the discounts in the wholesale market hurt the bottom line too much.

Singlaub says he's always thinking of future compatible products but adds, "We're nowhere near the end of the life cycle of this one." He also wants to be sure his distribution channels are in place and well understood before adding more products. The company is currently making some design adjustments to its bottle to make it slimmer and easier to expand while also considering additional color options.

Singlaub says he's driven by the desire to "create a brand out of this by reducing plastic waste and the amount of bottle water that is purchased." Over the two and half years since the bottle launched to market the founder says the company has had consistent growth. Hydaway team members work with sales reps, go to trade shows, and are constantly considering new distribution channels. The company is also adding additional products and accessories including carbon filters and travel cases. Hydaway is sold in Nordstrom, Ace Hardware, Brookstone, Bed Bath & Beyond, and in gift stores around the country.

Talisman Designs

Katherine Waymire started handmaking something she called "stylish stems," decorative wineglass identifiers—similar to the popular wine charms, just to feed her creative side. Her friends and family loved them and kept encouraging her to sell them. She figured she had nothing to lose, and since there wasn't much overhead, beyond some simple materials, she took a chance. Waymire made enough to take around to a few stores in Minneapolis, near where she lives. She went into three shops. "They all said yes." That was in 2002.

Waymire started handmaking more and more, and did so for about four months, until she realized it wasn't feasible to do it all on her own. "I started scaling immediately," she says. "You can't scale if you are handmaking every single piece." So, she worked with a local community of Hmong who were looking for work. Waymire brought them the glue, wire, and beads, and they helped to handcraft the wineglass embellishments. It wasn't long before she needed even more help.

Waymire discovered a nearby nonprofit that employed people who typically had difficulty finding jobs, and she had the stylish stems produced there. Months later she hit another wall. "While trying to scale the manufacturing, I was also trying to sell," she says. It was simply too much to do at once.

"You have to be able to ask for help," says Waymire. So she went to a friend who had experience manufacturing overseas. He traveled with her to China, and she found a factory that could produce what she wanted.

By 2005 Talisman Designs had introduced the Butter Boy, an adorable gadget for buttering corn that looks like a pudgy boy and keeps your fingers from getting greasy. "That was a massive hit," says Waymire. "From there, we started scaling product development." The company began adding multiple products a year, all in the category of giftable housewares, many of them for the kitchen. Waymire explains that the company is always looking to solve a problem with its products, be it cherries that need faster, simpler pit removal or a simpler way to zest a lime.

As time went on, Talisman kept getting its products into bigger stores, all while expanding its offerings.

"Sales and new products drive the cart," says Waymire, of the company's continued growth. She says she knows every product has a life cycle, so her team is always working on the next items. There have been years when Talisman Designs introduced 20 to 25 new products, and other years when it's been only 5. For Waymire, another aspect that has helped her to scale has been the relationship she has with her bank. She uses a local neighborhood bank in Minneapolis, where the bankers know her and she knows them. She says there have been times when she's gone in and asked for help, an extra line of credit, or something to get her through a production cycle or slump. "That doesn't happen at a big bank."

"I'm about incremental growth," says Waymire. "Ignore the shiny objects and chase the gold," she adds. Since she founded the company, Waymire has added about 200 products to her company.

She still works with the same factory in China where she began manufacturing, only she's added several others as well. The company sells to independent gift shops, Paper Source, Cost Plus, and many specialty shops.

CONCLUSION

There are two prominent questions that burn bright in the brains of aspiring entrepreneurs. After reading this book, they are likely on your mind as well.

"IS MY IDEA GOOD ENOUGH?"

If you put your idea through the paces outlined in Chapters 2 through 5, you will be far ahead of the pack. Frankly, most are paralyzed at the outset. One single but concrete step forward in pursuing an idea—no matter how wobbly—is worth more than one full month of rumination.

Alternately, many barrel ahead with no analysis. Before they know it, they are in the thick of a business that may or may not have solid underpinnings.

Do the work. Your future self will thank you.

A word of caution as you apply the concepts in Chapters 2 through 5. Every idea seems brilliant until you start researching it objectively. Then you find the flaws and weaknesses, and the bloom is off the rose. Some would-be entrepreneurs get sucked into an endless cycle of enthusiastically pursuing an idea until the obstacles surface, abandoning those ideas, only to pursue new ones, never being able to commit. I would rather see you abandon ideas than blindly pursue them, but keep this "familiarity breeds contempt" tendency in mind. When you find holes in your business idea, put them through these filters—which are all legitimate reasons to bail:

1. Is the market smaller than I thought?

2. Are there major regulatory or structural factors that cannot be addressed?

3. Is the cost to pursue this idea many multiples of what I imagined and want to take on?

4. Am I getting turned off by the general area itself? Is it honestly a product I want to live and breathe?

Regarding this process, here is an example: My oldest son started a business to provide a subscription service for delivery of quality, branded cannabis. He could see that the market was large and demand was clearly established. Legislative trends in the United States and globally were showing a quick pace to broad legalization. The current consumer-buying option—an inconvenient in-person visit to a dispensary—was inadequate. He likened it to going to an 1820s general store, where products were in bulk containers and you had to wait in line to consult with a person behind the counter. The product itself was confusing to assess, and there was no trusted "brand."

Those were all good things and indicated a very large opportunity. But along the way (in 2014–2015) he discovered that one of the core competencies he would have to develop in the business was navigating regulatory bodies. He was discouraged by seeing corruption in the industry even in the early days, and he found that disillusioning. He had started the business because he had a vision for building a great brand and service, but he had no stomach for the lobbying and "fighting City Hall" requirements of the business. He also found a particularly cautious investor population. Allen Morgan, a very experienced Silicon Valley startup "Sherpa," was an advisor to my son, and he told us that in 60 similar projects this was only one of a small handful for which he could not recruit angel investors. My son wisely moved on to his next venture. And he does appreciate that he helped define a new industry, even if he is no longer participating in it.

"AM I CUT OUT FOR BEING AN ENTREPRENEUR?"

Being a great entrepreneur has little to do with education or even intellect. It has more to do with tenacity and independence. Entrepreneurship is the Olympics of business. Here's the sports analogy I use: There are two skilled college athletes of equal caliber. They graduate. One takes a job, builds a family, and pursues her sport in her spare time. She is a weekend warrior with a conventional life, in the best sense. The other athlete sets her sights on the Olympics. She knowingly makes sacrifices in her personal and professional lives to train for the slim possibility of qualifying to compete for a gold medal. This athlete objectively faces steep odds, and trades away free time, income, and résumé growth—and pursues this goal anyway.

Founders are like the latter. The most famous definition of this career choice comes from my own Harvard Business School professor, Howard Stevenson: "Entrepreneurship is the pursuit of opportunity without regard to resources currently controlled."

I like this further explanation Stevenson gave in an interview with Eric Schurenberg, CEO of Mansueto Ventures. Eric writes:

> Back in 1983, he [Stevenson] told me, people tended to define entrepreneurship almost as a personality disorder, a kind of risk addiction. "But that didn't fit the entrepreneurs I knew," he said. "I never met an entrepreneur who got up in the morning saying, 'Where's the most risk in today's economy, and how can I get some?[']
> Most entrepreneurs I know are looking to lay risk off—on investors, partners, lenders, and anyone else." As for personality, he said, "The entrepreneurs I know are all different types. They're as likely to be wallflowers as to be the wild man of Borneo."

> By focusing on entrepreneurship as a process, his definition opened the term to all kinds of people. Plus,

it matched the one demographic fact HBS [Harvard Business School] researchers already knew about entrepreneurs—they were more likely to start out poor than rich. "They see an opportunity and don't feel constrained from pursuing it because they lack resources," says Stevenson. "They're *used* to making do without resources."[1]

It's nice to know that being poor is a benefit, and that resonates with me. Growing up I had wonderful parents, but I never had a financial safety net. I found that simple, stark reality very freeing in my adult life and as a founder. By getting myself through college and beyond, I learned that I could depend on myself to navigate most challenges. It does take a while—a long while—to transfer that confidence to yourself as a founder. The "first" time I did anything at The Grommet, it was pretty terrifying. The first investor pitch. The first hire. The first check I wrote. The first lawsuit (yes, there were those). The first time I had to let someone go.

But 10 years in, I usually think "bring it on" when new things arise. I know I can puzzle or push my way through an obstacle. I remember one investor told me, "I invested because I knew you would be a pit bull about this business. You would succeed. Or you would die trying." I feel like I have tasted both ends of that spectrum. Sometimes each in a single week.

So how can you know your personal capacity for tenacity? I would look for examples in your own life where you had two choices. One was more comfortable or safe, and the other represented a stretch or difficult choice—like the college athletes I described. Here are examples:

- Trying out for a play or chorus

- Running a marathon or any extreme physical challenge

- Moving far from home and family

- Getting a divorce or calling off an engagement

- Getting a degree while working full-time

- Taking a lateral job transfer to learn new skills, though the optics were not showing career progression

- Changing careers

- Being the person who shows up consistently when someone is sick

- Raising funds for a cause

- Leading a local charity or nonprofit

These are not classic measures of entrepreneurial talent. But until you have actually tried your hand at a business, you have to consider other indicators of your own ability to persevere and travel what is likely to be a lonely road.

Part and parcel of taking on the activities I listed is learning to conquer your own fear—and even embrace it. When it is associated with a decision or life change, fear is usually an indicator that you are on a growth edge. No one is fearless, but the people who manage to pursue their ambitions learn to recognize the fear and walk into it rather than practice avoidance. I can tell you from experience it does not feel good or comfortable. Far from it. In fact, the worst advice in the world is, "Follow your gut. If it feels right you will make the best decision." My observation is that the right decision often feels terrible, at least physically.

We all have a personal "tell" that signals, "Uh-oh, I am scared or excited about this situation." It might be insomnia, headaches, an elevated heartbeat, eczema, or overeating. My own tell is in my stomach—feelings ranging from butterflies to churning to nausea. I feel those sensations nearly every week, to this day. I have learned to say "There you are, my old friend. What are you here to teach me? What do I need to face down today?"

The final thought I would share about considering this journey and facing your fears is to think of the worst possible scenario of starting a business and failing. Rather than let insecurities and fears be vague and persistent companions, make them work hard. Imagine your concerns playing out into the worst possible scenario. If you start a business and it fails, what could happen?

Would you become unemployable? Unlikely. Very unlikely. In fact, I personally love hiring people who tried their hand at a now-shuttered business. They are wise and savvy and appreciate what it takes.

Would you burn through personal resources? Certainly—but Gerry Laybourne, creator of Oxygen and Nickelodeon and an investor in The Grommet, told me, "Just make sure you put some boundaries on your personal financial risk, so it is not devastating."

Would you be embarrassed about failure? That is guaranteed. But my observations on this are twofold. A wise friend, Irish venture capitalist Dermot Berkery, once told me, "Don't carry guilt about failure. As an investor, I lose money on most projects. All I really care about is, 'Did that founder do their best?' They will make mistakes, and some could be fatal, but did they give it all they could to grow the business and my money? They should not carry any more burden than that simple expectation." Nor should you.

The second reality of a business failure is that no one really cares. It sounds harsh, but it's true. People are busy. Someone else's career and finances are not that important to them. Friends and family are sympathetic for the requisite single conversation, and then they immediately move on to, "So what are you going to do next?" They will probably start helping you find your next business opportunity or job. By virtue of the fact that you tried, you have signaled a strength of conviction and purpose that most people lack. The only true failure is not trying.

NOTES

Chapter 1

1. http://www.wipo.int/edocs/pubdocs/en/wipo_pub_941_2017 -chapter2.pdf.
2. Vikram Alexei Kansara, "Chris Anderson Says the 'Maker' Movement is the Next Industrial Revolution," *Business of Fashion*, November 6, 2012, https://www.businessoffashion.com/articles/long-view/the-long-view -chris-anderson-says-the-maker-movement-is-the-next-industrial -revolution.

Chapter 3

1. Jeff Haden. "22 Years Ago Steve Jobs Said 1 Thing Separates People Who Achieve from Those Who Only Dream," *Inc.* magazine, 2017, https://www.inc.com/jeff-haden/22-years-ago-steve-jobs-said-1-thing -separates-people-who-achieve-from-those-who-only-dream.html.
2. Ibid.
3. Guy Raz, "Ben & Jerry's: Ben Cohen and Jerry Greenfield," *How I Built This*, podcast, 2017, https://www.npr.org/podcasts/510313/how-i-built -this.
4. Guy Raz, "Framebridge: Susan Tynan," *How I Built This*, podcast, 2017, https://www.npr.org/podcasts/510313/how-i-built-this.
5. Alison Wood Brooks and Francesca Gino, Harvard Business School; Maurice E. Schweitzer, Wharton School, University of Pennsylvania, "Smart People Ask for (My) Advice: Seeking Advice Boosts Perceptions of Competence," 2015.

Chapter 4

1. Sarah Coffey, "The Field Guide to Maker Spaces in All 50 States," blog, *Front + Main*, 2016, https://blog.westelm.com/2016/06/21/maker-space -guide/.
2. https://www.ponyride.org/what-we-do/.
3. Micheline Maynard, "Can Fashion Help Detroit Make a Comeback?" *New York Times*, March 2018, https://www.nytimes.com/2018/03/02 /business/can-fashion-help-detroit-make-a-comeback.html.

4. Janet Napolitano, "Why Universities are the New Startup Incubators," *Medium*, October 2016, https://medium.com/@UofCalifornia/why-universities-are-the-new-startup-incubators-be877f3c4cc4.
5. https://www.facebook.com/groups/librarymaker/about/.
6. Amandine Richardot, "18 of the Best Hardware Accelerators to Launch Your Business," blog, *Sculpteo*, 2017, https://www.sculpteo.com/blog/2017/05/03/18-of-the-best-hardware-accelerators-to-launch-your-business/.
7. Alex Konrad, "The Best Startup Accelerators of 2017," *Forbes*, 2017, https://www.forbes.com/sites/alexkonrad/2017/06/07/best-accelerators-of-2017/#58a8f1d610cb.

Chapter 5

1. Christopher Mims, "Why There Are More Consumer Goods Than Ever," *Wall Street Journal*, 2016, https://www.wsj.com/articles/why-there-are-more-consumer-goods-than-ever-1461556860.
2. Guy Raz, "LÄRABAR: Lara Merriken," *How I Built This*, podcast, March 2018, https://www.npr.org/templates/transcript/transcript.php?storyId=594357259.

Chapter 7

1. Jon Emont, Robert McMillan, and Laura Stevens, "Amazon Investigates Employees Leaking Data for Bribes," *Wall Street Journal*, September 2018, https://www.wsj.com/articles/amazon-investigates-employees-leaking-data-for-bribes-1537106401.

Chapter 8

1. Rikke Dam and Teo Siang, "Design Thinking: Get Started with Prototyping," *Interaction Design*, 2018, https://www.interaction-design.org/literature/article/design-thinking-get-started-with-prototyping.
2. Guy Raz, "Dyson: James Dyson," *How I Built This*, podcast, February 12, 2018, https://www.npr.org/templates/transcript/transcript.php?storyId=584331881.

Chapter 9

1. Roxanne Quimby and Susan Donovan, "How I Did It: Roxanne Quimby," *Inc.* magazine, 2004, https://www.inc.com/magazine/20040101/howididit.html.

Chapter 10

1. Alex Conrad, "CircleUp Fund Brings Moneyball to Consumer Brands," *Forbes*, October 2017, https://www.forbes.com/sites/alexkonrad

/2017/10/31/circleup-fund-brings-moneyball-to-consumer-brands/
#2d09f3932a82.

2. Guy Raz, "Kate Spade: Kate & Andy Spade," *How I Built This*, podcast, 2017, https://one.npr.org/?sharedMediaId=513311127:513326948.

3. Harvard Business School 2016, https://entrepreneurship.hbs.edu /founders/Pages/profile.aspx?num=294.

Chapter 14

1. Carlos Waters, What America's Mall Decline Means for Social Space," VOX, video, April 2018, https://www.youtube.com/watch?v= oooVC3zfDc8&feature=youtu.be.

2. "Ecommerce Share of Retail Sales in US," https://www.statista .com/statistics/379112/e-commerce-share-of-retail-sales-in-us/; Mary Meeker, "Internet Trends," May 2018, https://www.recode.net/2018 /5/30/17385116/mary-meeker-slides-internet-trends-code-conference -2018.

3. Shira Ovide, "How Amazon's Bottom Appetite Became Corporate America's Nightmare," Bloomberg, March 2018, https://www .bloomberg.com/graphics/2018-amazon-industry-displacement/.

4. Wade Shepard, "Amazon and Ebay Opened up a Pandora's Box for Counterfeiters and Now Don't Know What to Do," *Forbes*, October 2017, https://www.forbes.com/sites/wadeshepard/2017/10/28/amazon-and -ebay-opened-pandoras-box-of-chinese-counterfeits-and-now-dont -know-what-to-do/2/#17c7b5c32270.

5. David Marino-Nachison, "Amazon: A $25 Billion Private Label Business?" *Forbes*, June 2018, https://www.barrons.com/articles/amazon -a-25-billion-private-label-business-1528131628.

6. https://www.prospershow.com/are-amazon-chargebacks-eating-into -your-profits-8-reasons-why-and-what-you-can-do-about-it/.

7. William Lewis, "Manufacturer Suggest Retail Price (MSRP) vs Minimum Advertised Price (MAP) - Explained," Nuvonium blog, February 2013, https://www.nuvonium.com/blog/view/manufacturer-suggest -retail-price-msrp-vs-minimum-advertised-price-map-expl.

8. "The Multiplier Effect of Independent Local Businesses," https://www .amiba.net/resources/multiplier-effect/.

Chapter 15

1. "We Analyzed Nine of the Biggest Direct-to-Consumer Success Stories to Figure Out the Secrets to Their Growth—Here's What We Learned," CBInsights, December 2017, https://www.cbinsights.com/research /direct-to-consumer-retail-strategies/.

2. Jeff Kauflin, "Exclusive Sneaker Startup Allbirds Lands $17.5M in New Funding," *Forbes*, September 2017, https://www.forbes.com/sites /jeffkauflin/2017/09/05/exclusive-sneaker-startup-allbirds-lands-17 -5-million-in-new-funding/#148715545368.
3. "We Analyzed Nine of the Biggest Direct-to-Consumer Success Stories," CBInsights.

Chapter 16
1. Jillian Hufford, "Are Fulfillment By Amazon (FBA) Costs Worth It?," NChannel blog, January 2018, https://www.nchannel.com/blog/is -fulfillment-by-amazon-fba-worth-the-cost/.

Chapter 21
1. Robert Valerio, Quora, April 2015, https://www.quora.com/What-does -an-international-distributor-add-to-the-price-of-a-retail-product.
2. Randy Meyers, "How to Find an Overseas Distributor," *Entrepreneur*, May 2010, https://www.entrepreneur.com/article/206810.

Conclusion
1. Eric Schurenberg, "What Is an Entrepreneur? The Best Answer Ever," *Inc.* magazine, January 2012, https://www.inc.com/eric-schurenberg /the-best-definition-of-entepreneurship.html.

ABOUT THE MAKING OF THE BOOK COVER

The cover was designed by lead Grommet designer Stacey Bakaj. Stacey set out to make the words themselves physical entities, so each was individually fabricated. These items where then assembled and photographed by Grommet photographer Timothy Renzi.

HOW WE: laser cut out of wood

Made by Grommet employee Zack Williamson. The wood is walnut, finished with mineral oil. Prior to cutting, the wood was covered in transfer paper to prevent scorch marks. The laser used was the Glowforge Basic model.

Make: handmade out of clay

Crafted by Stacey Bakaj. Made with Crayola Air Clay. Finished with a light coat of Krylon Crystal Clear Acrylic Coating 1303.

STUFF: 3D printed out of plastic

Fabricated by Scott Janousek at Artisan's Asylum. Material used was PLA (polylactide), a very common thermoplastic for rapid 3D print prototyping. The printer used was the FlashForge Creator Pro.

NOW: fabricated out of metal

Fabricated at Big Blue Saw. The material used was 304 Stainless Steel with a brushed finish. It was cut on a Techni Waterjet X3.

Here's a close-up of the cover in real life:

Here's Stacey inspecting her work and ensuring everything is just right before the photo shoot:

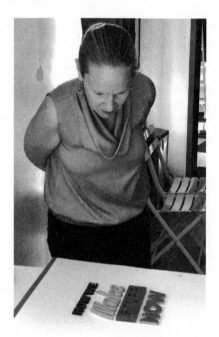

INDEX

ABOUT THE AUTHOR

 **Jules Pieri** is cofounder and CEO of The Grommet, a site that has launched more than 2,000 consumer products since 2008. The company's Citizen Commerce™ movement is reshaping how products are discovered, shared, and bought.

Jules started her career as an industrial designer for technology companies and was an executive at Keds, Stride Rite, and Playskool. The Grommet is her third startup, following roles as VP at Design Continuum and President of Ziggs.com.

She was named one of Fortune's Most Powerful Women Entrepreneurs in 2013 and one of Goldman Sachs' 100 Most Interesting Entrepreneurs in 2014. She is currently an Entrepreneur in Residence at Harvard Business School.

Jules is frequently asked to speak on consumer trends and technologies, design, and entrepreneurship. She has presented at HBS, SCAD, MIT, and at conferences, including SXSW, PwC Women's Conference, Internet Retailer, and the Conference on World Affairs. She's been featured in the *New York Times*, the *Wall Street Journal*, *Forbes*, *Fortune*, and many other media outlets.

Visit thegrommet.com.